CAST OF CHARACTERS

TATSU

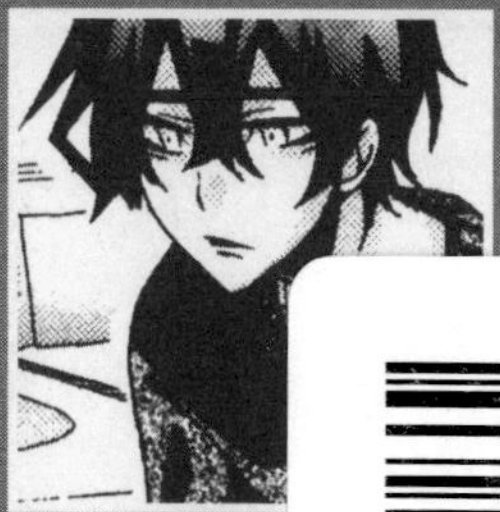

The owner of the house. High school boy. He's good at cooking and household chores.

KASUMI

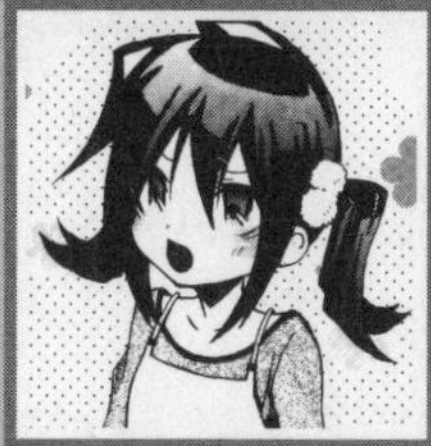

Tatsumi's little sister. Loves her big brother very much, and so resents Wakasa.

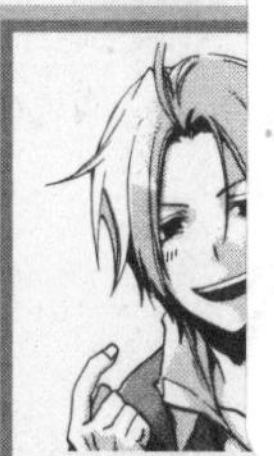

Tatsumi's friend. He has two older sisters.

UNCLE HISATORA

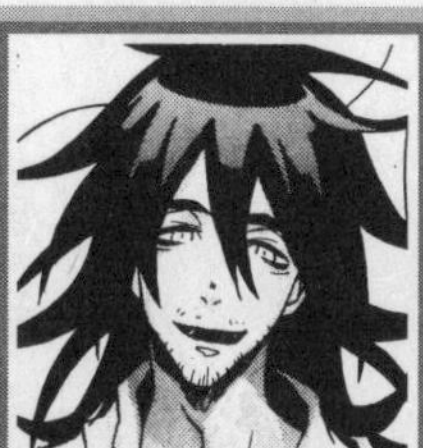

Tatsumi's uncle. He develops suspicious medicines and has Tatsumi test them out.

WAKASA

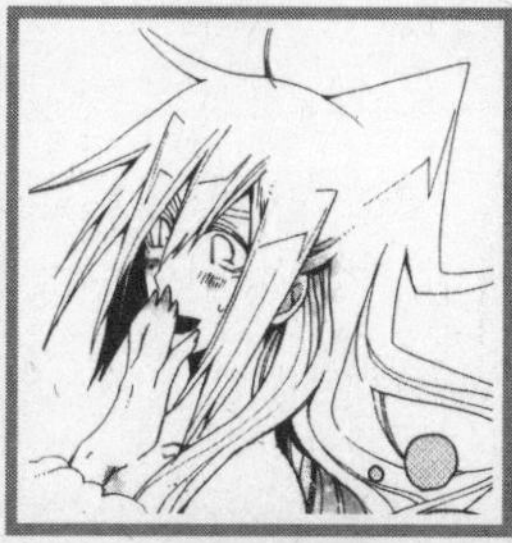

The free-loading fish of Tatsumi's house. His age... don't ask.

MAKI

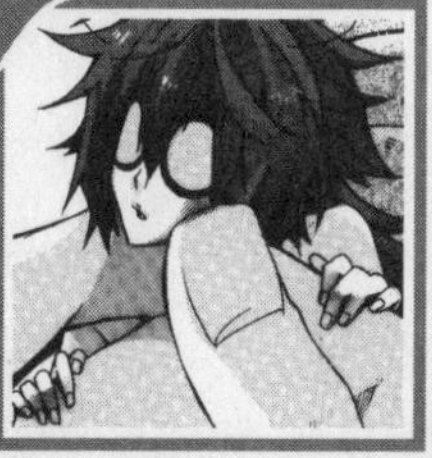

A snail that appears quietly at the bath. Super near-sighted and self-loathing.

TAKASU

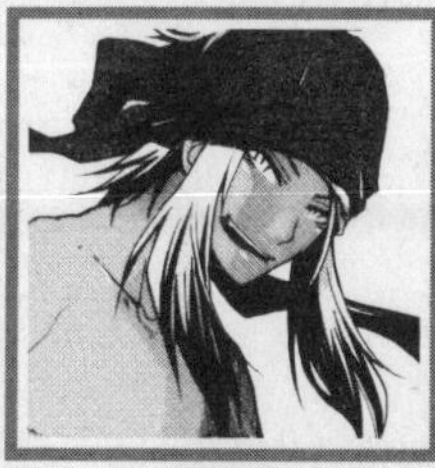

An octopus that sometimes appears in the bath. Seems to be long-time friends with Wakasa. He's good at massages.

MIKUNI

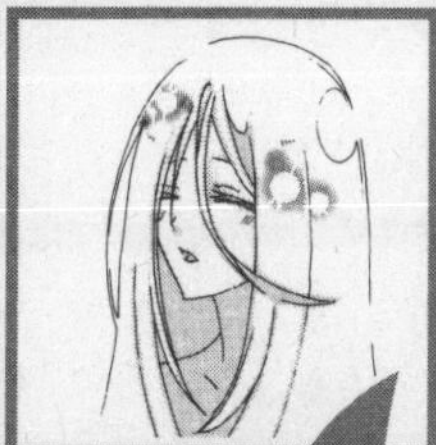

A jellyfish that wanders into the bath. His body is 99% water. He loves Aquarius.

GOROMARU

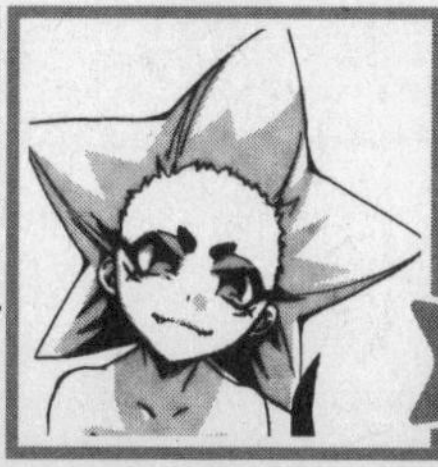

A starfish that appears in the house and often goes unnoticed. He is skilled at clinging.

AGARI

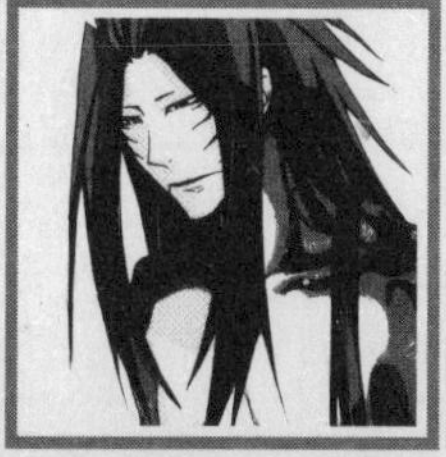

A shark that suddenly appears in the bath. It seems he is Wakasa's senpai.

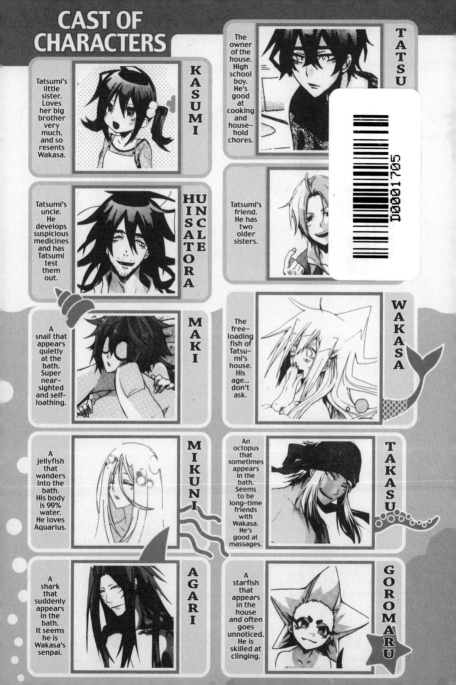

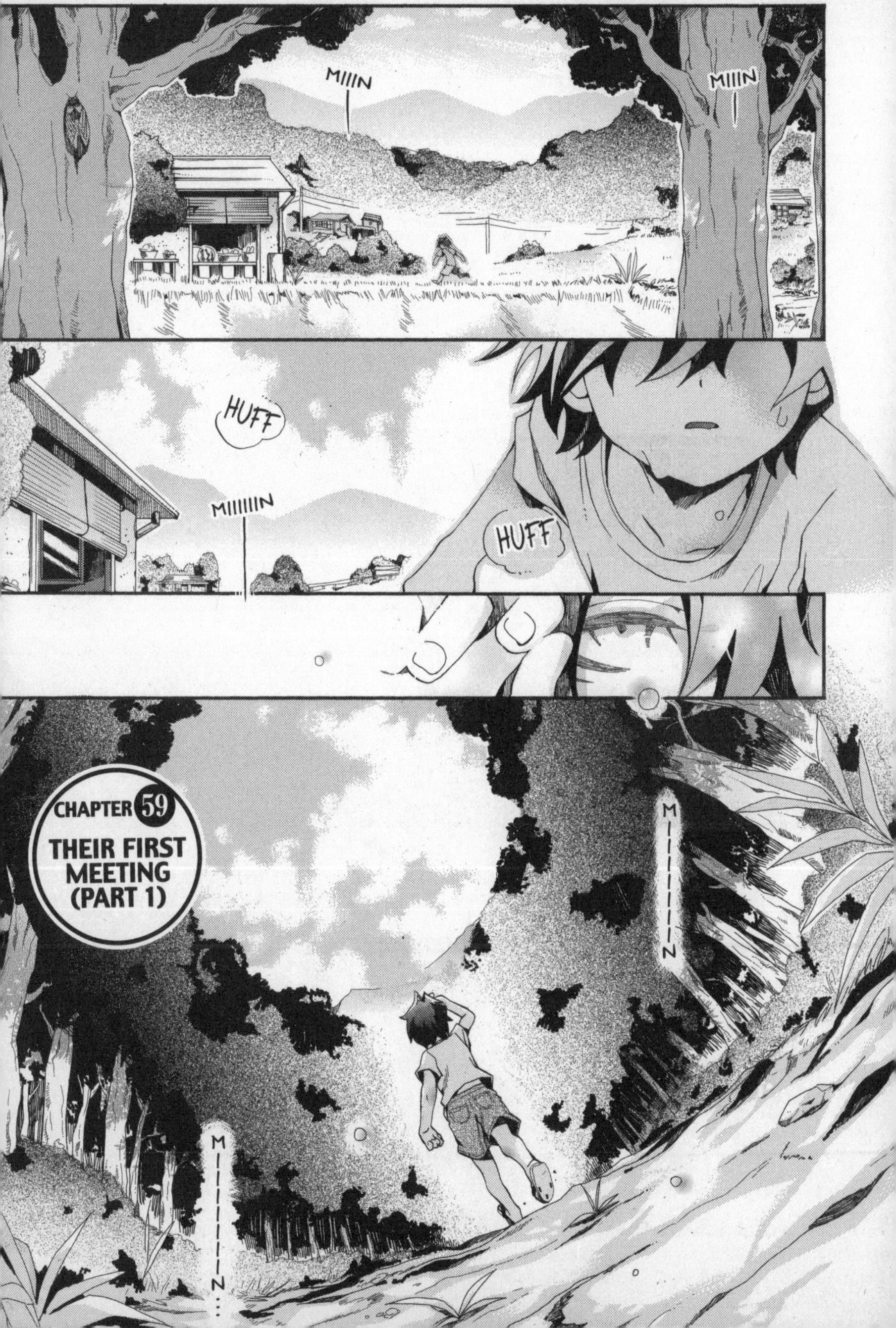
MIIIN
MIIIN
HUFF
HUFF
MIIIIIIN
CHAPTER 59
THEIR FIRST MEETING (PART 1)
M————N
M————N...

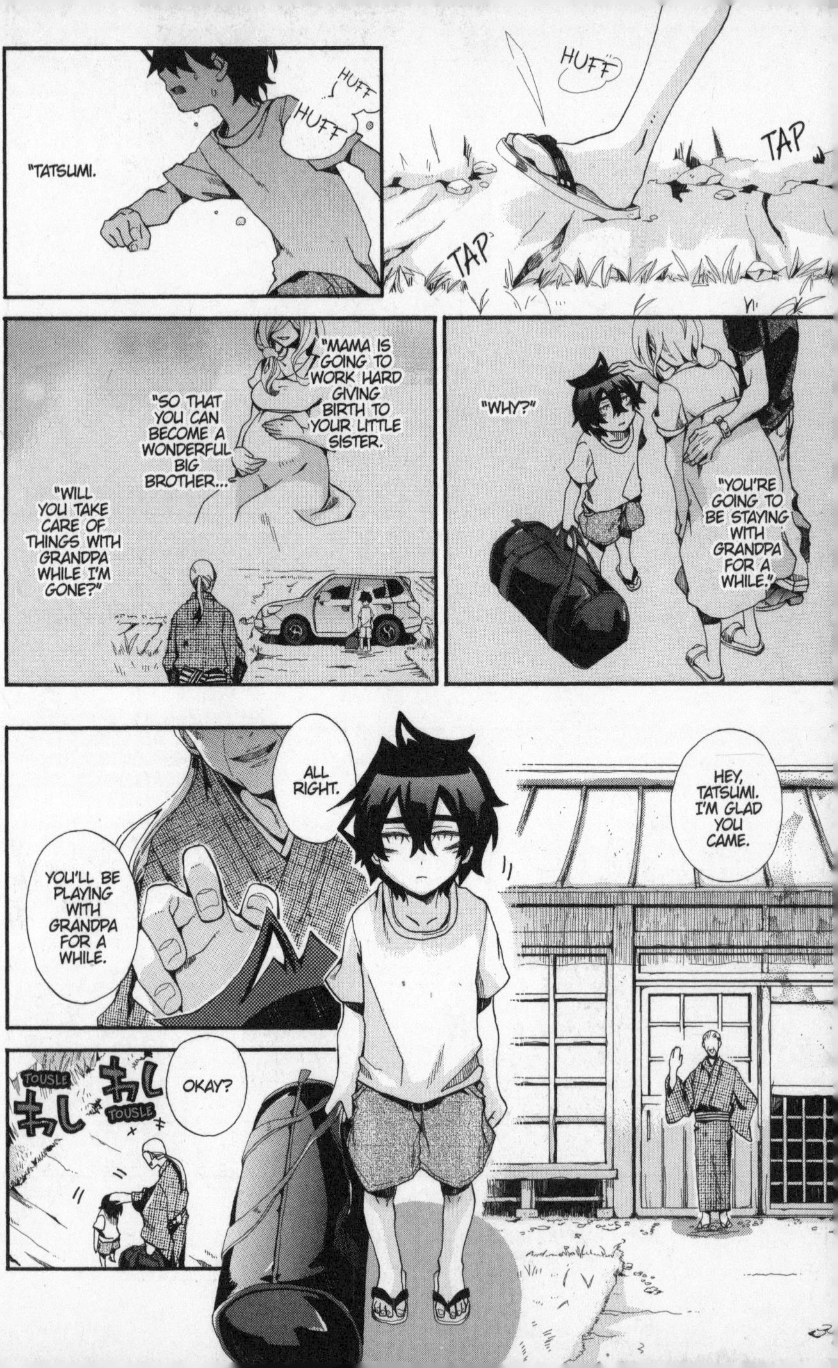
HUFF
TAP
TAP
HUFF HUFF
"TATSUMI.
"WHY?"
"YOU'RE GOING TO BE STAYING WITH GRANDPA FOR A WHILE."
"MAMA IS GOING TO WORK HARD GIVING BIRTH TO YOUR LITTLE SISTER.
"SO THAT YOU CAN BECOME A WONDERFUL BIG BROTHER...
"WILL YOU TAKE CARE OF THINGS WITH GRANDPA WHILE I'M GONE?"
HEY, TATSUMI. I'M GLAD YOU CAME.
ALL RIGHT.
YOU'LL BE PLAYING WITH GRANDPA FOR A WHILE.
OKAY?
わし TOUSLE
わし TOUSLE

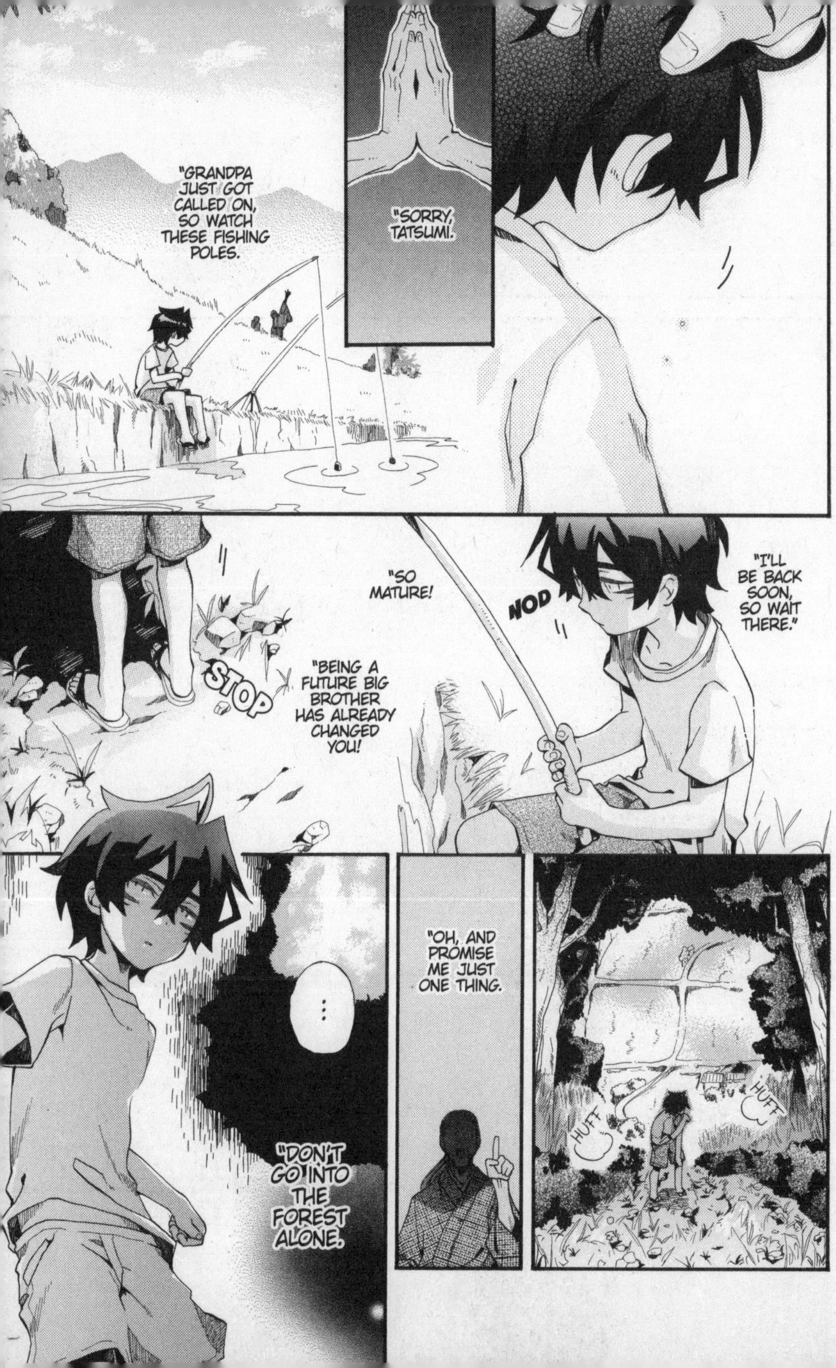
"SORRY, TATSUMI.
"GRANDPA JUST GOT CALLED ON, SO WATCH THESE FISHING POLES.
"I'LL BE BACK SOON, SO WAIT THERE."
NOD
"SO MATURE!
"BEING A FUTURE BIG BROTHER HAS ALREADY CHANGED YOU!
STOP
HUFF
HUFF
"OH, AND PROMISE ME JUST ONE THING.
...
"DON'T GO INTO THE FOREST ALONE.

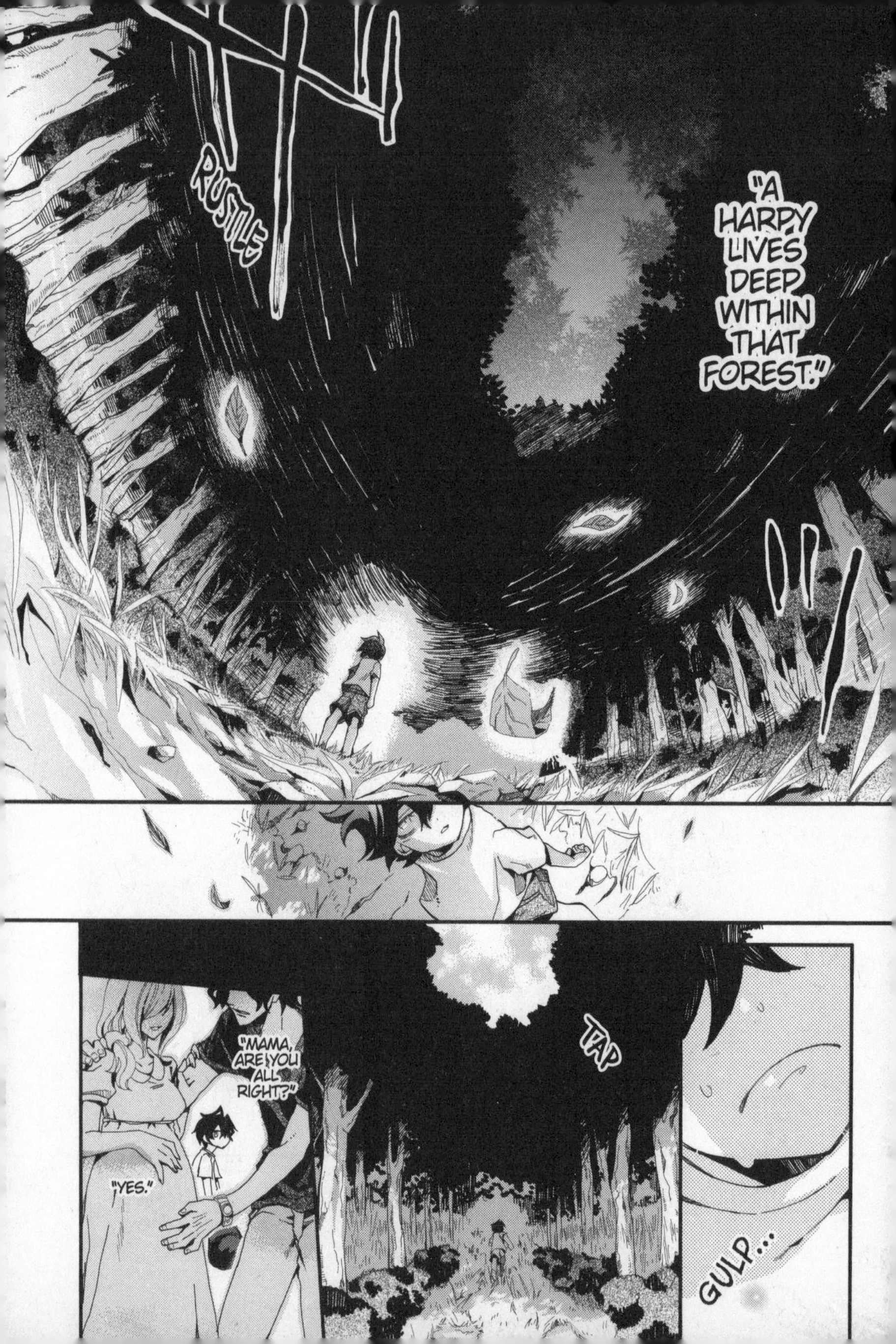
"A HARPY LIVES DEEP WITHIN THAT FOREST."
RUSTLE
GULP...
TAP
"MAMA, ARE YOU ALL RIGHT?"
"YES."

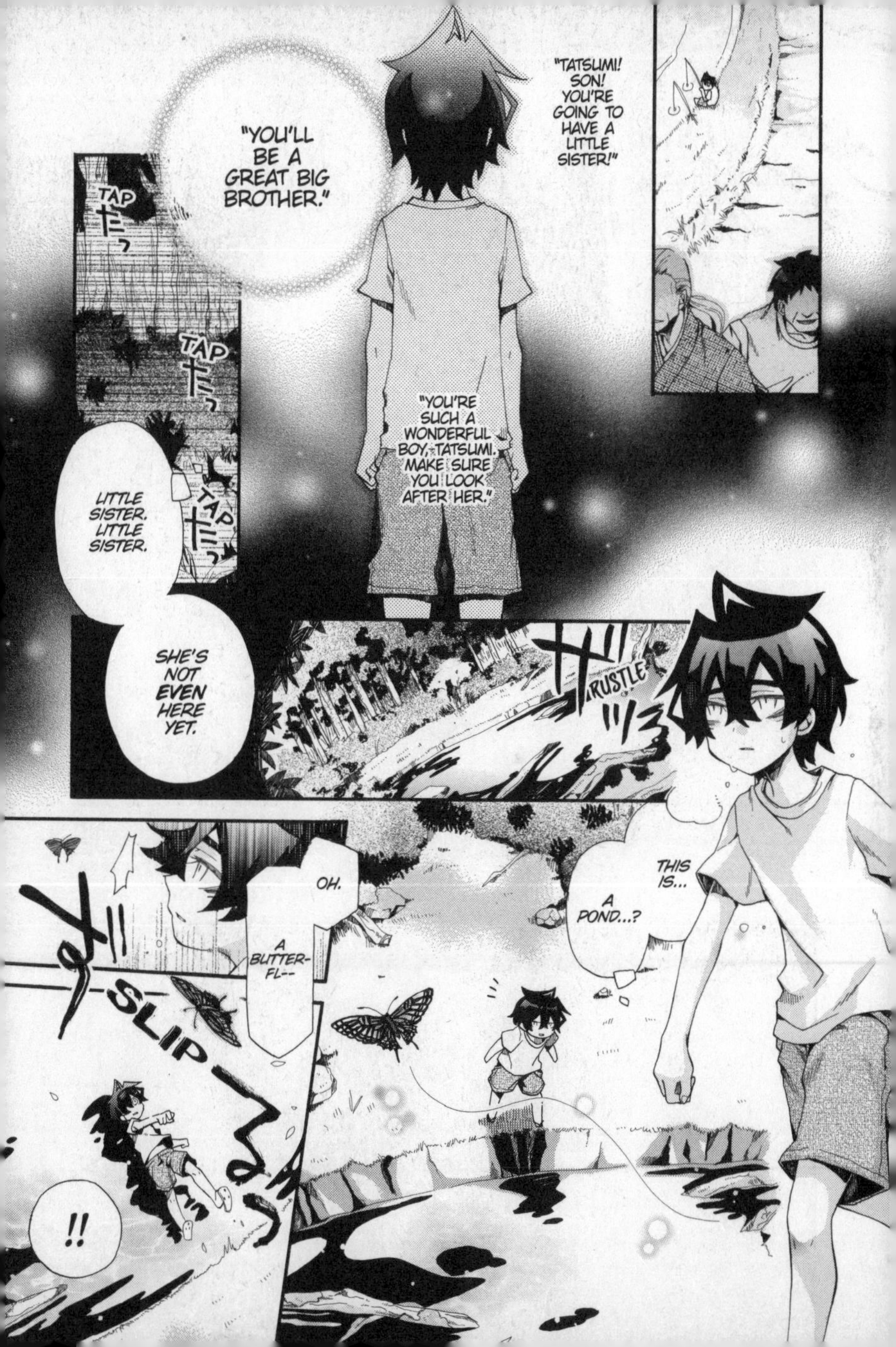
"TATSUMI! SON! YOU'RE GOING TO HAVE A LITTLE SISTER!"
"YOU'LL BE A GREAT BIG BROTHER."
"YOU'RE SUCH A WONDERFUL BOY, TATSUMI. MAKE SURE YOU LOOK AFTER HER."
TAP
TAP
TAP
LITTLE SISTER. LITTLE SISTER.
SHE'S NOT EVEN HERE YET.
RUSTLE
THIS IS...
A POND...?
OH.
A BUTTER-FL--
SLIP
!!

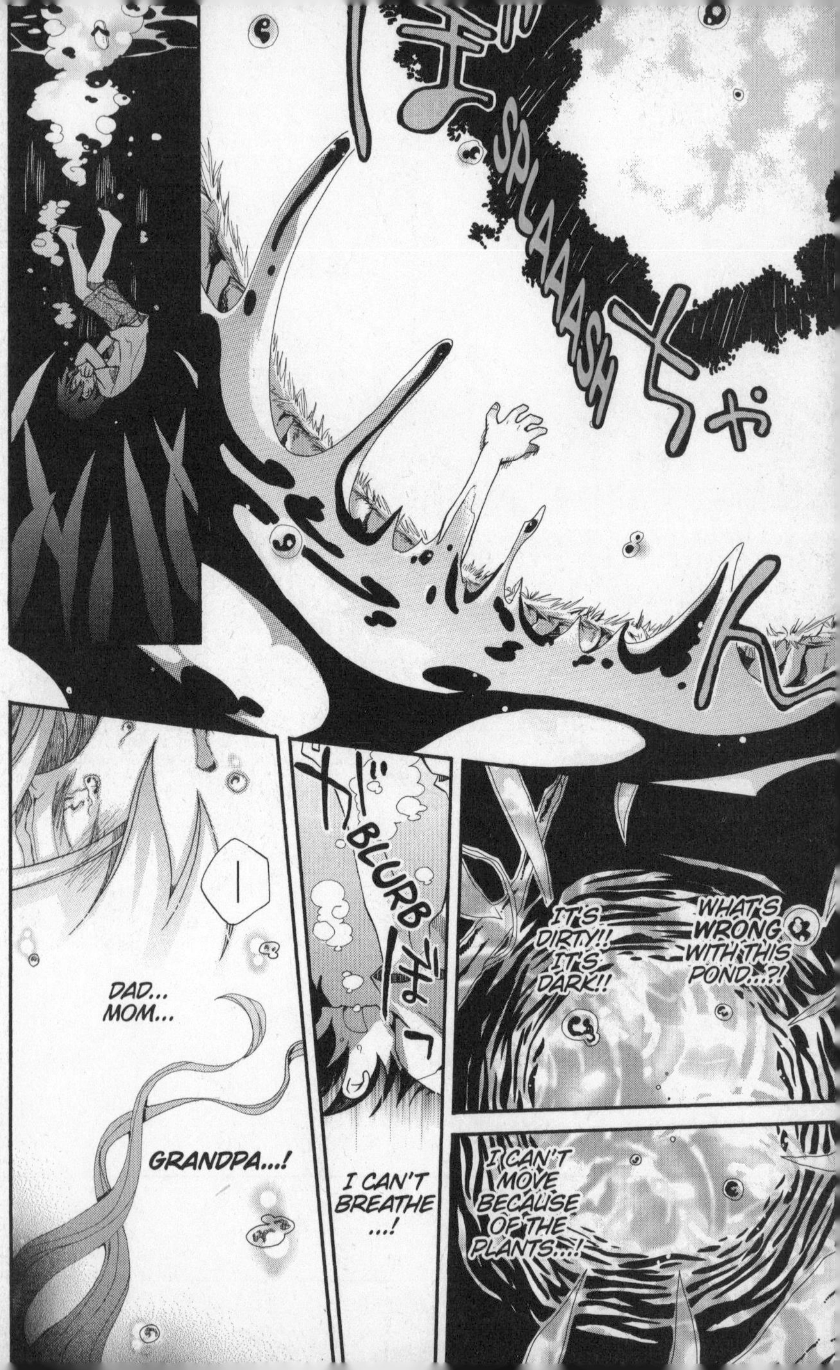
SPLAASH
WHAT'S WRONG WITH THIS POND...?!
IT'S DIRTY!! IT'S DARK!!
I CAN'T MOVE BECAUSE OF THE PLANTS...!
BLURB
I CAN'T BREATHE...!
DAD... MOM...
GRANDPA...!

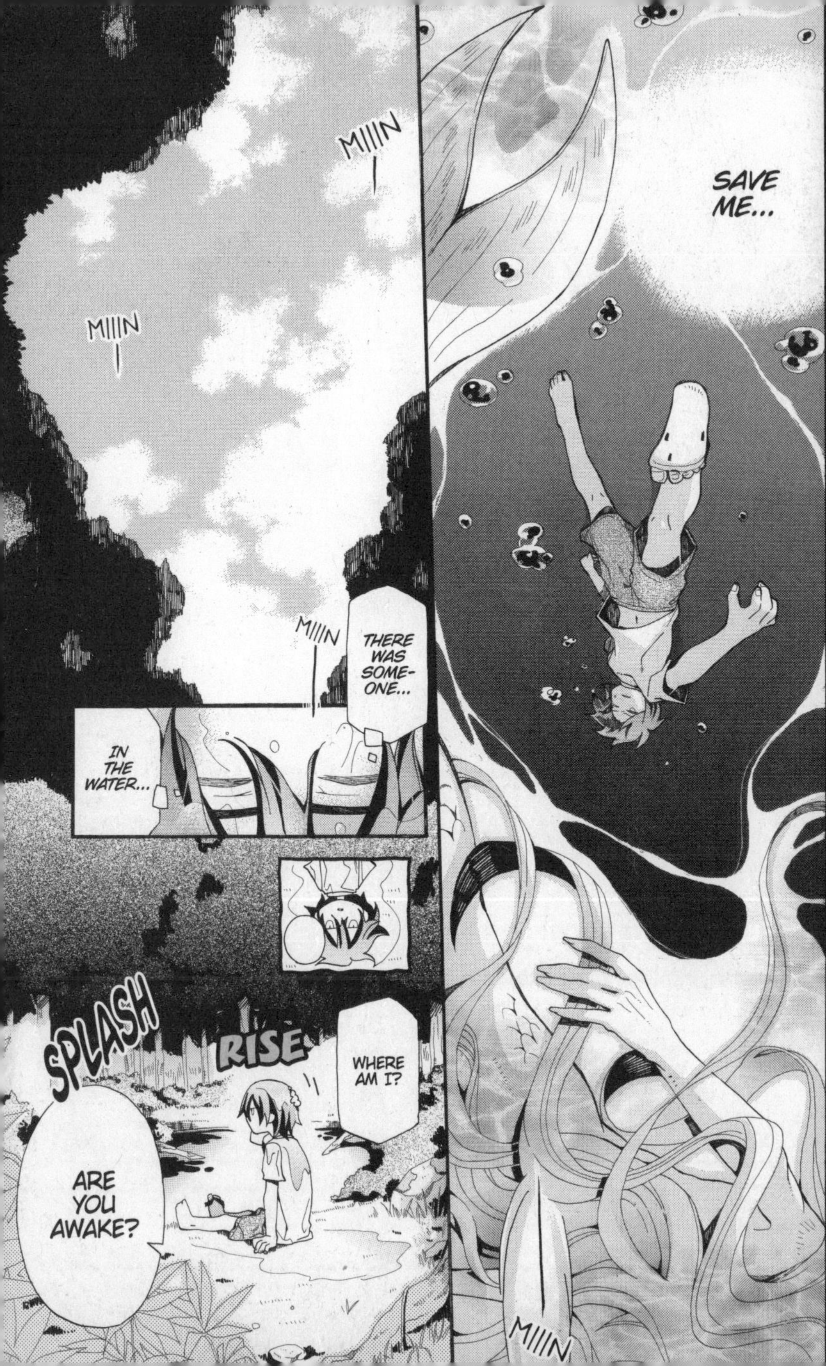
SAVE ME...
MIIIN
MIIIN
MIIIN
MIIIN
THERE WAS SOME-ONE...
IN THE WATER...
WHERE AM I?
RISE
SPLASH
ARE YOU AWAKE?

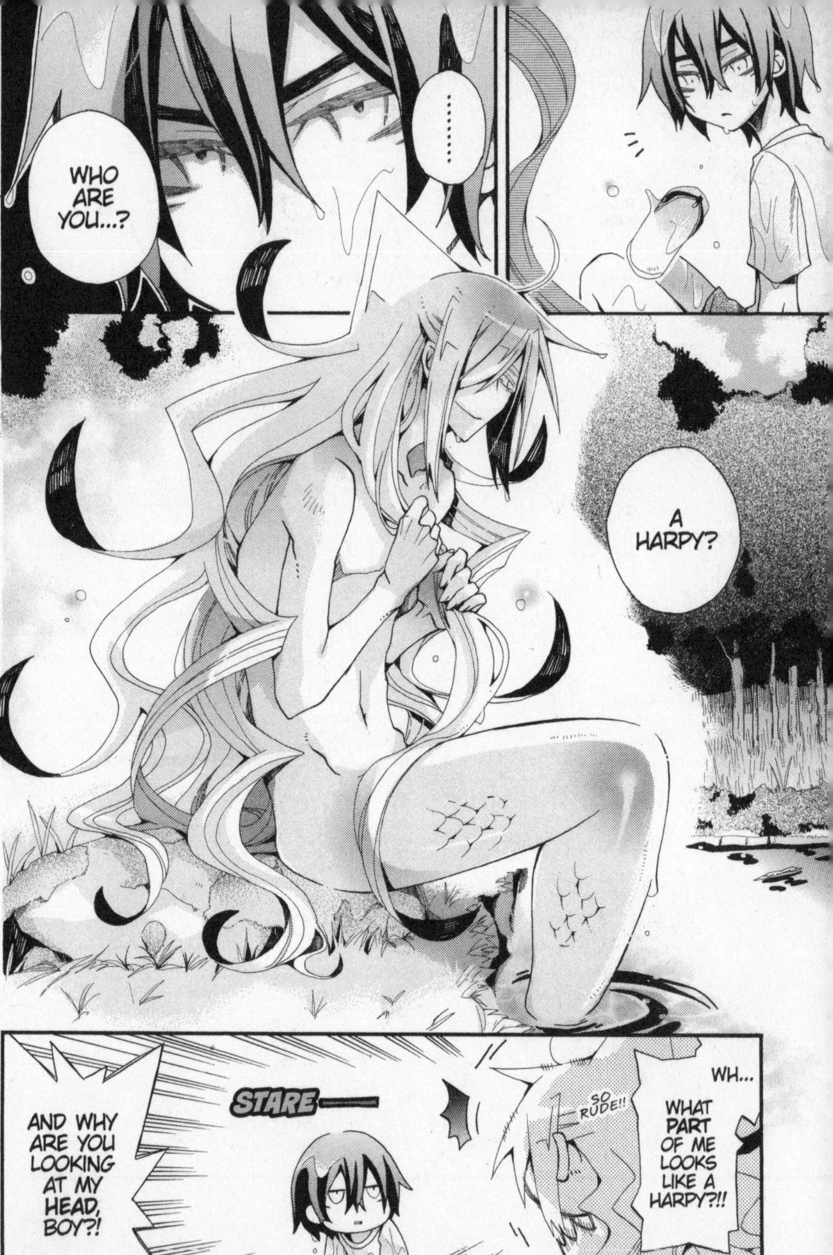
......
WHO ARE YOU...?
A HARPY?
WH...
WHAT PART OF ME LOOKS LIKE A HARPY?!!
SO RUDE!!
STARE——
AND WHY ARE YOU LOOKING AT MY HEAD, BOY?!

CHAPTER 60
THEIR FIRST MEETING (PART 2)

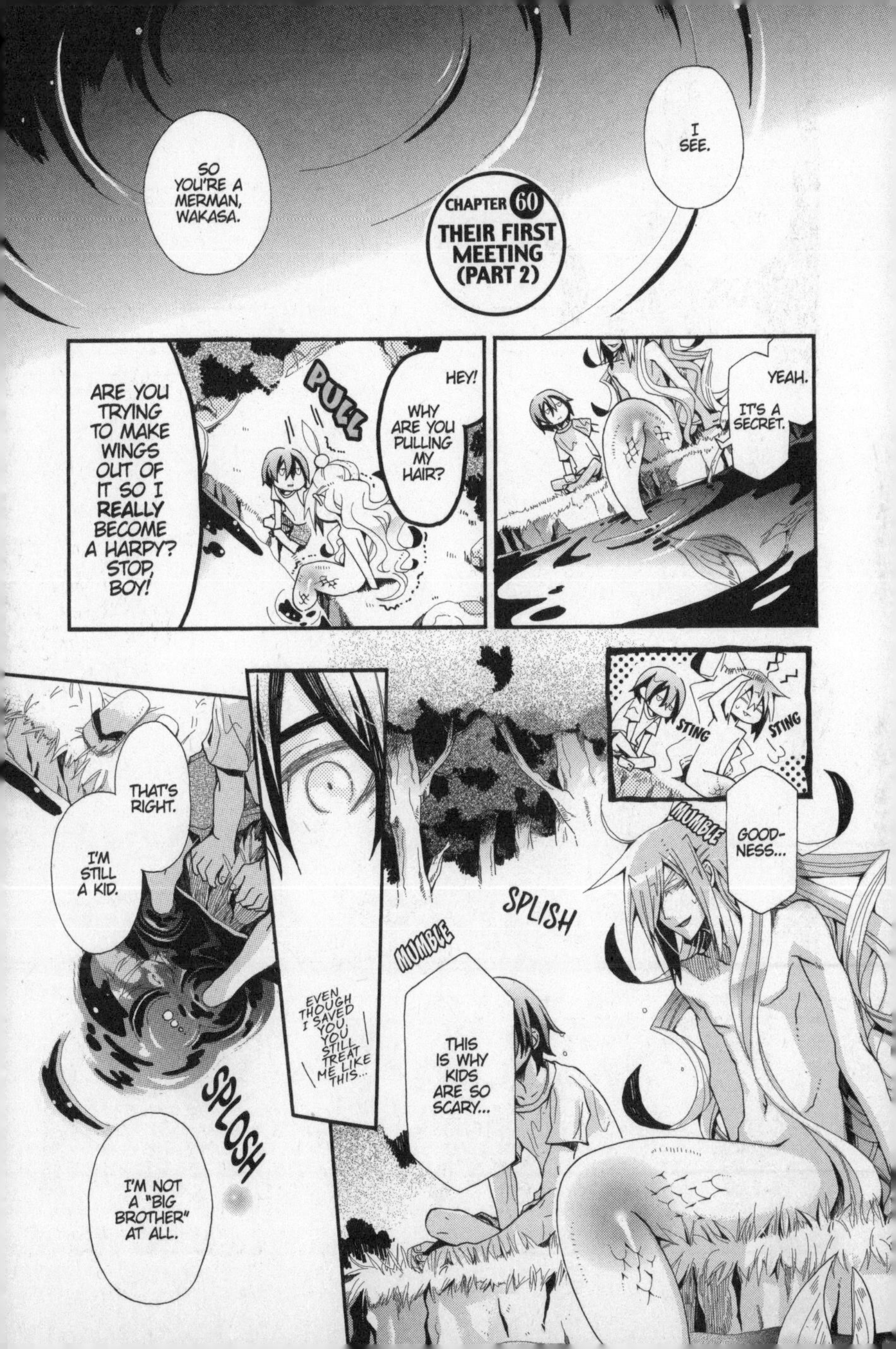
I SEE.
SO YOU'RE A MERMAN, WAKASA.
YEAH.
IT'S A SECRET.
HEY!
WHY ARE YOU PULLING MY HAIR?
PULL
ARE YOU TRYING TO MAKE WINGS OUT OF IT SO I REALLY BECOME A HARPY? STOP, BOY!
STING
STING
GOOD-NESS...
MUMBLE
SPLISH
MUMBLE
THIS IS WHY KIDS ARE SO SCARY...
EVEN THOUGH I SAVED YOU, YOU STILL TREAT ME LIKE THIS...
THAT'S RIGHT.
I'M STILL A KID.
SPLOSH
I'M NOT A "BIG BROTHER" AT ALL.

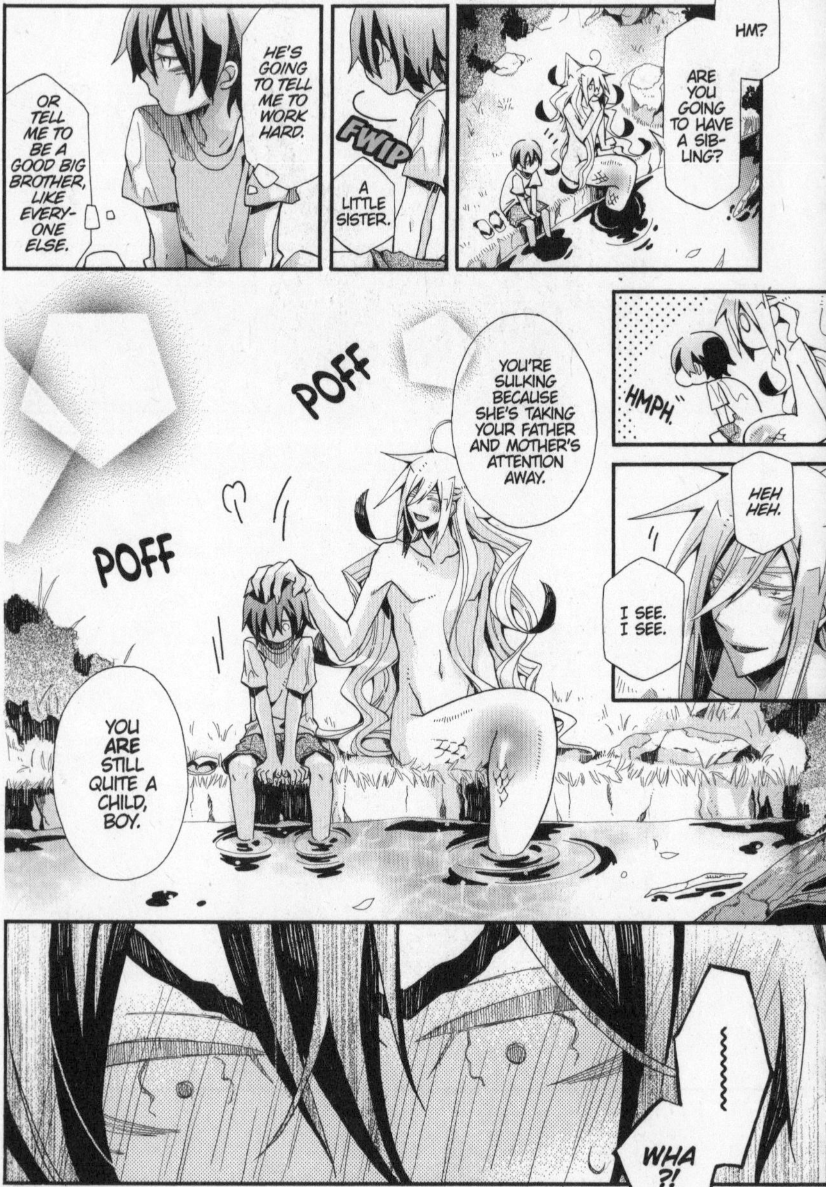
HM?
ARE YOU GOING TO HAVE A SIB-LING?
FWIP
A LITTLE SISTER.
HE'S GOING TO TELL ME TO WORK HARD.
OR TELL ME TO BE A GOOD BIG BROTHER, LIKE EVERY-ONE ELSE.
HMPH.
HEH HEH.
I SEE. I SEE.
YOU'RE SULKING BECAUSE SHE'S TAKING YOUR FATHER AND MOTHER'S ATTENTION AWAY.
POFF
POFF
YOU ARE STILL QUITE A CHILD, BOY.
......
WHA ?!

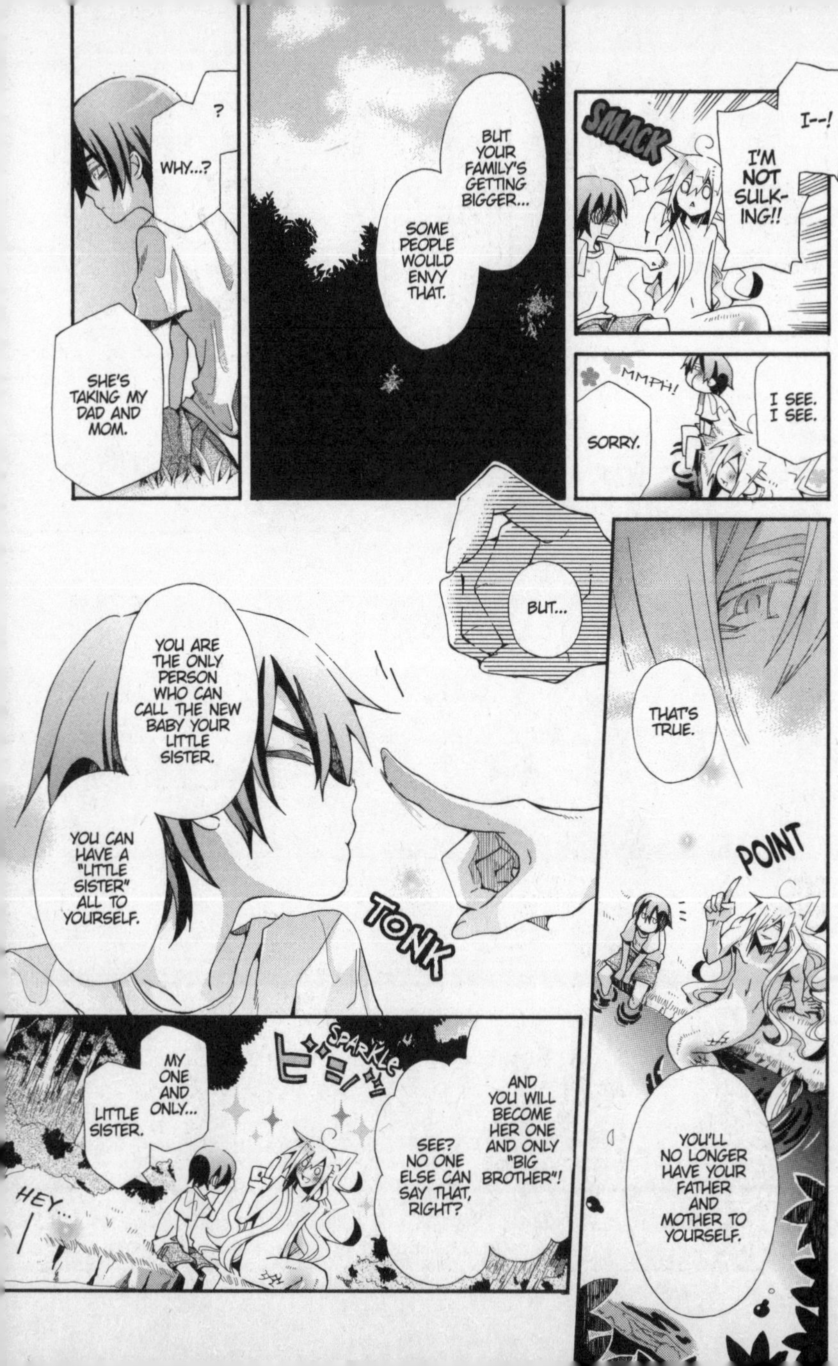
SMACK
I--!
I'M NOT SULKING!!
I SEE. I SEE.
MMPH!
SORRY.
BUT YOUR FAMILY'S GETTING BIGGER...
SOME PEOPLE WOULD ENVY THAT.
?
WHY...?
SHE'S TAKING MY DAD AND MOM.
THAT'S TRUE.
POINT
YOU'LL NO LONGER HAVE YOUR FATHER AND MOTHER TO YOURSELF.
BUT...
YOU ARE THE ONLY PERSON WHO CAN CALL THE NEW BABY YOUR LITTLE SISTER.
YOU CAN HAVE A "LITTLE SISTER" ALL TO YOURSELF.
TONK
AND YOU WILL BECOME HER ONE AND ONLY "BIG BROTHER"!
SEE? NO ONE ELSE CAN SAY THAT, RIGHT?
SPARKLE
MY ONE AND ONLY...
LITTLE SISTER.
HEY...

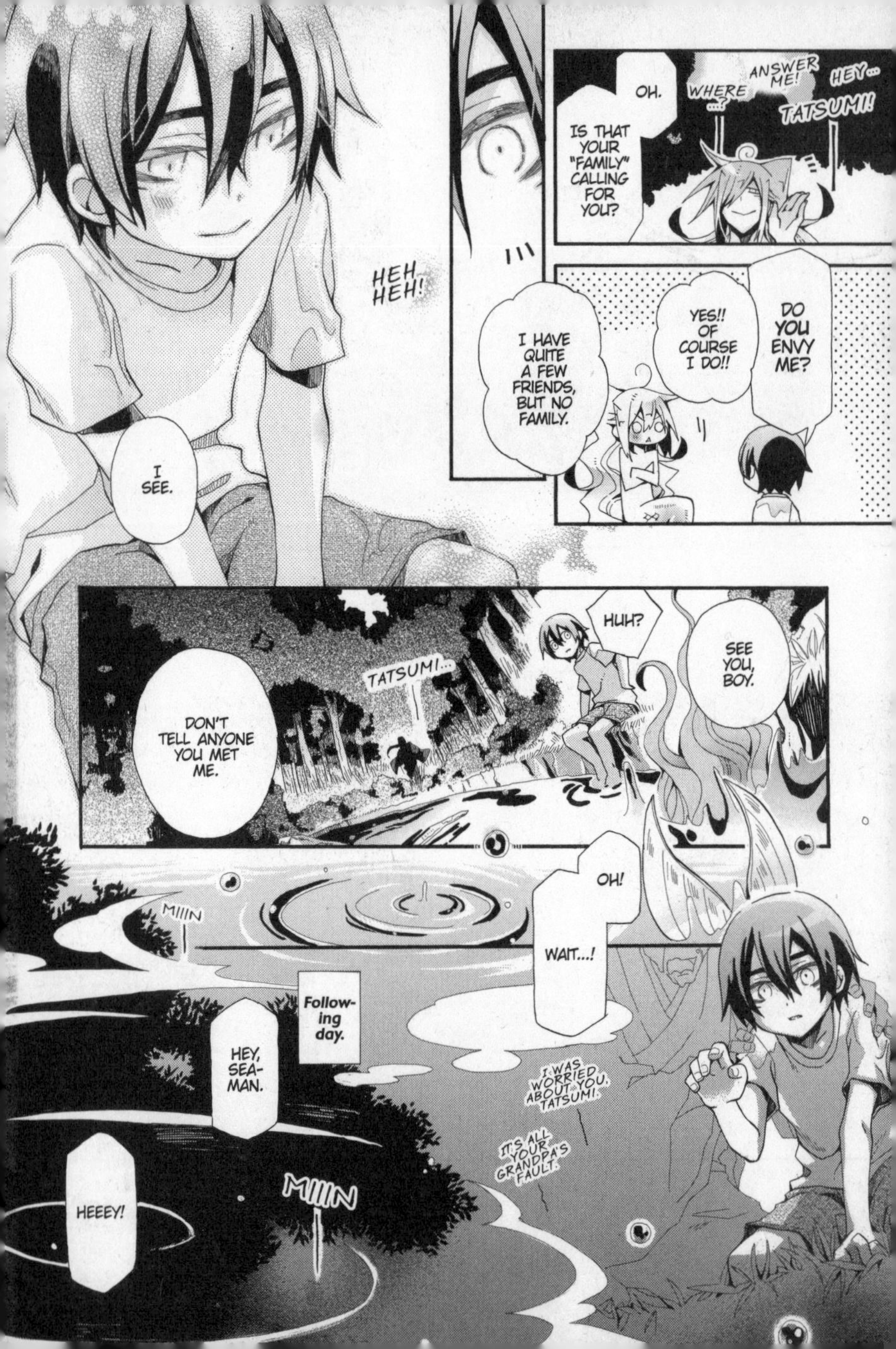
HEY... TATSUMI!
ANSWER ME!
WHERE ...?
OH.
IS THAT YOUR "FAMILY" CALLING FOR YOU?
DO YOU ENVY ME?
YES!! OF COURSE I DO!!
I HAVE QUITE A FEW FRIENDS, BUT NO FAMILY.
HEH HEH!
I SEE.
SEE YOU, BOY.
HUH?
TATSUMI...
DON'T TELL ANYONE YOU MET ME.
OH!
WAIT...!
I WAS WORRIED ABOUT YOU, TATSUMI.
IT'S ALL YOUR GRANDPA'S FAULT.
MIIIN
Follow-ing day.
HEY, SEA-MAN.
MIIIN
HEEEY!

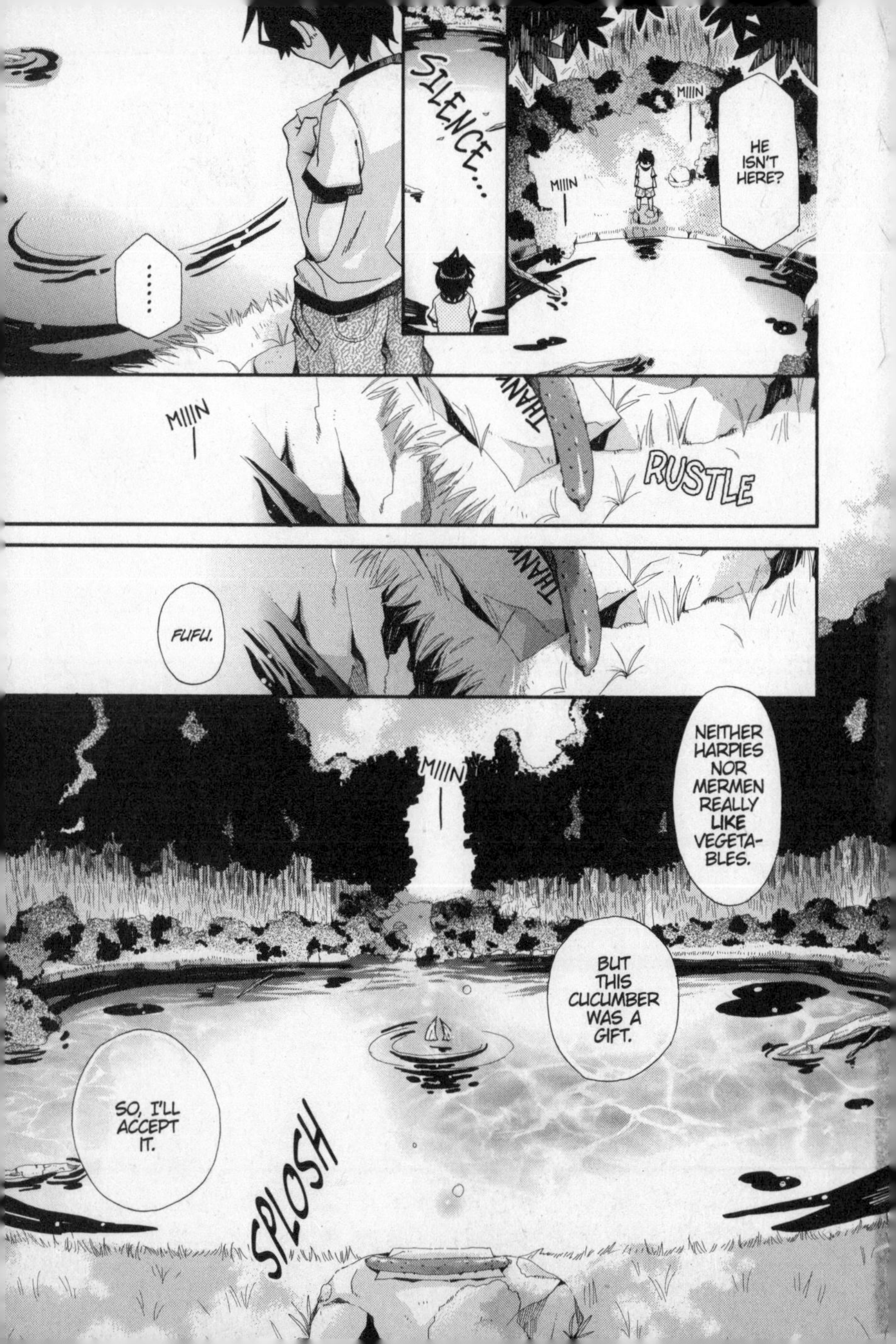
MIIIN
HE ISN'T HERE?
MIIIN
SILENCE...
......
RUSTLE
MIIIN
FUFU.
NEITHER HARPIES NOR MERMEN REALLY LIKE VEGETA-BLES.
MIIIN
BUT THIS CUCUMBER WAS A GIFT.
SO, I'LL ACCEPT IT.
SPLOSH

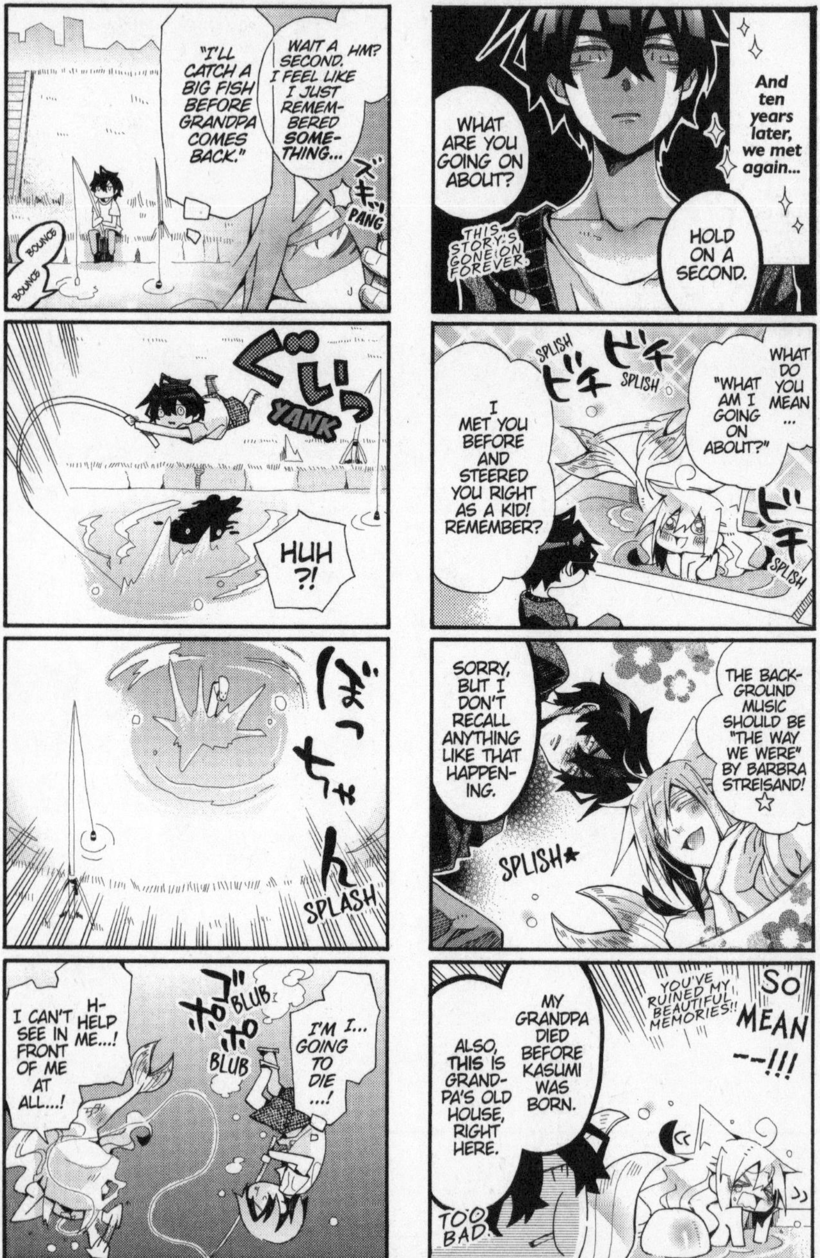
And ten years later, we met again...
HOLD ON A SECOND.
WHAT ARE YOU GOING ON ABOUT?
THIS STORY'S GONE ON FOREVER.
WHAT DO YOU MEAN ... "WHAT AM I GOING ON ABOUT?"
ビチビチ SPLISH SPLISH
I MET YOU BEFORE AND STEERED YOU RIGHT AS A KID! REMEMBER?
ビチ SPLISH
THE BACKGROUND MUSIC SHOULD BE "THE WAY WE WERE" BY BARBRA STREISAND! ☆
SORRY, BUT I DON'T RECALL ANYTHING LIKE THAT HAPPENING.
SPLISH★
So MEAN--!!!
YOU'VE RUINED MY BEAUTIFUL MEMORIES!!
MY GRANDPA DIED BEFORE KASUMI WAS BORN.
ALSO, THIS IS GRANDPA'S OLD HOUSE, RIGHT HERE.
TOO BAD.
HM? WAIT A SECOND. I FEEL LIKE I JUST REMEMBERED SOMETHING...
ズキッ PANG
"I'LL CATCH A BIG FISH BEFORE GRANDPA COMES BACK."
BOUNCE BOUNCE BOUNCE
ぐいっ YANK
HUH?!
ぼっちゃん SPLASH
I... I'M GOING TO DIE...!
ゴボゴボ BLUB BLUB
H-HELP ME...!
I CAN'T SEE IN FRONT OF ME AT ALL...!

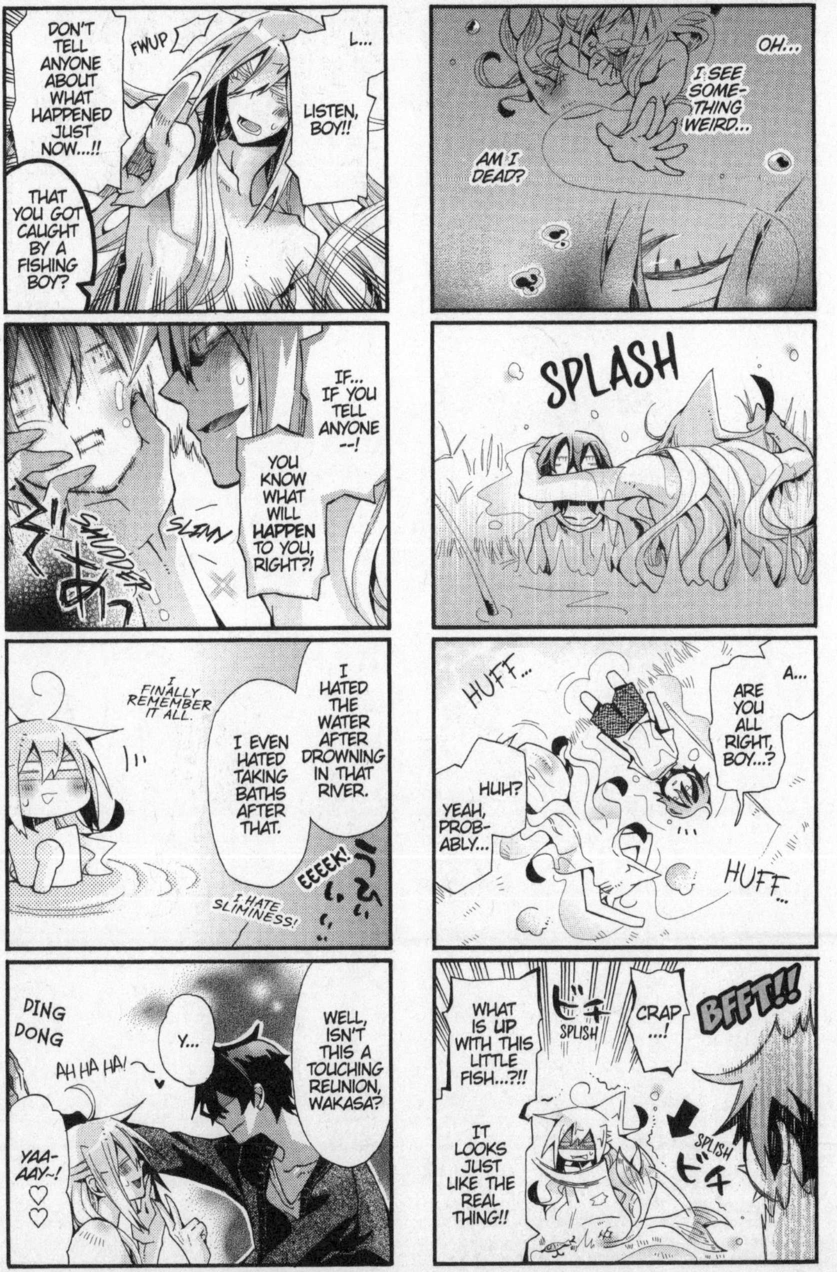
OH...
I SEE SOME-THING WEIRD...
AM I DEAD?
SPLASH
HUFF...
A...
ARE YOU ALL RIGHT, BOY...?
HUH? YEAH, PROB-ABLY...
HUFF...
BFFT!!
CRAP...!
ビチ
SPLISH
WHAT IS UP WITH THIS LITTLE FISH...?!!
IT LOOKS JUST LIKE THE REAL THING!!
SPLISH
ビチ
L...
LISTEN, BOY!!
FWUP
DON'T TELL ANYONE ABOUT WHAT HAPPENED JUST NOW...!!
THAT YOU GOT CAUGHT BY A FISHING BOY?
IF... IF YOU TELL ANYONE --!
YOU KNOW WHAT WILL HAPPEN TO YOU, RIGHT?!
SLIMY
SHUDDER
I HATED THE WATER AFTER DROWNING IN THAT RIVER.
I EVEN HATED TAKING BATHS AFTER THAT.
I FINALLY REMEMBER IT ALL.
EEEEK!
I HATE SLIMINESS!
WELL, ISN'T THIS A TOUCHING REUNION, WAKASA?
Y...
DING DONG
AH HA HA!~
YAAA-AAY~! ♡ ♡

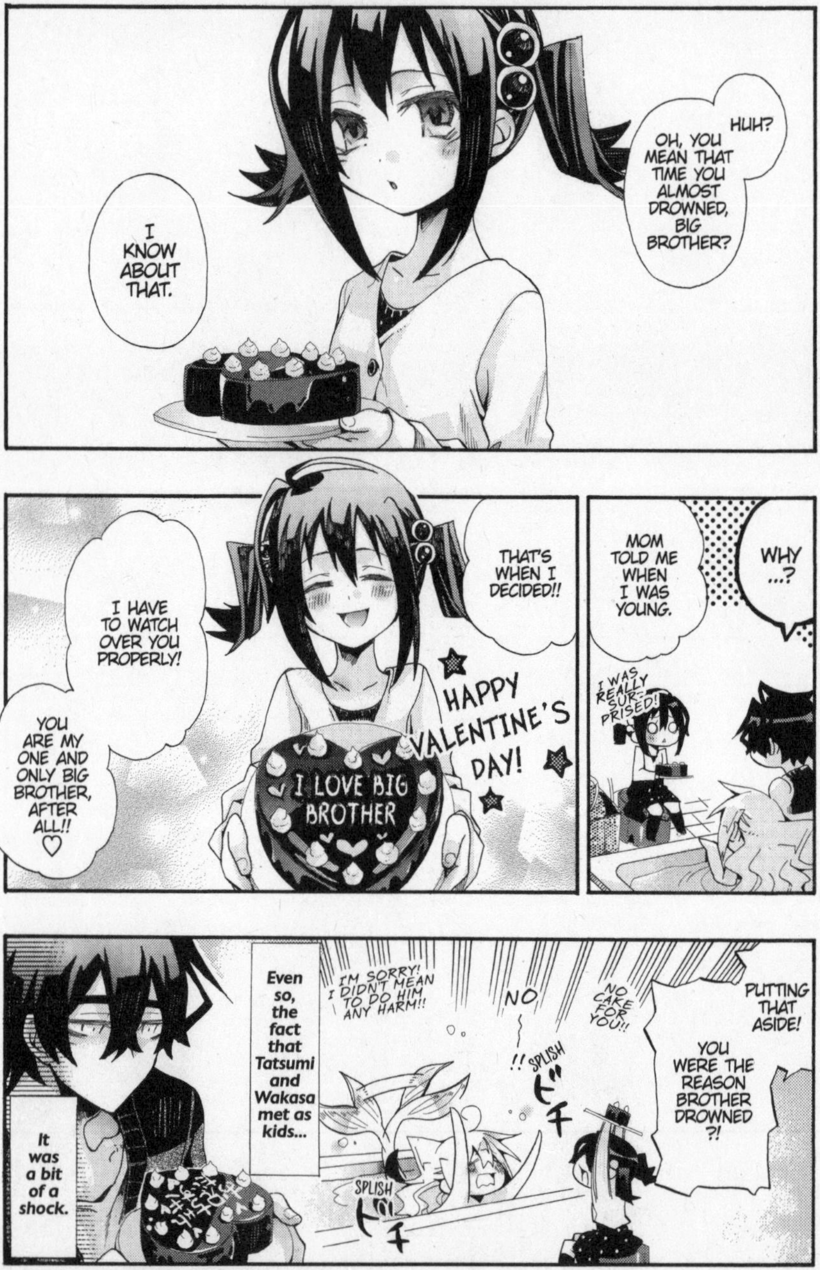
HUH? OH, YOU MEAN THAT TIME YOU ALMOST DROWNED, BIG BROTHER?
I KNOW ABOUT THAT.
WHY ...?
MOM TOLD ME WHEN I WAS YOUNG.
I WAS REALLY SUR-PRISED!
THAT'S WHEN I DECIDED!!
I HAVE TO WATCH OVER YOU PROPERLY!
YOU ARE MY ONE AND ONLY BIG BROTHER, AFTER ALL!! ♡
HAPPY VALENTINE'S DAY!
I LOVE BIG BROTHER
PUTTING THAT ASIDE!
YOU WERE THE REASON BROTHER DROWNED ?!
NO CAKE FOR YOU!!
NO
!! SPLISH
I'M SORRY! I DIDN'T MEAN TO DO HIM ANY HARM!!
SPLISH
Even so, the fact that Tatsumi and Wakasa met as kids...
It was a bit of a shock.

Merman
My Tub

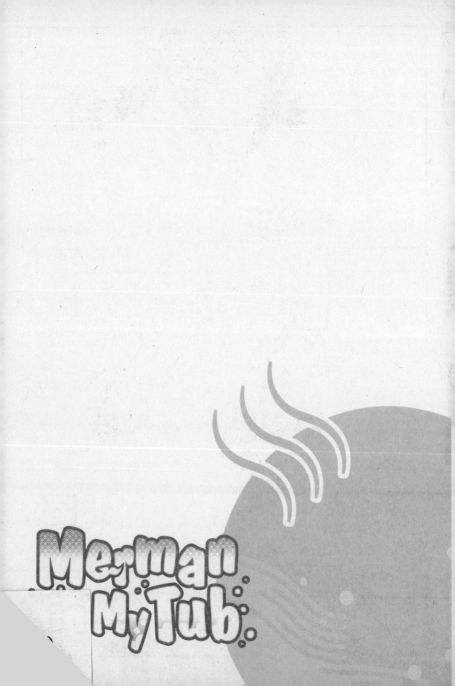

オレん家のフロ事情

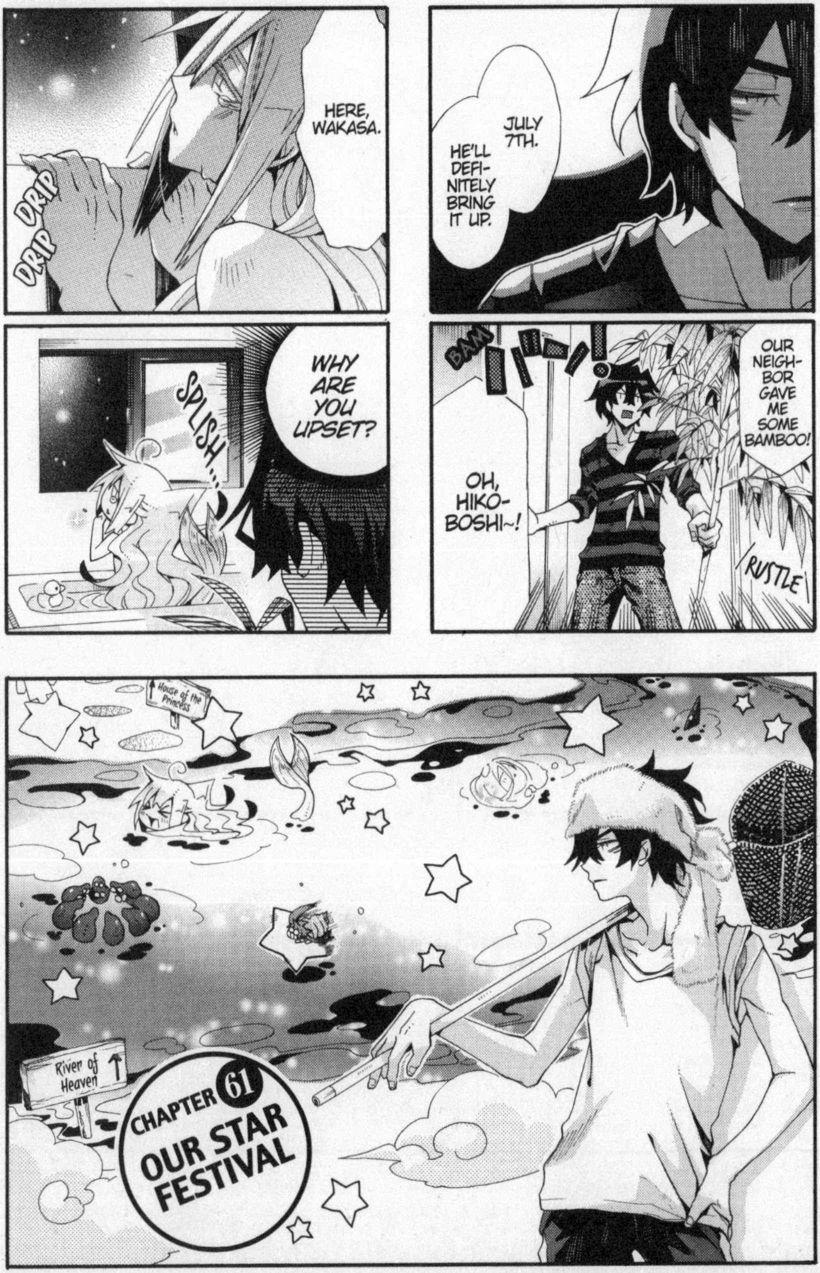
JULY 7TH.
HE'LL DEFINITELY BRING IT UP.
HERE, WAKASA.
DRIP DRIP
OUR NEIGHBOR GAVE ME SOME BAMBOO!
BAM
OH, HIKOBOSHI~!
RUSTLE
WHY ARE YOU UPSET?
SPLISH...
House of the Princess
River of Heaven
CHAPTER 61
OUR STAR FESTIVAL

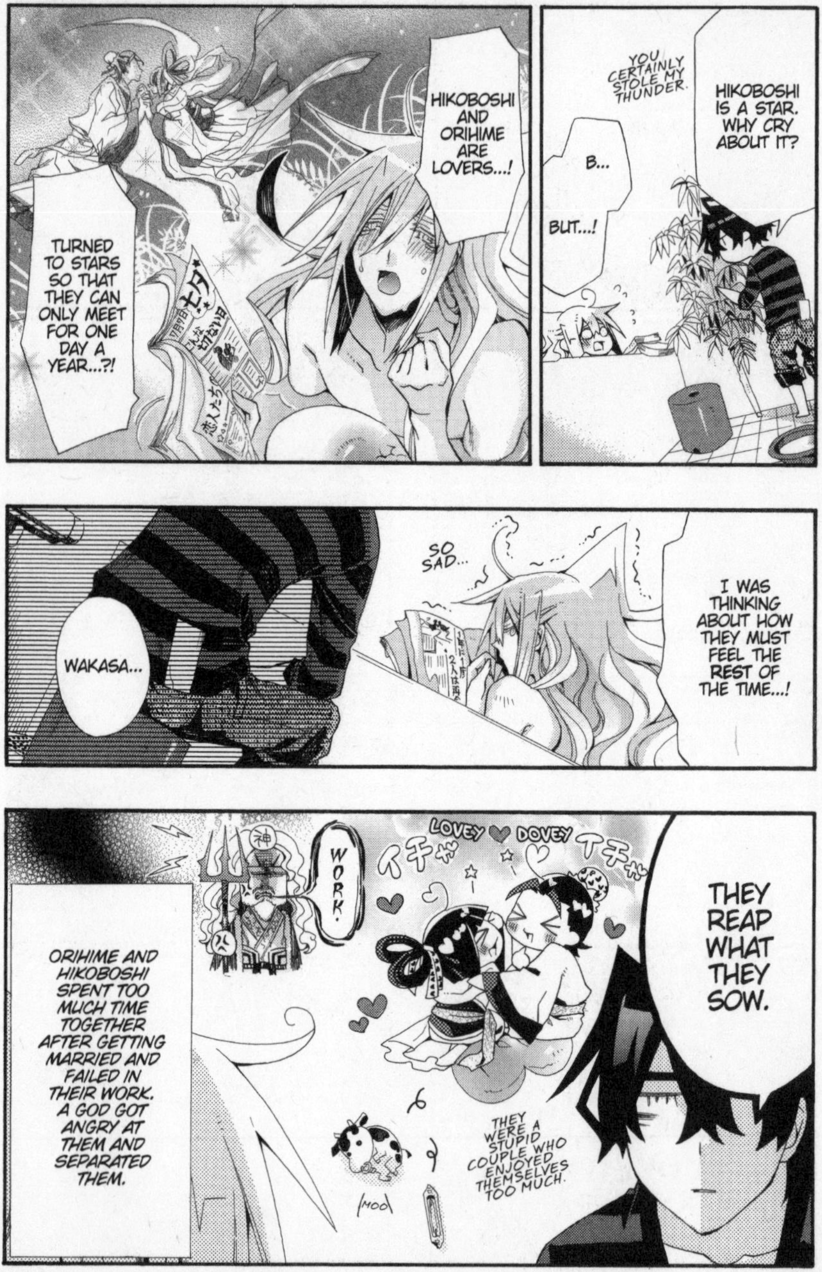
HIKOBOSHI IS A STAR. WHY CRY ABOUT IT?
YOU CERTAINLY STOLE MY THUNDER.
B...
BUT...!
HIKOBOSHI AND ORIHIME ARE LOVERS...!
TURNED TO STARS SO THAT THEY CAN ONLY MEET FOR ONE DAY A YEAR...?!
I WAS THINKING ABOUT HOW THEY MUST FEEL THE REST OF THE TIME...!
SO SAD...
WAKASA...
THEY REAP WHAT THEY SOW.
LOVEY ♥ DOVEY
イチャ イチャ
神
WORK.
THEY WERE A STUPID COUPLE WHO ENJOYED THEMSELVES TOO MUCH.
MOO
ORIHIME AND HIKOBOSHI SPENT TOO MUCH TIME TOGETHER AFTER GETTING MARRIED AND FAILED IN THEIR WORK. A GOD GOT ANGRY AT THEM AND SEPARATED THEM.

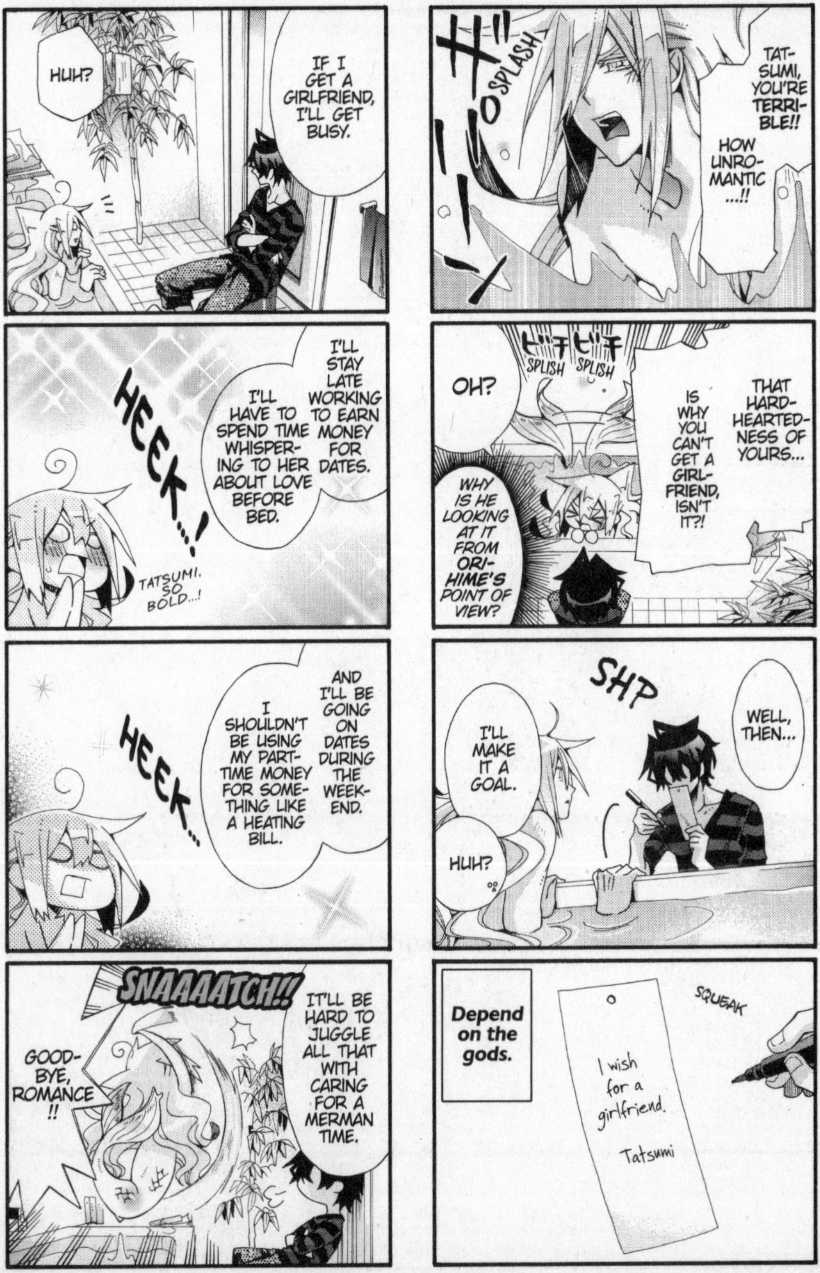

SPLASH
TAT-SUMI, YOU'RE TERRI-BLE!!
HOW UNRO-MANTIC ...!!
ビチビチ
SPLISH SPLISH
OH?
THAT HARD-HEARTED-NESS OF YOURS...
IS WHY YOU CAN'T GET A GIRL-FRIEND, ISN'T IT?!
WHY IS HE LOOKING AT IT FROM ORI-HIME'S POINT OF VIEW?
SHP
WELL, THEN...
I'LL MAKE IT A GOAL.
HUH?
Depend on the gods.
SQUEAK
I wish for a girlfriend.
Tatsumi
HUH?
IF I GET A GIRLFRIEND, I'LL GET BUSY.
I'LL STAY LATE WORKING TO EARN MONEY FOR DATES.
I'LL HAVE TO SPEND TIME WHISPER-ING TO HER ABOUT LOVE BEFORE BED.
HEEK...!
TATSUMI, SO BOLD...!
AND I'LL BE GOING ON DATES DURING THE WEEK-END.
I SHOULDN'T BE USING MY PART-TIME MONEY FOR SOME-THING LIKE A HEATING BILL.
HEEK...
SNAAAATCH!!
IT'LL BE HARD TO JUGGLE ALL THAT WITH CARING FOR A MERMAN TIME.
GOOD-BYE, ROMANCE !!

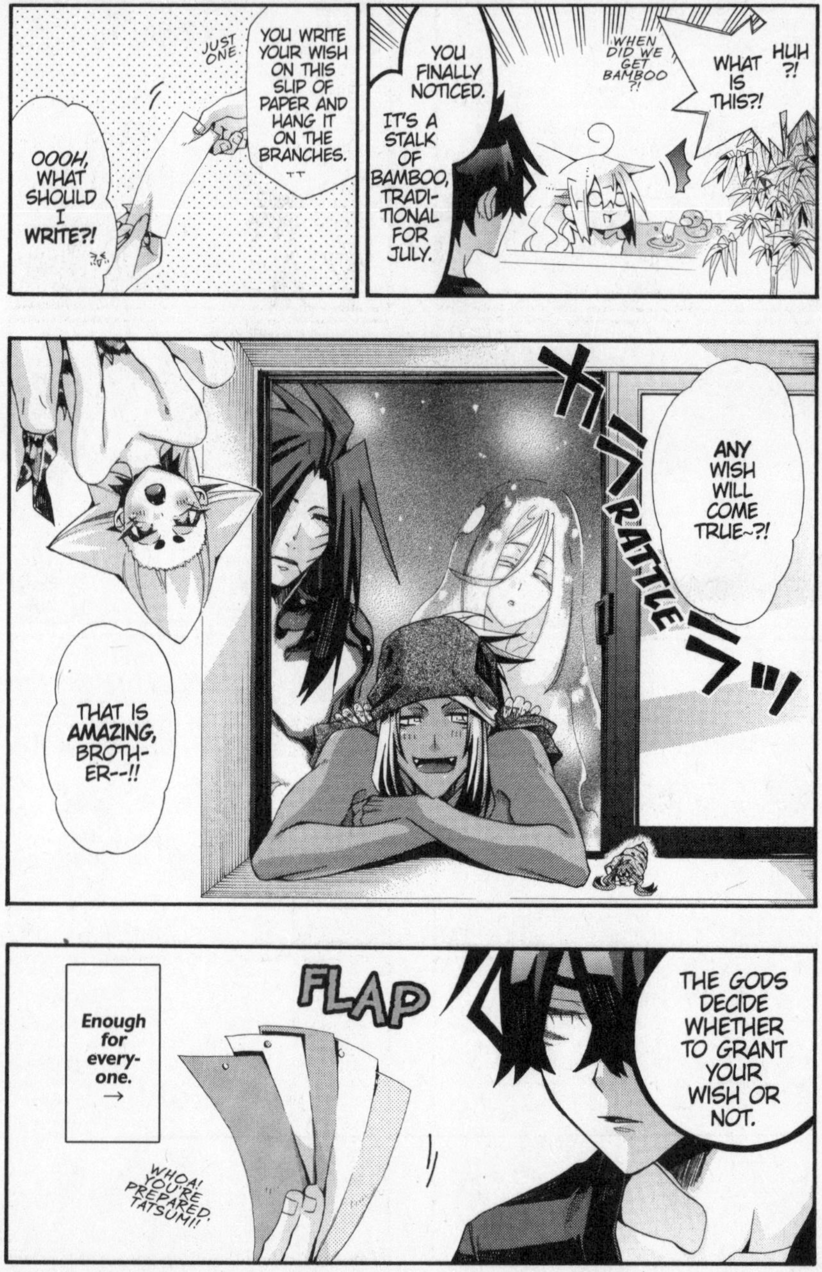
HUH?!
WHAT IS THIS?!
WHEN DID WE GET BAMBOO?!
YOU FINALLY NOTICED.
IT'S A STALK OF BAMBOO, TRADITIONAL FOR JULY.
YOU WRITE YOUR WISH ON THIS SLIP OF PAPER AND HANG IT ON THE BRANCHES.
JUST ONE.
OOOH, WHAT SHOULD I WRITE?!
ANY WISH WILL COME TRUE~?!
RATTLE
THAT IS AMAZING, BROTHER--!!
THE GODS DECIDE WHETHER TO GRANT YOUR WISH OR NOT.
FLAP
Enough for everyone. →
WHOA! YOU'RE PREPARED, TATSUMI!

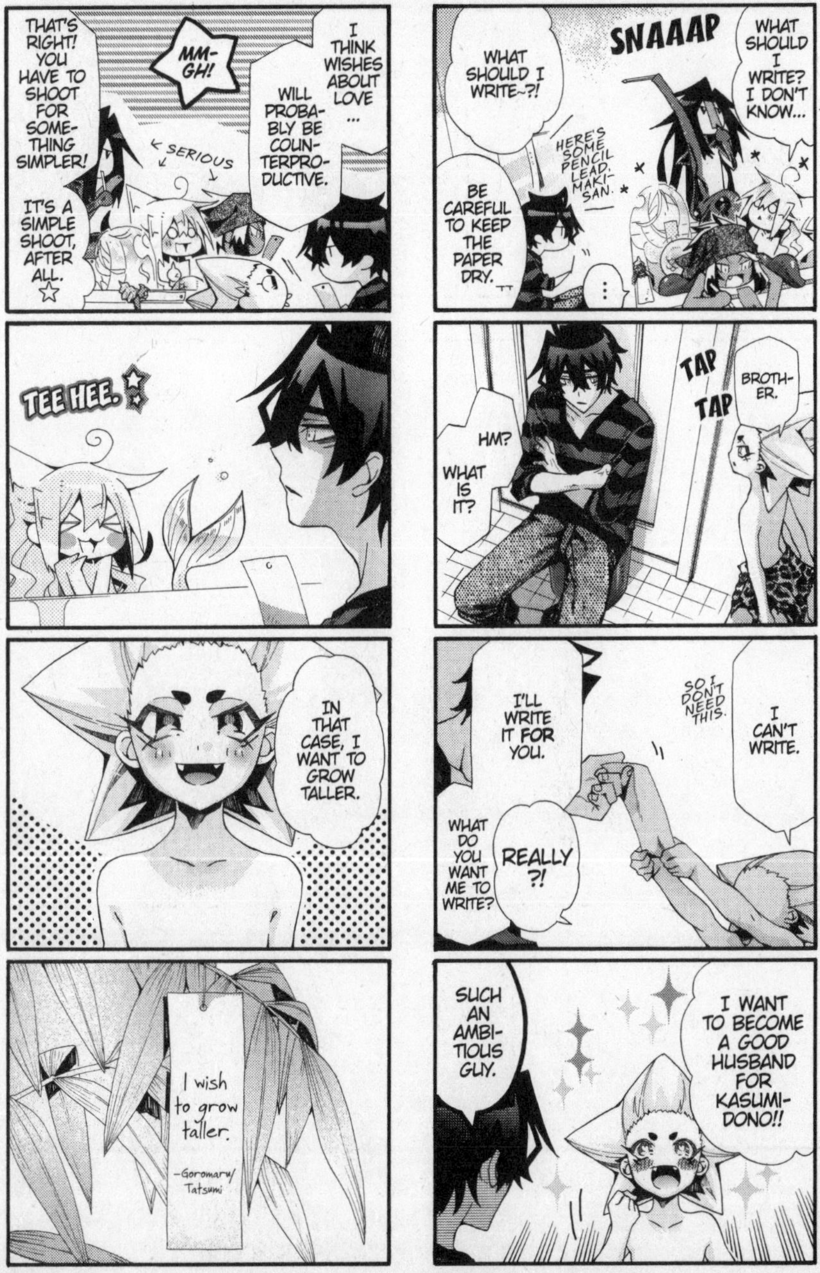
WHAT SHOULD I WRITE? I DON'T KNOW...
SNAAAP
WHAT SHOULD I WRITE~?!
HERE'S SOME PENCIL LEAD, MAKI-SAN.
BE CAREFUL TO KEEP THE PAPER DRY.
...
I THINK WISHES ABOUT LOVE...
WILL PROBABLY BE COUNTERPRODUCTIVE.
MM-GH!
THAT'S RIGHT! YOU HAVE TO SHOOT FOR SOMETHING SIMPLER!
SERIOUS
IT'S A SIMPLE SHOOT, AFTER ALL. ☆
TAP
TAP
BROTHER.
HM?
WHAT IS IT?
TEE HEE.
I CAN'T WRITE.
SO I DON'T NEED THIS.
I'LL WRITE IT FOR YOU.
REALLY?!
WHAT DO YOU WANT ME TO WRITE?
IN THAT CASE, I WANT TO GROW TALLER.
I WANT TO BECOME A GOOD HUSBAND FOR KASUMI-DONO!!
SUCH AN AMBITIOUS GUY.
I wish to grow taller.
—Goromaru/Tatsumi

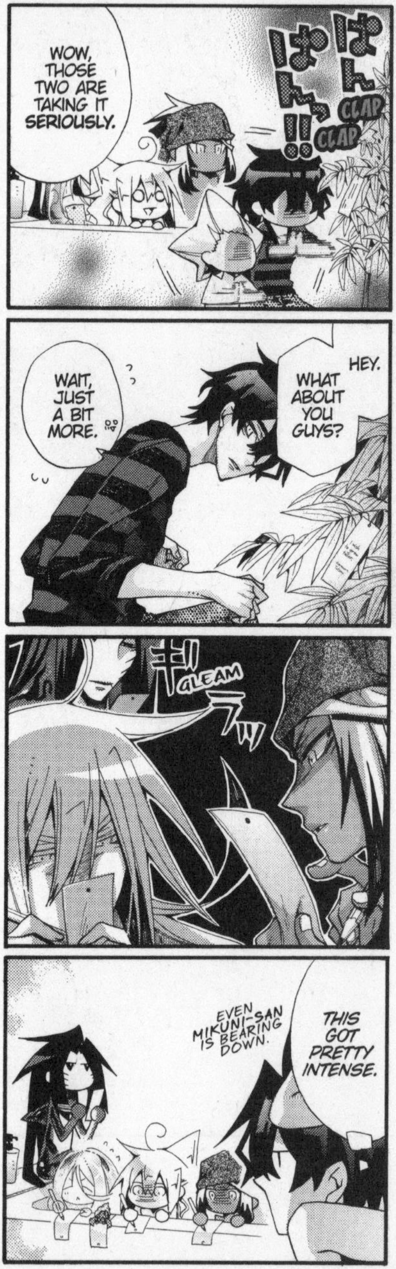
ぱんぱんっ!!
CLAP
CLAP
WOW, THOSE TWO ARE TAKING IT SERIOUSLY.
HEY. WHAT ABOUT YOU GUYS?
WAIT, JUST A BIT MORE.
ギラッ
GLEAM
THIS GOT PRETTY INTENSE.
EVEN MIKUNI-SAN IS BEARING DOWN.
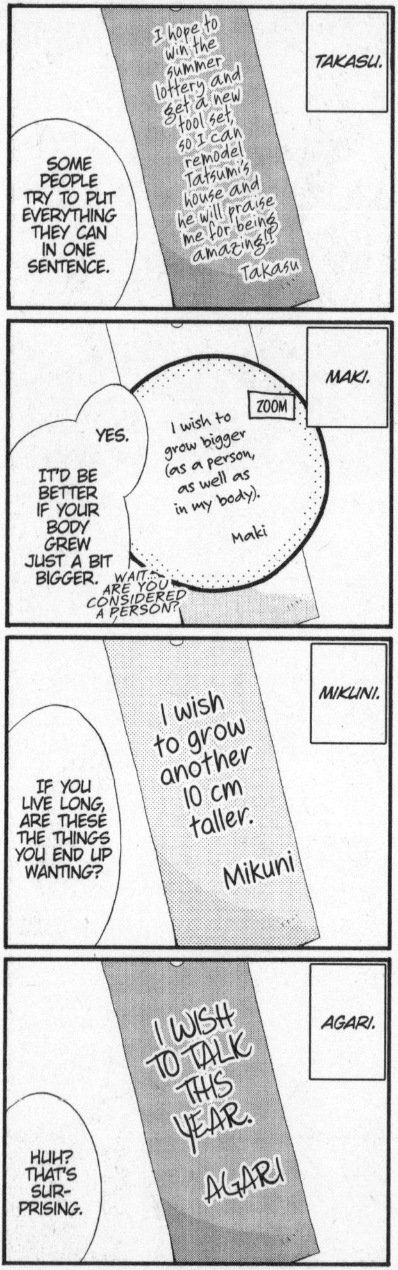
TAKASU.
I hope to win the summer lottery and get a new tool set, so I can remodel Tatsumi's house and he will praise me for being amazing!!
Takasu
SOME PEOPLE TRY TO PUT EVERYTHING THEY CAN IN ONE SENTENCE.
MAKI.
ZOOM
I wish to grow bigger (as a person, as well as in my body).
Maki
YES.
IT'D BE BETTER IF YOUR BODY GREW JUST A BIT BIGGER.
WAIT... ARE YOU CONSIDERED A PERSON?
MIKUNI.
I wish to grow another 10 cm taller.
Mikuni
IF YOU LIVE LONG, ARE THESE THE THINGS YOU END UP WANTING?
AGARI.
I WISH TO TALK THIS YEAR.
AGARI
HUH? THAT'S SUR-PRISING.

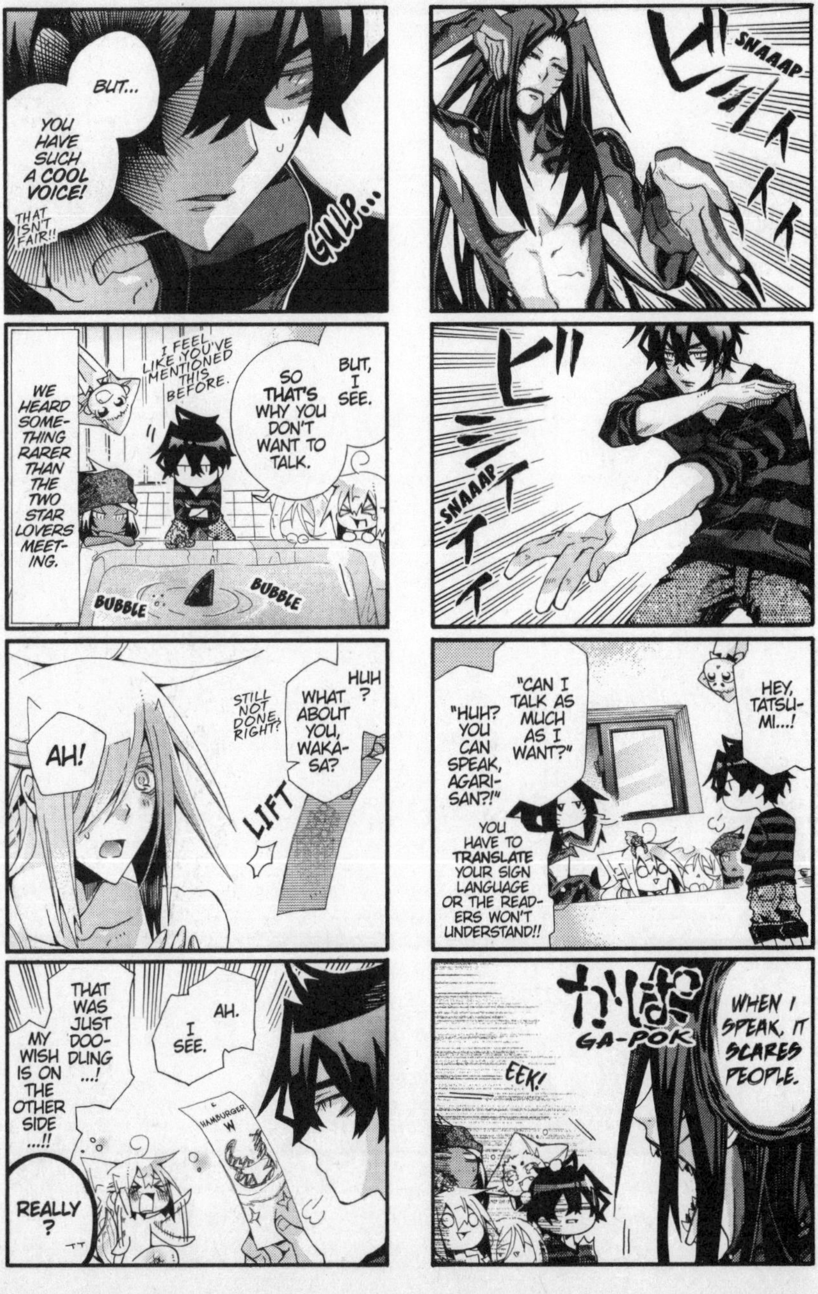

SNAAAP
SNAAAP
HEY, TATSUMI...!
"CAN I TALK AS MUCH AS I WANT?"
"HUH? YOU CAN SPEAK, AGARI-SAN?!"
YOU HAVE TO TRANSLATE YOUR SIGN LANGUAGE OR THE READERS WON'T UNDERSTAND!!
GA-POK
WHEN I SPEAK, IT SCARES PEOPLE.
EEK!
BUT... YOU HAVE SUCH A COOL VOICE!
THAT ISN'T FAIR!!
GULP...
BUT, I SEE.
SO THAT'S WHY YOU DON'T WANT TO TALK.
I FEEL LIKE YOU'VE MENTIONED THIS BEFORE.
WE HEARD SOMETHING RARER THAN THE TWO STAR LOVERS MEETING.
BUBBLE
BUBBLE
HUH?
WHAT ABOUT YOU, WAKASA?
STILL NOT DONE, RIGHT?
LIFT
AH!
AH. I SEE.
THAT WAS JUST DOODLING...!
MY WISH IS ON THE OTHER SIDE...!!
HAMBURGER
REALLY?

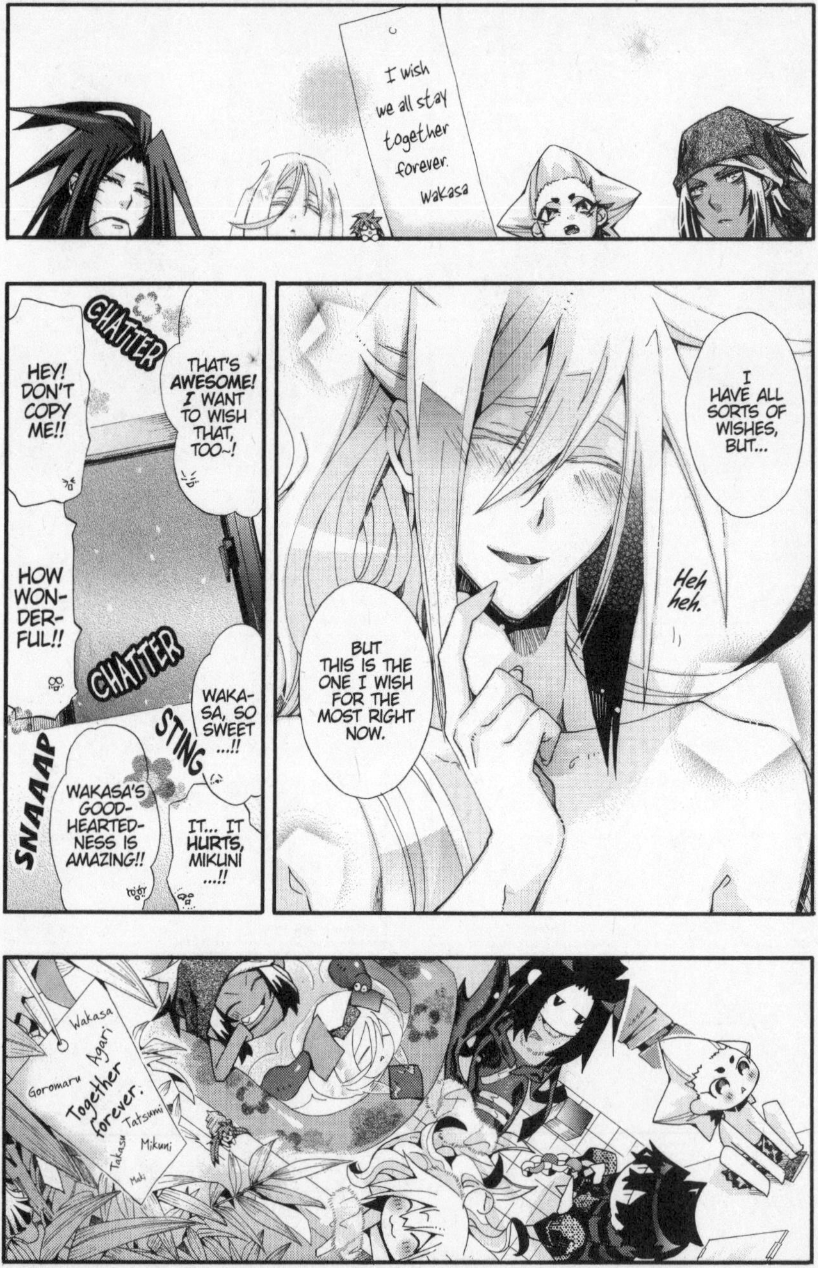
I wish we all stay together forever. Wakasa
I HAVE ALL SORTS OF WISHES, BUT...
Heh heh.
BUT THIS IS THE ONE I WISH FOR THE MOST RIGHT NOW.
THAT'S AWESOME! I WANT TO WISH THAT, TOO~!
CHATTER
HEY! DON'T COPY ME!!
WAKA-SA, SO SWEET...!!
CHATTER
HOW WON-DER-FUL!!
STING
IT... IT HURTS, MIKUNI...!!
WAKASA'S GOOD-HEARTED-NESS IS AMAZING!!
SNAAAP
Wakasa
Agari
Goromaru
Together forever.
Tatsumi
Mikuni
Takasu
Maki

Merman in My Tub

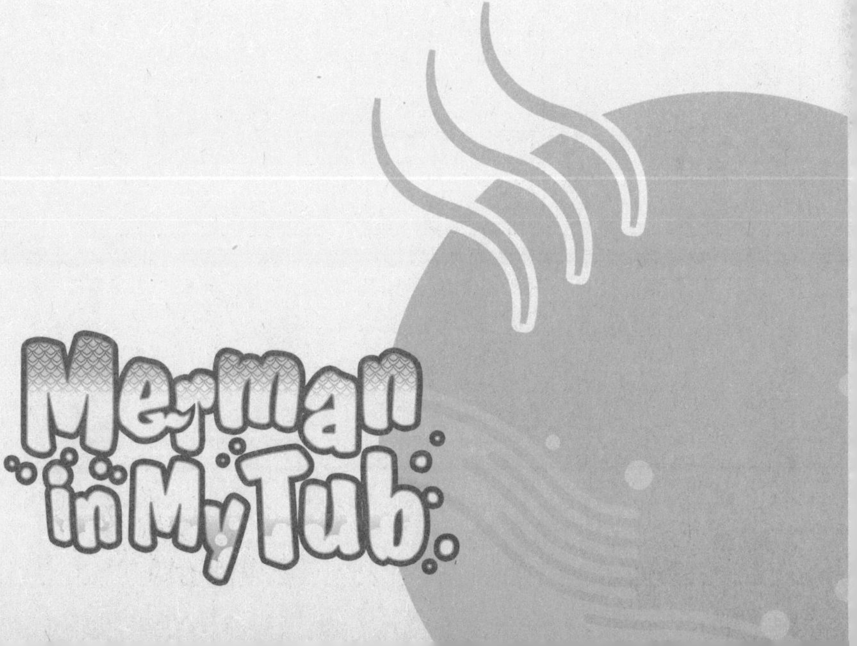

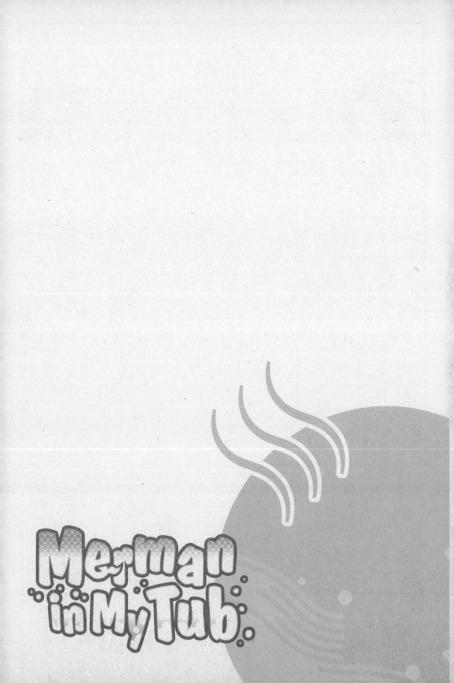

オレんち家のフロ事情

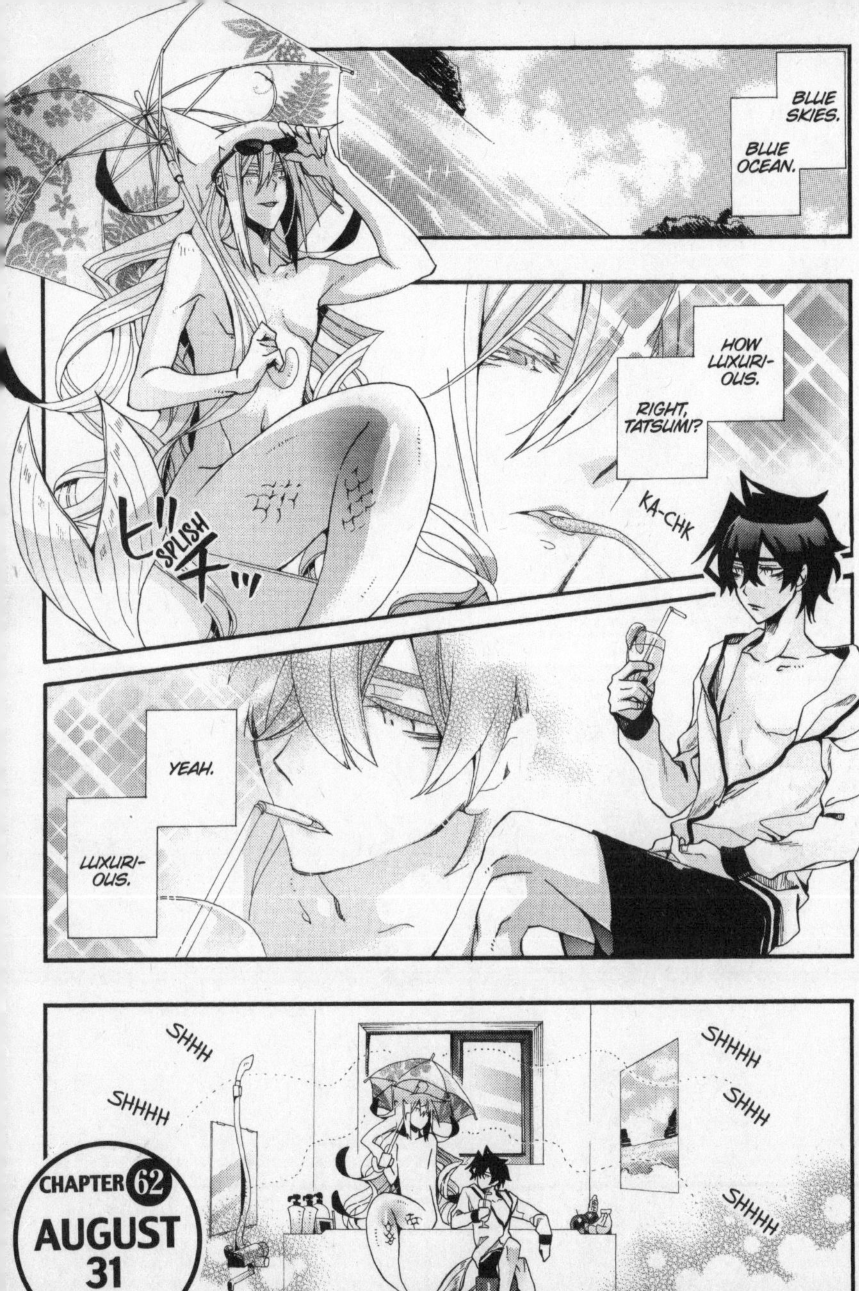
BLUE SKIES.
BLUE OCEAN.
HOW LUXURI-OUS.
RIGHT, TATSUMI?
KA-CHK
SPLISH
YEAH.
LUXURI-OUS.
SHHHH
SHHH
SHHHH
SHHH
SHHHH
CHAPTER 62
AUGUST 31

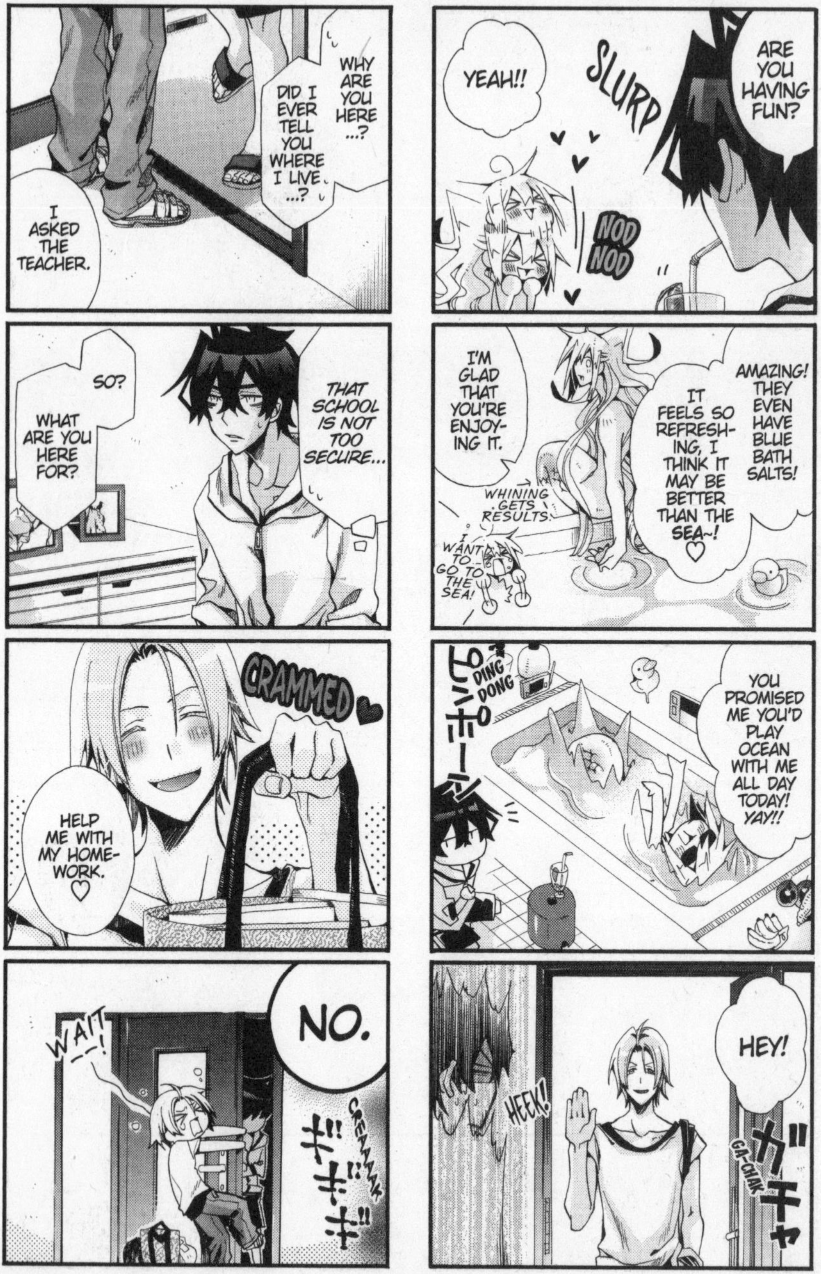
ARE YOU HAVING FUN?
SLURP
YEAH!!
NOD NOD
AMAZING! THEY EVEN HAVE BLUE BATH SALTS!
IT FEELS SO REFRESH-ING, I THINK IT MAY BE BETTER THAN THE SEA~! ♡
I'M GLAD THAT YOU'RE ENJOY-ING IT.
WHINING GETS RESULTS.
I WANT TO GO TO THE SEA!
YOU PROMISED ME YOU'D PLAY OCEAN WITH ME ALL DAY TODAY! YAY!!
ピンポーン
DING DONG
HEY!
ガチャ
GA-CHAK
HEEK!
WHY ARE YOU HERE ...?
DID I EVER TELL YOU WHERE I LIVE ...?
I ASKED THE TEACHER.
THAT SCHOOL IS NOT TOO SECURE...
SO?
WHAT ARE YOU HERE FOR?
CRAMMED
HELP ME WITH MY HOME-WORK. ♡
NO.
ギ!! ギ!! ギ!!
CREAAAAK
WAIT—!

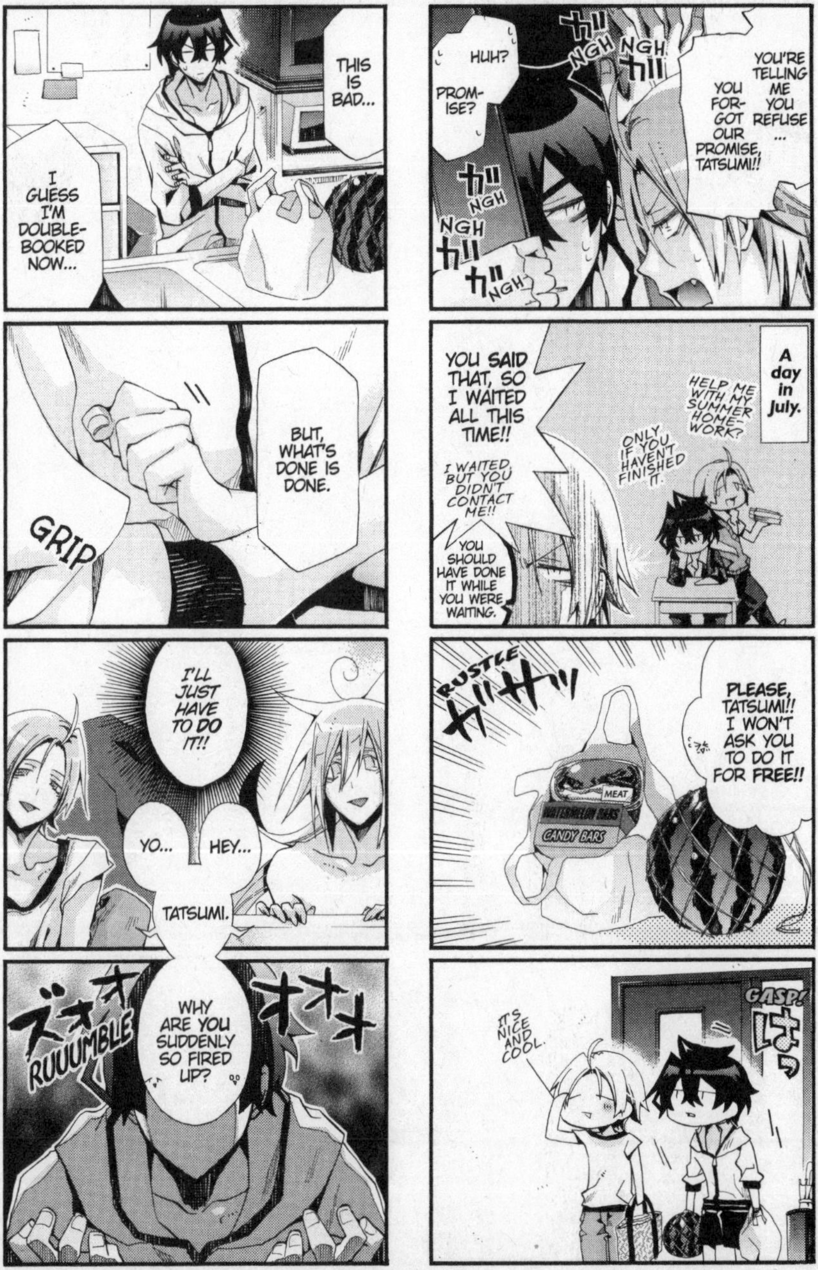
YOU'RE TELLING ME YOU REFUSE ... YOU FORGOT OUR PROMISE, TATSUMI!!
NGH NGH
HUH? PROMISE?
NGH NGH NGH
A day in July.
HELP ME WITH MY SUMMER HOMEWORK?
ONLY IF YOU HAVEN'T FINISHED IT.
YOU SAID THAT, SO I WAITED ALL THIS TIME!!
I WAITED, BUT YOU DIDN'T CONTACT ME!!
YOU SHOULD HAVE DONE IT WHILE YOU WERE WAITING.
PLEASE, TATSUMI!! I WON'T ASK YOU TO DO IT FOR FREE!!
RUSTLE
MEAT
WATERMELON BARS
CANDY BARS
GASP!
IT'S NICE AND COOL.
THIS IS BAD...
I GUESS I'M DOUBLE-BOOKED NOW...
BUT, WHAT'S DONE IS DONE.
GRIP
I'LL JUST HAVE TO DO IT!!
YO... HEY...
TATSUMI.
WHY ARE YOU SUDDENLY SO FIRED UP?
RUUUMBLE

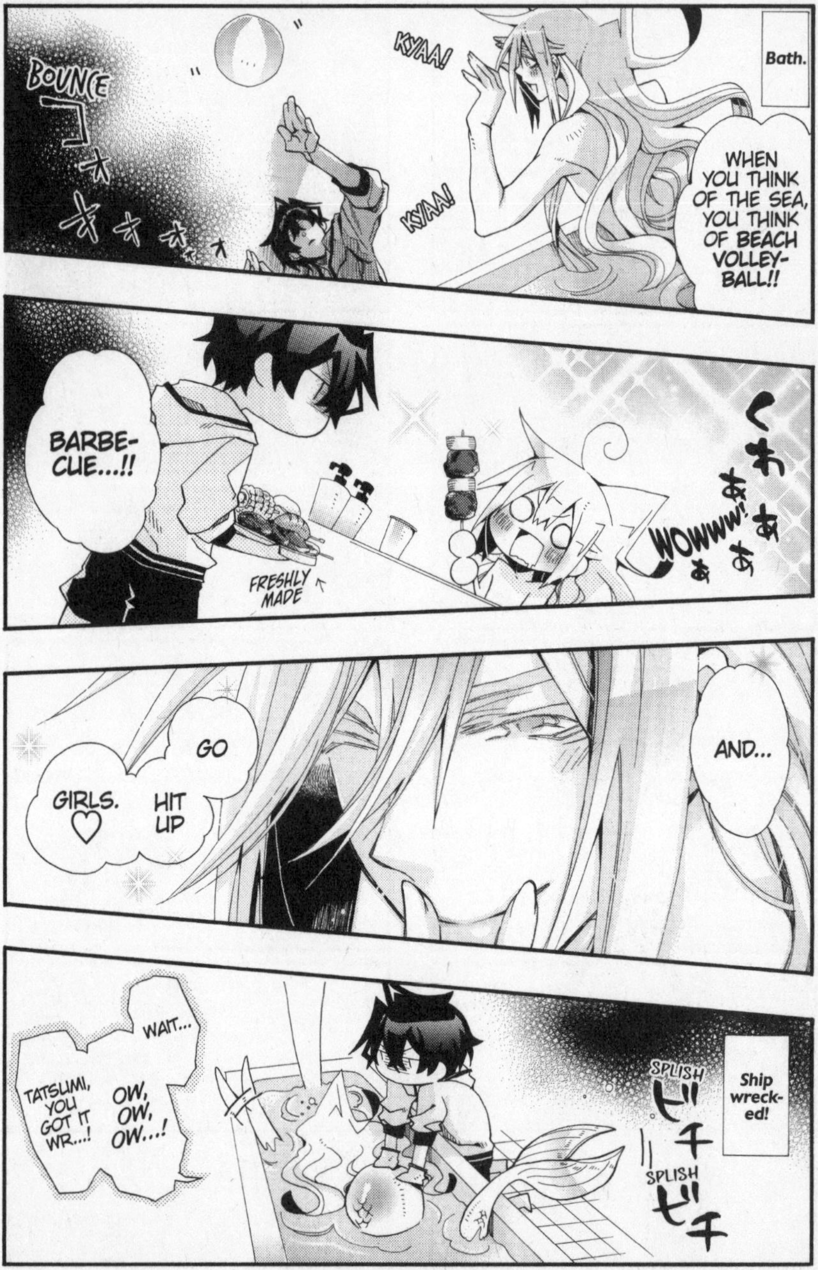

Bath.
WHEN YOU THINK OF THE SEA, YOU THINK OF BEACH VOLLEY-BALL!!
KYAA!
KYAA!
BOUNCE
WOWWW!
BARBE-CUE...!!
FRESHLY MADE
AND...
GO HIT UP GIRLS. ♡
Ship wreck-ed!
SPLISH
SPLISH
WAIT...
OW, OW, OW...!
TATSUMI, YOU GOT IT WR...!

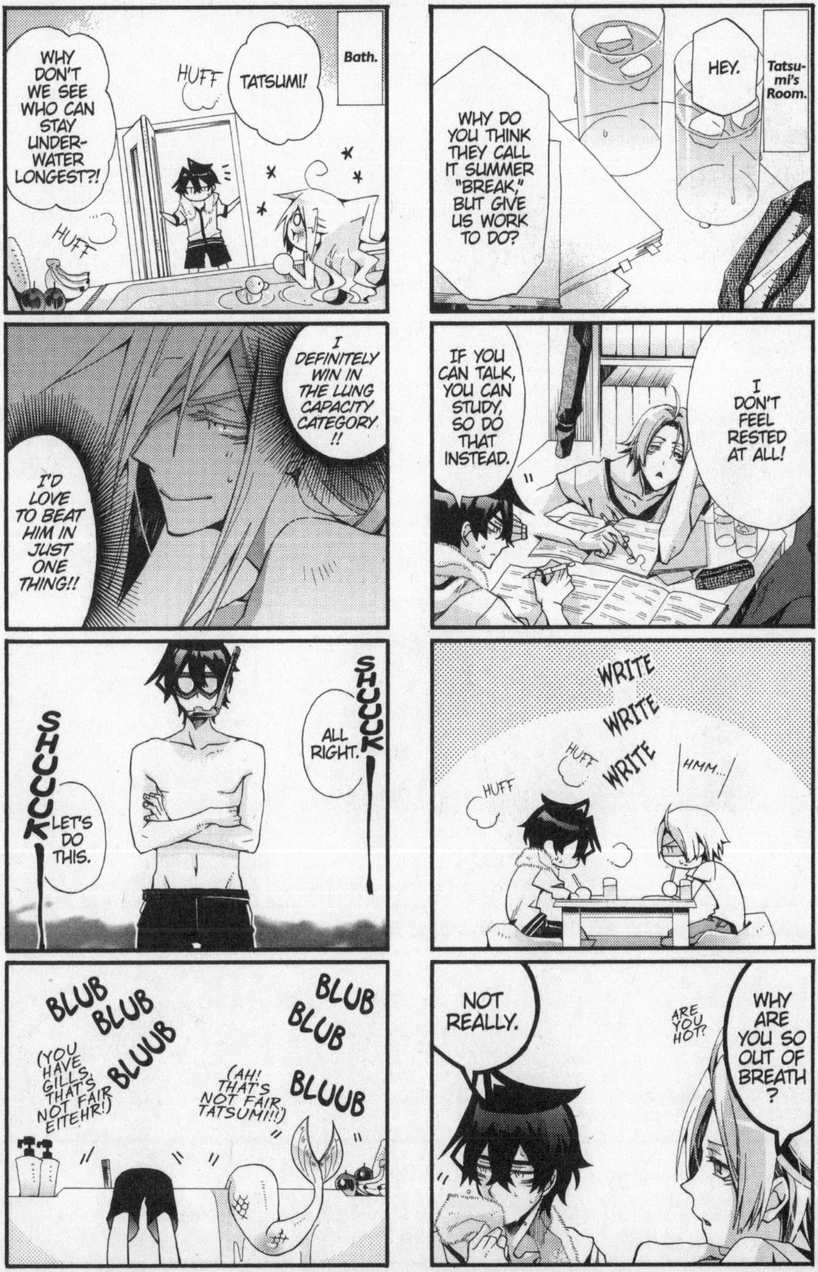
Tatsumi's Room.
HEY.
WHY DO YOU THINK THEY CALL IT SUMMER "BREAK," BUT GIVE US WORK TO DO?
I DON'T FEEL RESTED AT ALL!
IF YOU CAN TALK, YOU CAN STUDY, SO DO THAT INSTEAD.
WRITE
WRITE
WRITE
HMM...
HUFF
HUFF
WHY ARE YOU SO OUT OF BREATH?
ARE YOU HOT?
NOT REALLY.
Bath.
TATSUMI!
HUFF
WHY DON'T WE SEE WHO CAN STAY UNDER-WATER LONGEST?!
HUFF
I DEFINITELY WIN IN THE LUNG CAPACITY CATEGORY!!
I'D LOVE TO BEAT HIM IN JUST ONE THING!!
SHUUUK
ALL RIGHT.
SHUUUK
LET'S DO THIS.
BLUB
BLUB
BLUUB
(AH! THAT'S NOT FAIR, TATSUMI!!)
BLUB
BLUB
BLUUB
(YOU HAVE GILLS, THAT'S NOT FAIR EITEHR!)

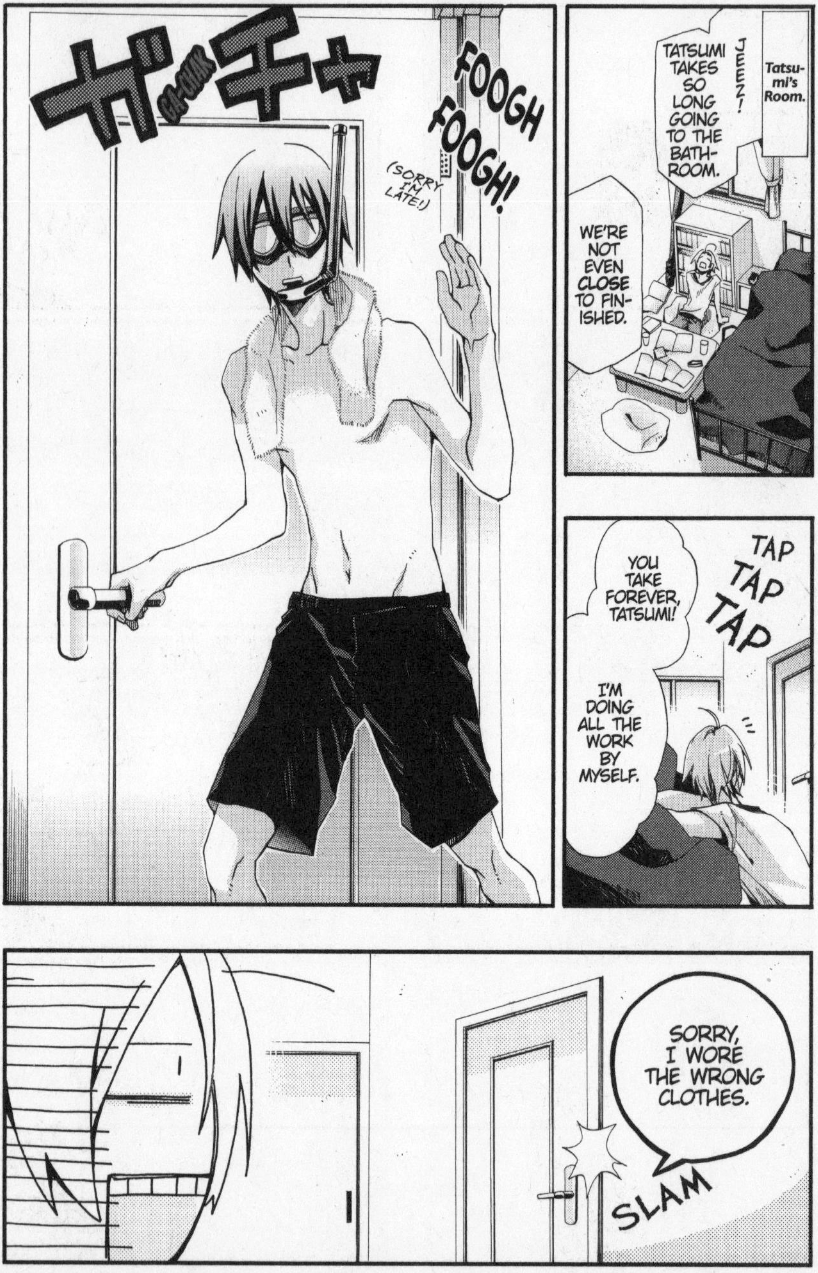
Tatsumi's Room.
JEEZ!
TATSUMI TAKES SO LONG GOING TO THE BATHROOM.
WE'RE NOT EVEN CLOSE TO FINISHED.
TAP TAP TAP
YOU TAKE FOREVER, TATSUMI!
I'M DOING ALL THE WORK BY MYSELF.
ガチャ
GA-CHAK
FOOGH FOOGH!
(SORRY I'M LATE!)
SORRY, I WORE THE WRONG CLOTHES.
SLAM

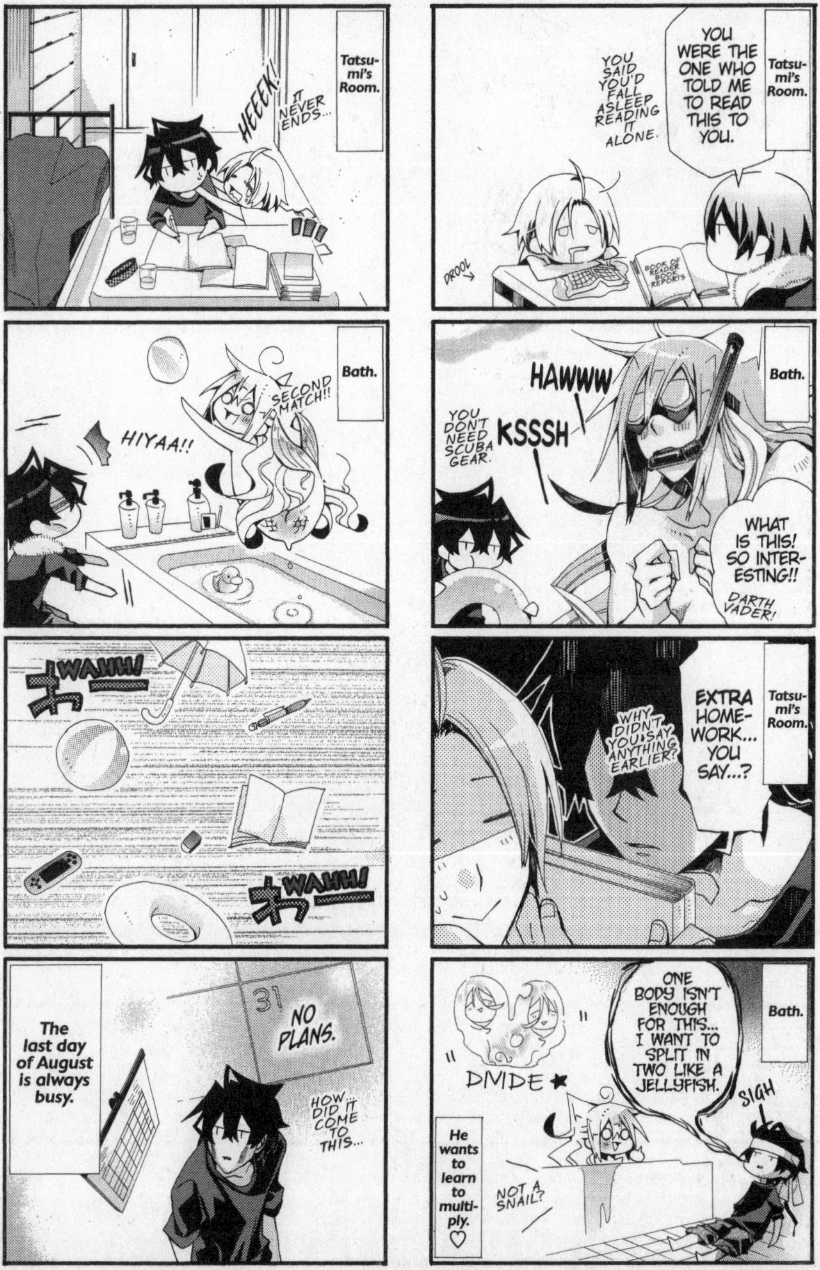
Tatsu-mi's Room.
YOU WERE THE ONE WHO TOLD ME TO READ THIS TO YOU.
YOU SAID YOU'D FALL ASLEEP READING IT ALONE.
BOOK OF READER BOOK REPORTS
DROOL
Tatsu-mi's Room.
HEEEK!!
IT NEVER ENDS...
Bath.
HAWWW
KSSSH
YOU DON'T NEED SCUBA GEAR.
WHAT IS THIS! SO INTER-ESTING!!
DARTH VADER!
Bath.
SECOND MATCH!!
HIYAA!!
Tatsu-mi's Room.
EXTRA HOME-WORK... YOU SAY...?
WHY DIDN'T YOU SAY ANYTHING EARLIER?
WAHH!
わー
WAHH!
わー
Bath.
ONE BODY ISN'T ENOUGH FOR THIS... I WANT TO SPLIT IN TWO LIKE A JELLYFISH.
SIGH
DIVIDE ★
NOT A SNAIL?
He wants to learn to multi-ply. ♡
The last day of August is always busy.
31
NO PLANS.
HOW... DID IT COME TO THIS...

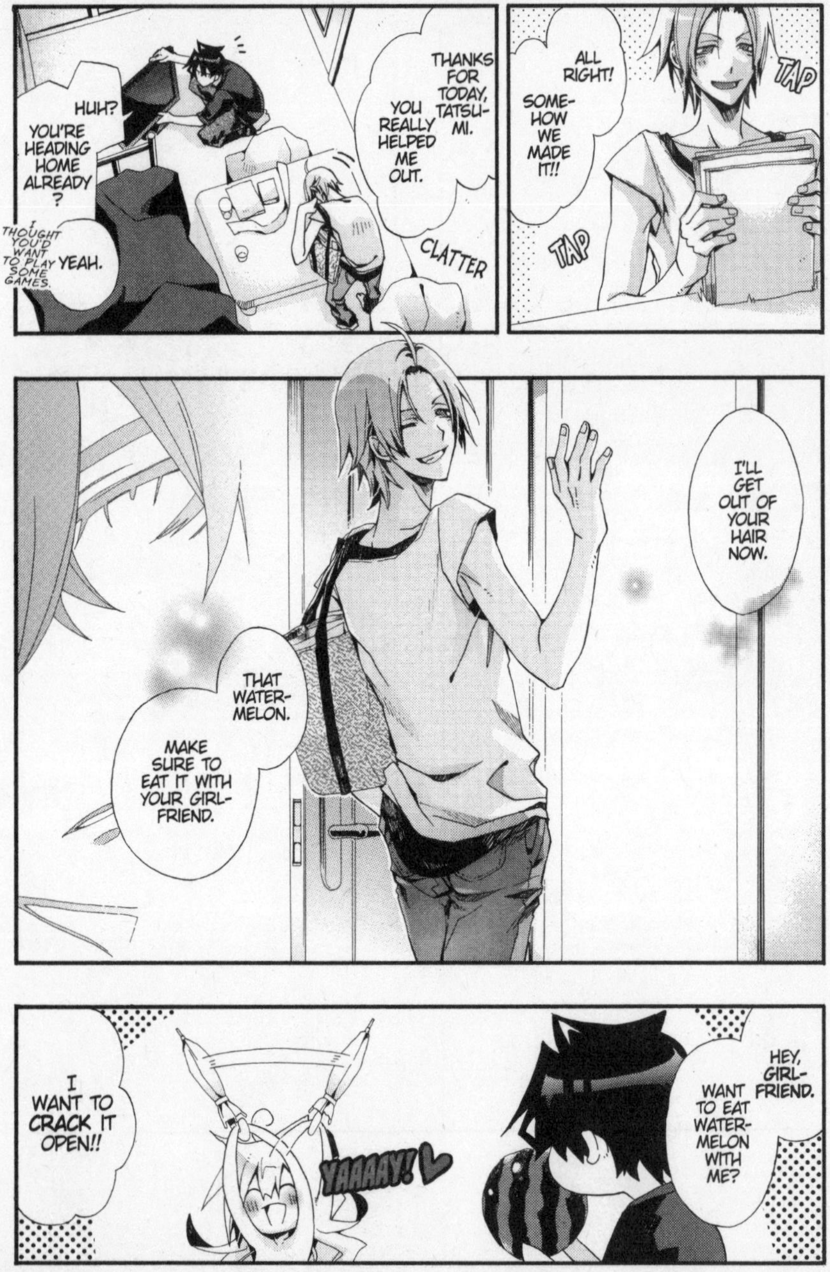
ALL RIGHT!
SOMEHOW WE MADE IT!!
TAP
TAP
THANKS FOR TODAY, TATSUMI.
YOU REALLY HELPED ME OUT.
CLATTER
HUH?
YOU'RE HEADING HOME ALREADY?
I THOUGHT YOU'D WANT TO PLAY SOME GAMES.
YEAH.
I'LL GET OUT OF YOUR HAIR NOW.
THAT WATERMELON.
MAKE SURE TO EAT IT WITH YOUR GIRLFRIEND.
HEY, GIRLFRIEND.
WANT TO EAT WATERMELON WITH ME?
YAAAAY! ♥
I WANT TO CRACK IT OPEN!!

Merman in My Tub

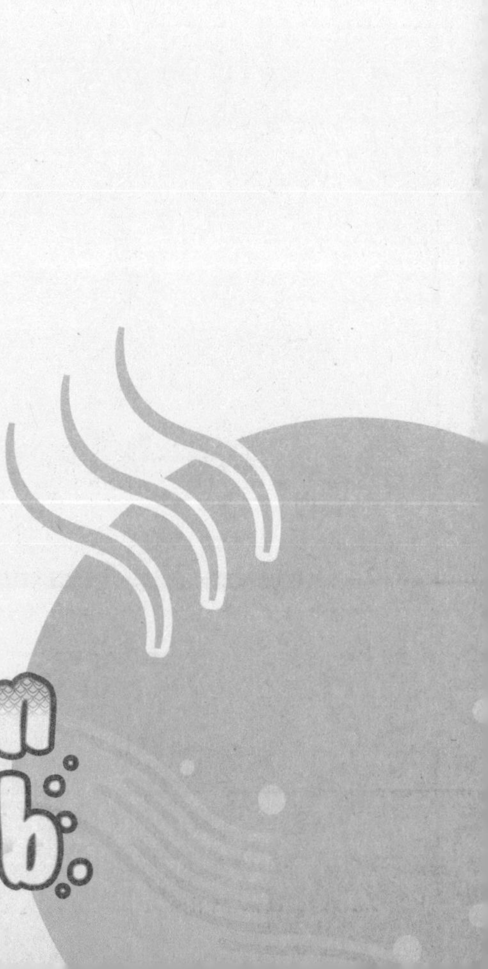

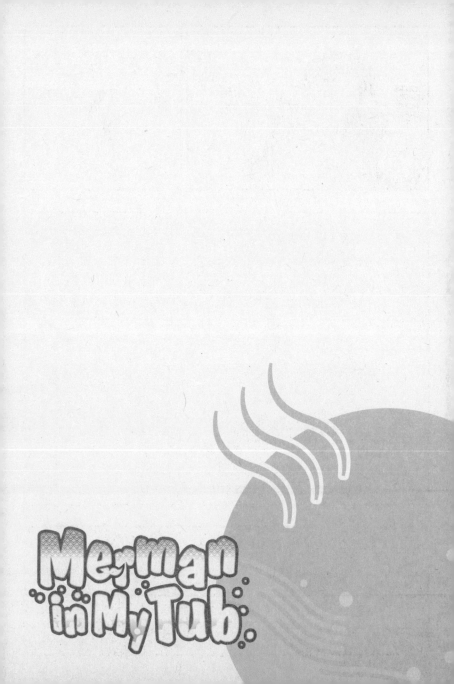

オレん家のフロ事情

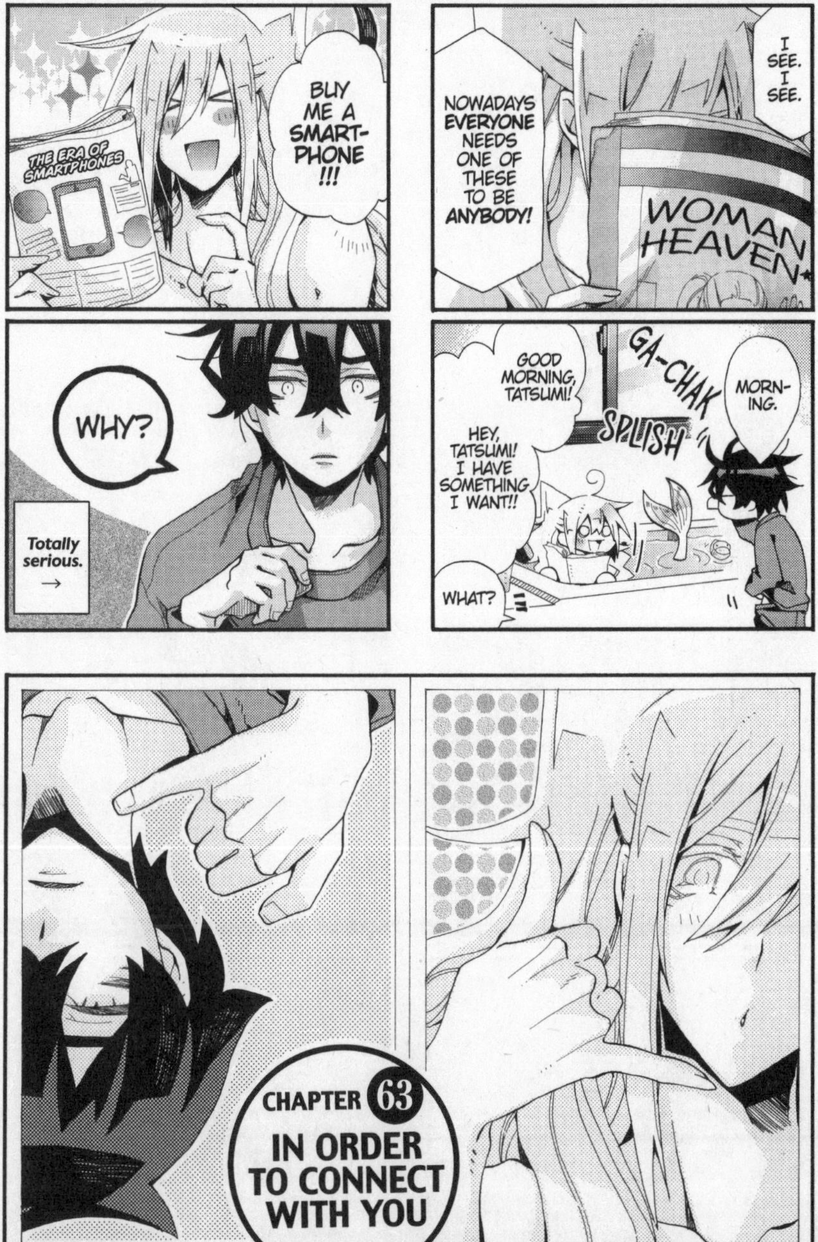

I SEE. I SEE.
NOWADAYS EVERYONE NEEDS ONE OF THESE TO BE ANYBODY!
WOMAN HEAVEN
BUY ME A SMART-PHONE!!!
THE ERA OF SMARTPHONES
MORN-ING.
GA-CHAK
GOOD MORNING, TATSUMI!
SPLISH
HEY, TATSUMI! I HAVE SOMETHING I WANT!!
WHAT?
WHY?
Totally serious. →
CHAPTER 63
IN ORDER TO CONNECT WITH YOU

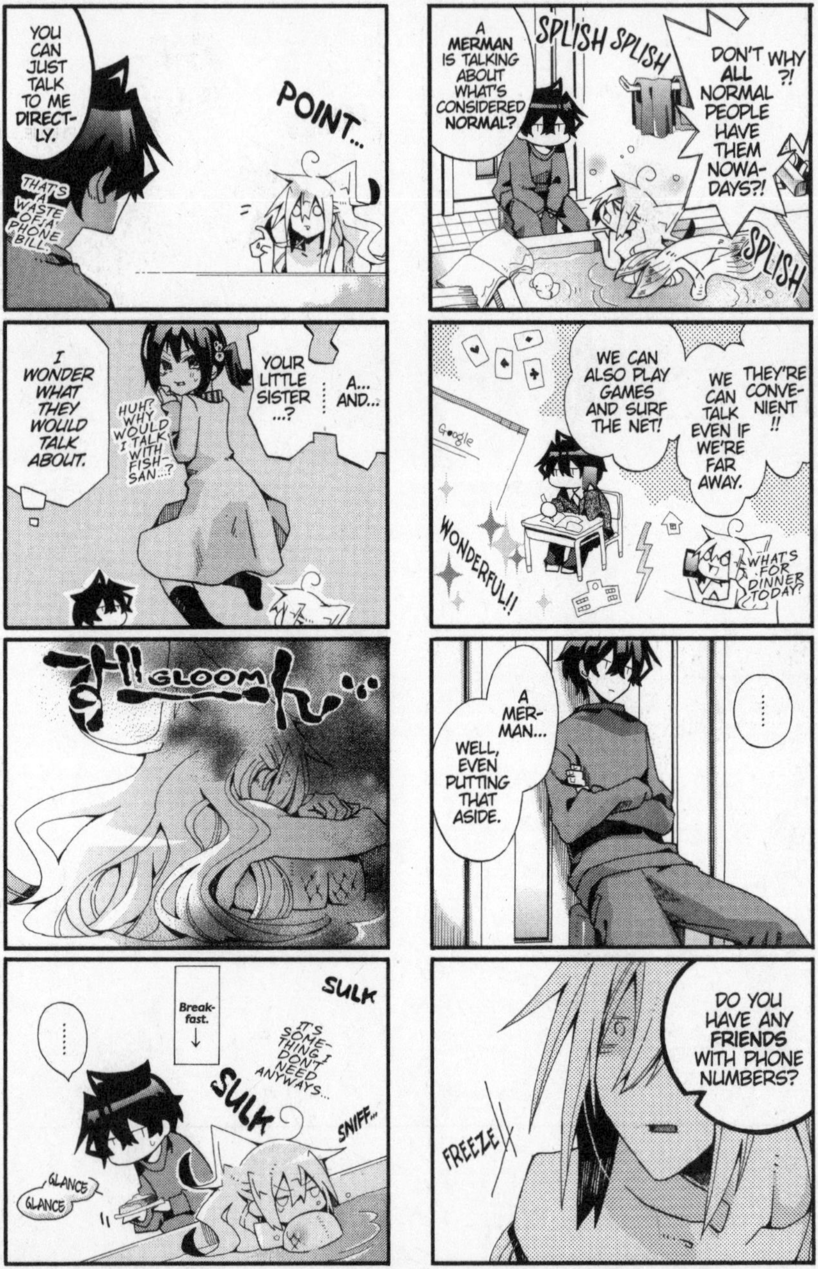
WHY?!
DON'T ALL NORMAL PEOPLE HAVE THEM NOWADAYS?!
SPLISH SPLISH
A MERMAN IS TALKING ABOUT WHAT'S CONSIDERED NORMAL?
SPLISH
THEY'RE CONVENIENT!!
WE CAN TALK EVEN IF WE'RE FAR AWAY.
WE CAN ALSO PLAY GAMES AND SURF THE NET!
Google
WONDERFUL!!
WHAT'S FOR DINNER TODAY?
......
A MERMAN...
WELL, EVEN PUTTING THAT ASIDE.
DO YOU HAVE ANY FRIENDS WITH PHONE NUMBERS?
FREEZE
POINT...
YOU CAN JUST TALK TO ME DIRECTLY.
THAT'S A WASTE OF A PHONE BILL.
A... AND...
......
YOUR LITTLE SISTER...?
HUH? WHY WOULD I TALK WITH FISH-SAN...?
I WONDER WHAT THEY WOULD TALK ABOUT.
GLOOM
SULK
Break-fast.
IT'S SOMETHING I DON'T NEED ANYWAYS...
......
SULK
SNIFF...
GLANCE
GLANCE

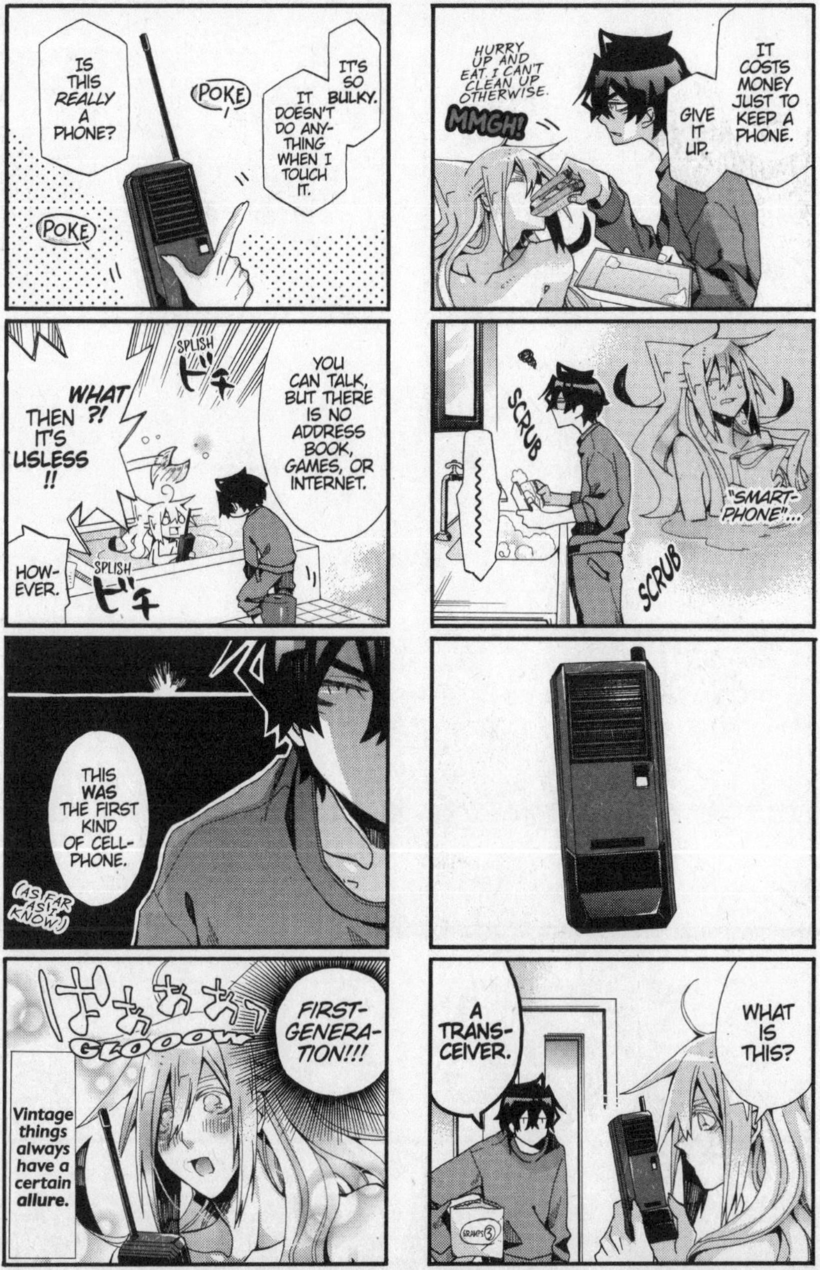
IT COSTS MONEY JUST TO KEEP A PHONE.
GIVE IT UP.
HURRY UP AND EAT. I CAN'T CLEAN UP OTHERWISE.
MMGH!
SCRUB
"SMART-PHONE"...
SCRUB
WHAT IS THIS?
A TRANS-CEIVER.
GRAMPS 3
IT'S SO BULKY.
IT DOESN'T DO ANY-THING WHEN I TOUCH IT.
POKE
IS THIS REALLY A PHONE?
POKE
YOU CAN TALK, BUT THERE IS NO ADDRESS BOOK, GAMES, OR INTERNET.
SPLISH
WHAT ?!
THEN IT'S USLESS !!
HOW-EVER.
SPLISH
THIS WAS THE FIRST KIND OF CELL-PHONE.
(AS FAR AS I KNOW.)
FIRST-GENERATION!!!
GLOOOW
Vintage things always have a certain allure.

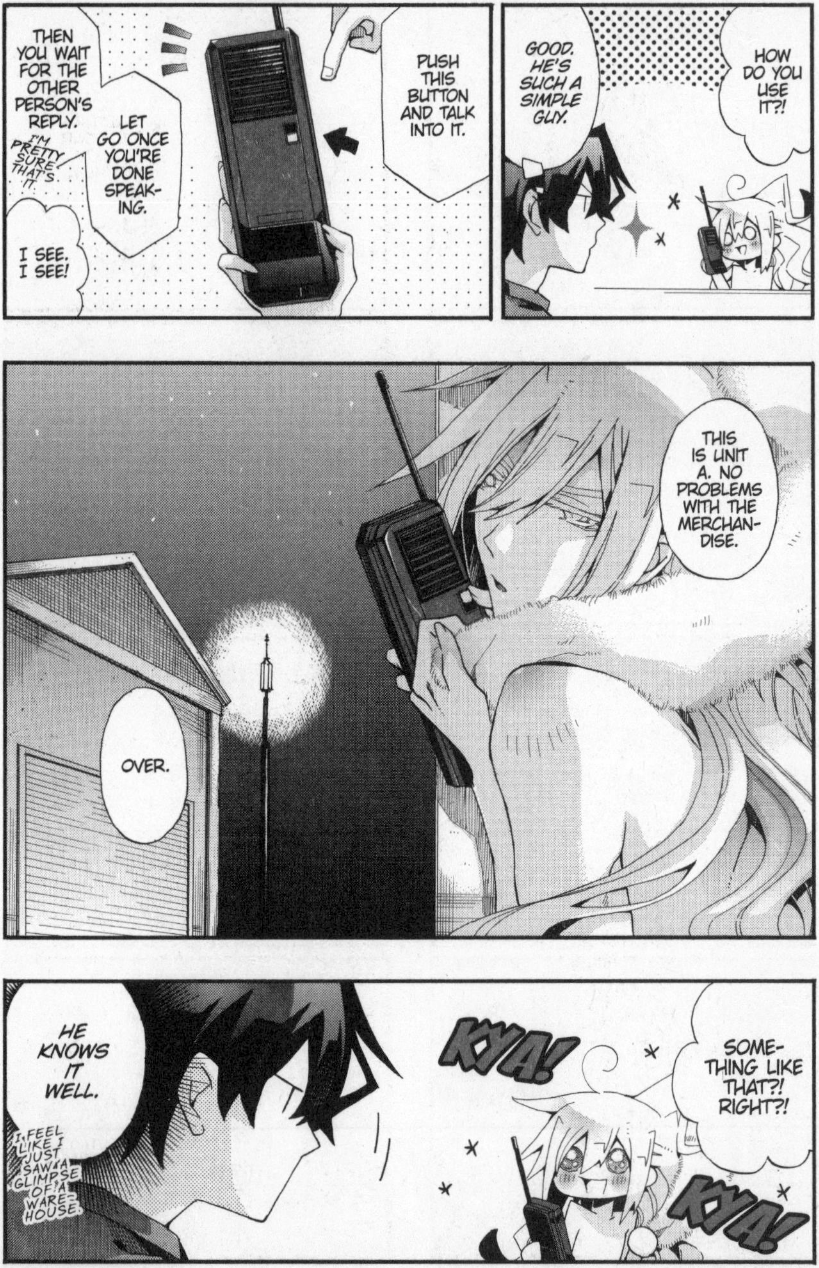
HOW DO YOU USE IT?!
GOOD. HE'S SUCH A SIMPLE GUY.
PUSH THIS BUTTON AND TALK INTO IT.
LET GO ONCE YOU'RE DONE SPEAKING.
THEN YOU WAIT FOR THE OTHER PERSON'S REPLY.
I'M PRETTY SURE THAT'S IT.
I SEE. I SEE!
THIS IS UNIT A. NO PROBLEMS WITH THE MERCHANDISE.
OVER.
SOMETHING LIKE THAT?! RIGHT?!
KYA!
KYA!
HE KNOWS IT WELL.
I FEEL LIKE I JUST SAW A GLIMPSE OF A WAREHOUSE.

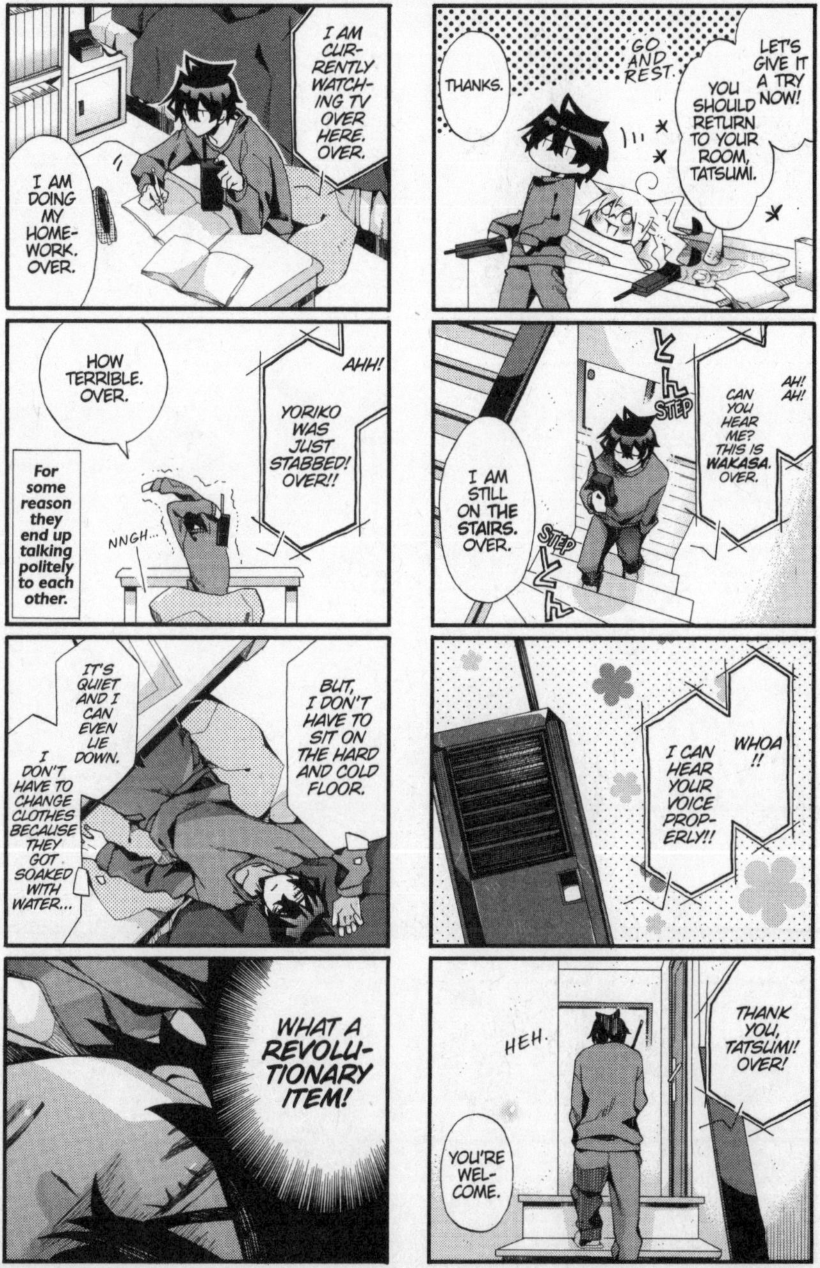
LET'S GIVE IT A TRY NOW!
YOU SHOULD RETURN TO YOUR ROOM, TATSUMI.
GO AND REST.
THANKS.
AH! AH! CAN YOU HEAR ME? THIS IS WAKASA. OVER.
STEP
I AM STILL ON THE STAIRS. OVER.
STEP
WHOA!!
I CAN HEAR YOUR VOICE PROPERLY!!
THANK YOU, TATSUMI! OVER!
HEH.
YOU'RE WELCOME.
I AM CURRENTLY WATCHING TV OVER HERE. OVER.
I AM DOING MY HOMEWORK. OVER.
AHH!
YORIKO WAS JUST STABBED! OVER!!
HOW TERRIBLE. OVER.
NNGH...
For some reason they end up talking politely to each other.
BUT, I DON'T HAVE TO SIT ON THE HARD AND COLD FLOOR.
IT'S QUIET AND I CAN EVEN LIE DOWN.
I DON'T HAVE TO CHANGE CLOTHES BECAUSE THEY GOT SOAKED WITH WATER...
WHAT A REVOLUTIONARY ITEM!

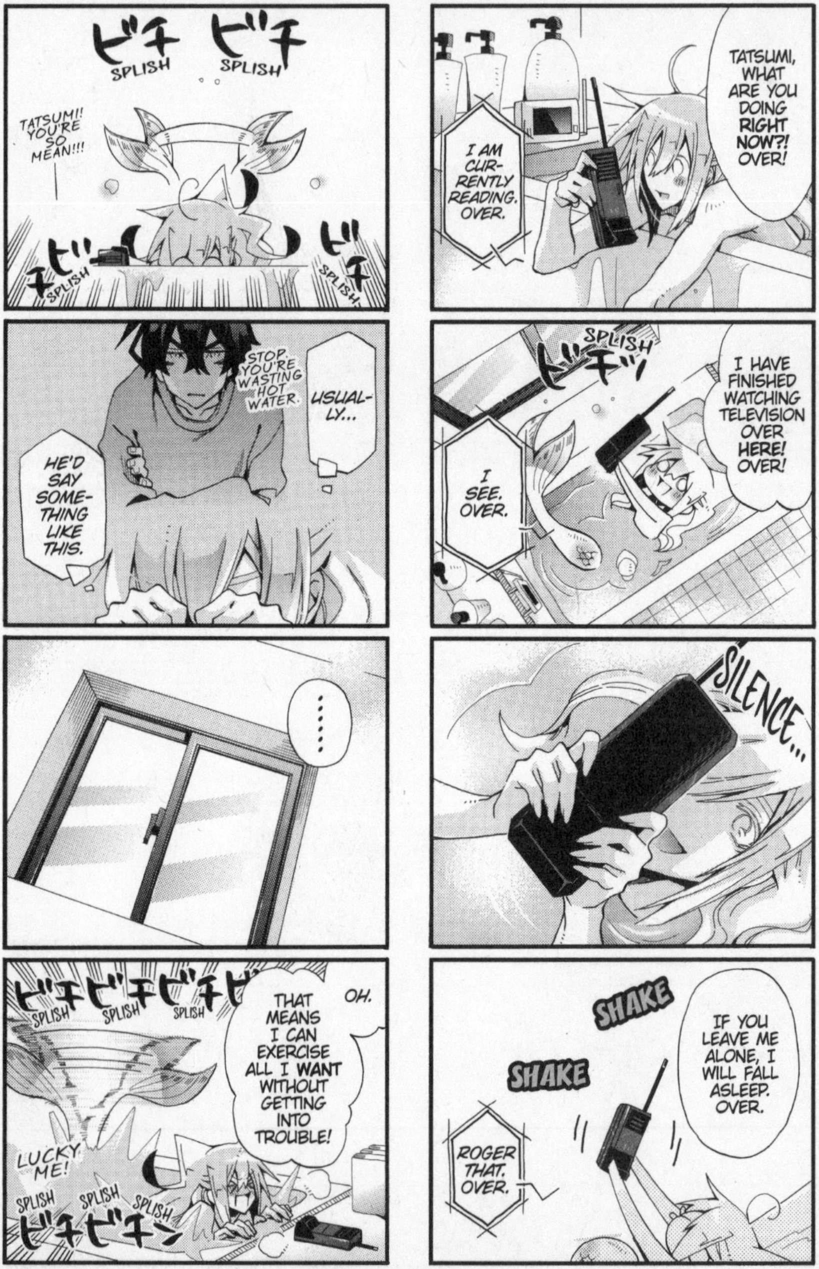
TATSUMI, WHAT ARE YOU DOING RIGHT NOW?! OVER!
I AM CURRENTLY READING. OVER.
SPLISH
I HAVE FINISHED WATCHING TELEVISION OVER HERE! OVER!
I SEE. OVER.
SILENCE...
SHAKE
SHAKE
IF YOU LEAVE ME ALONE, I WILL FALL ASLEEP. OVER.
ROGER THAT. OVER.
ビチ ビチ
SPLISH SPLISH
TATSUMI!! YOU'RE SO MEAN!!!
SPLISH
SPLISH
USUALLY...
STOP. YOU'RE WASTING HOT WATER.
HE'D SAY SOMETHING LIKE THIS.
......
ビチビチビチ
SPLISH SPLISH SPLISH
OH.
THAT MEANS I CAN EXERCISE ALL I WANT WITHOUT GETTING INTO TROUBLE!
LUCKY ME!
SPLISH SPLISH SPLISH

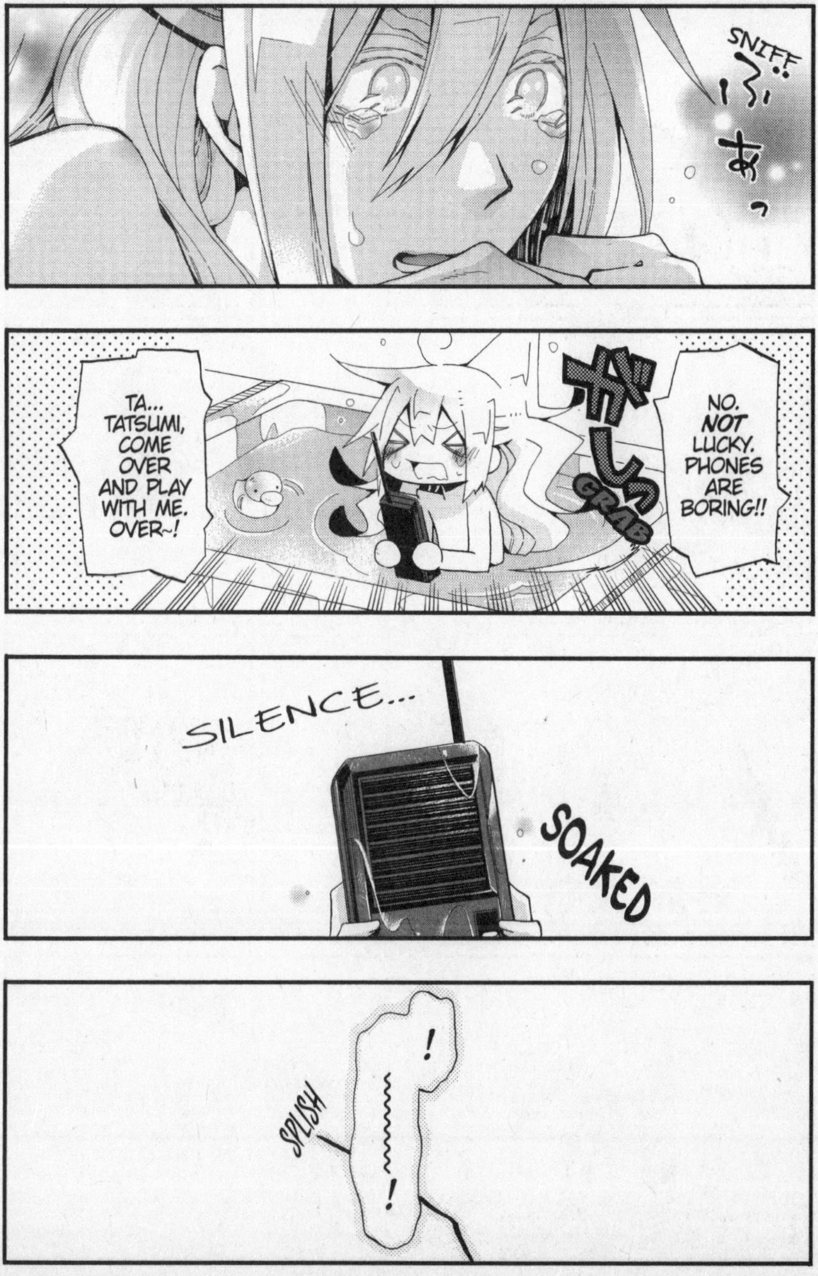
SNIFF
ぶあっ
NO. NOT LUCKY. PHONES ARE BORING!!
がしっ
GRAB
TA... TATSUMI, COME OVER AND PLAY WITH ME. OVER~!
SILENCE...
SOAKED
!
~~~~!
SPLISH
~~~~

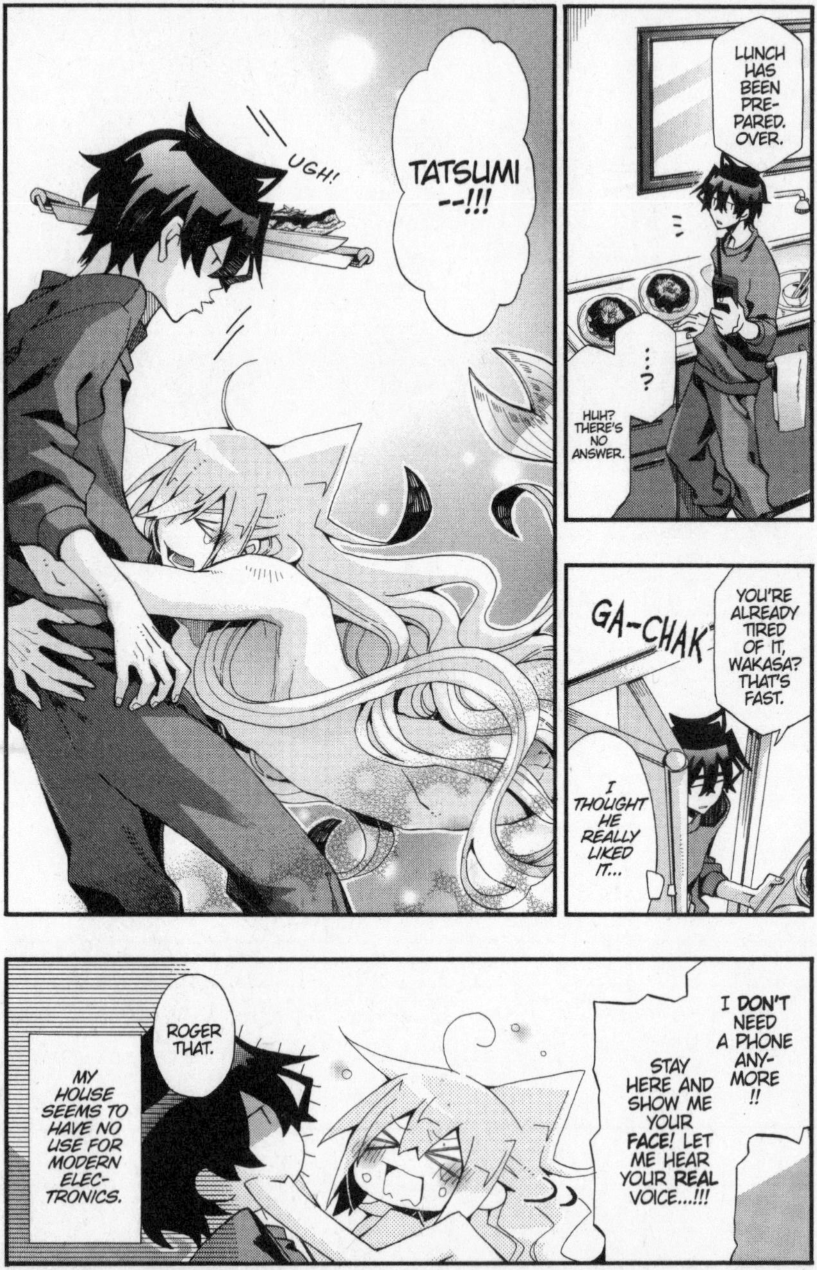
LUNCH HAS BEEN PRE-PARED. OVER.
...?
HUH? THERE'S NO ANSWER.
YOU'RE ALREADY TIRED OF IT, WAKASA? THAT'S FAST.
GA-CHAK
I THOUGHT HE REALLY LIKED IT...
TATSUMI --!!!
UGH!
I DON'T NEED A PHONE ANY-MORE !!
STAY HERE AND SHOW ME YOUR FACE! LET ME HEAR YOUR REAL VOICE...!!!
ROGER THAT.
MY HOUSE SEEMS TO HAVE NO USE FOR MODERN ELEC-TRONICS.

Merman in My Tub

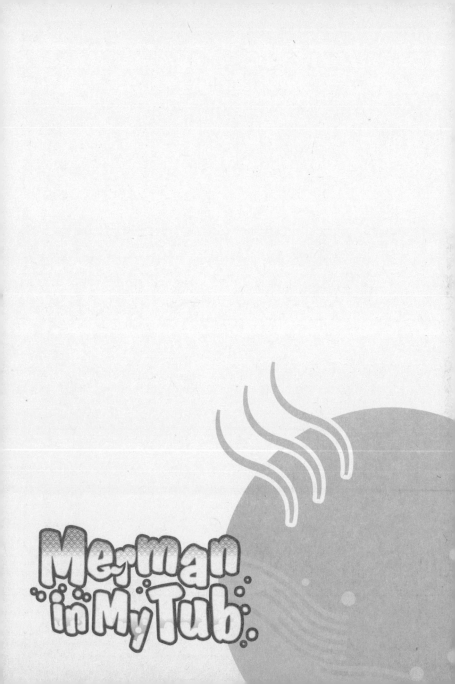

オレん家（ち）のフロ事情

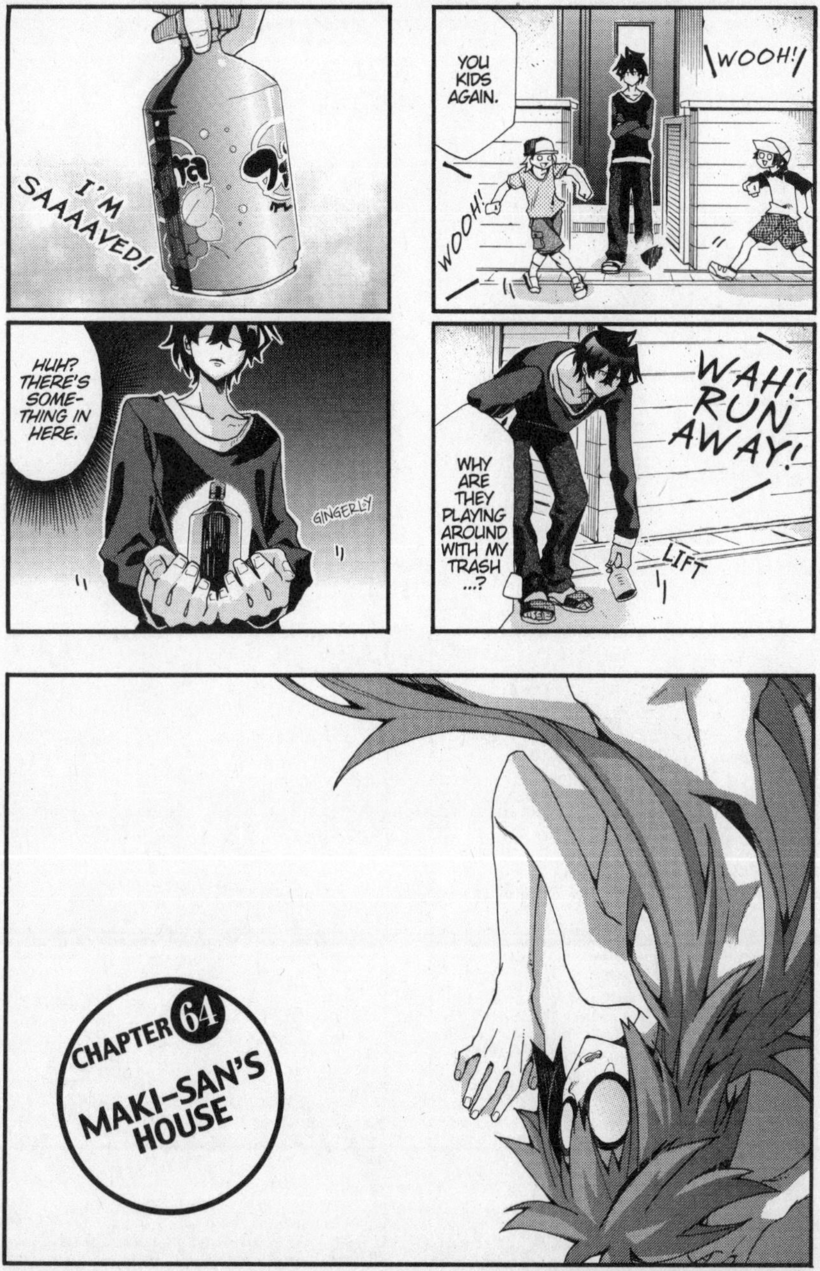
WOOH!
YOU KIDS AGAIN.
WOOH!
I'M SAAAAVED!
WAH! RUN AWAY!
WHY ARE THEY PLAYING AROUND WITH MY TRASH ...?
LIFT
HUH? THERE'S SOME-THING IN HERE.
GINGERLY
CHAPTER 64
MAKI-SAN'S HOUSE

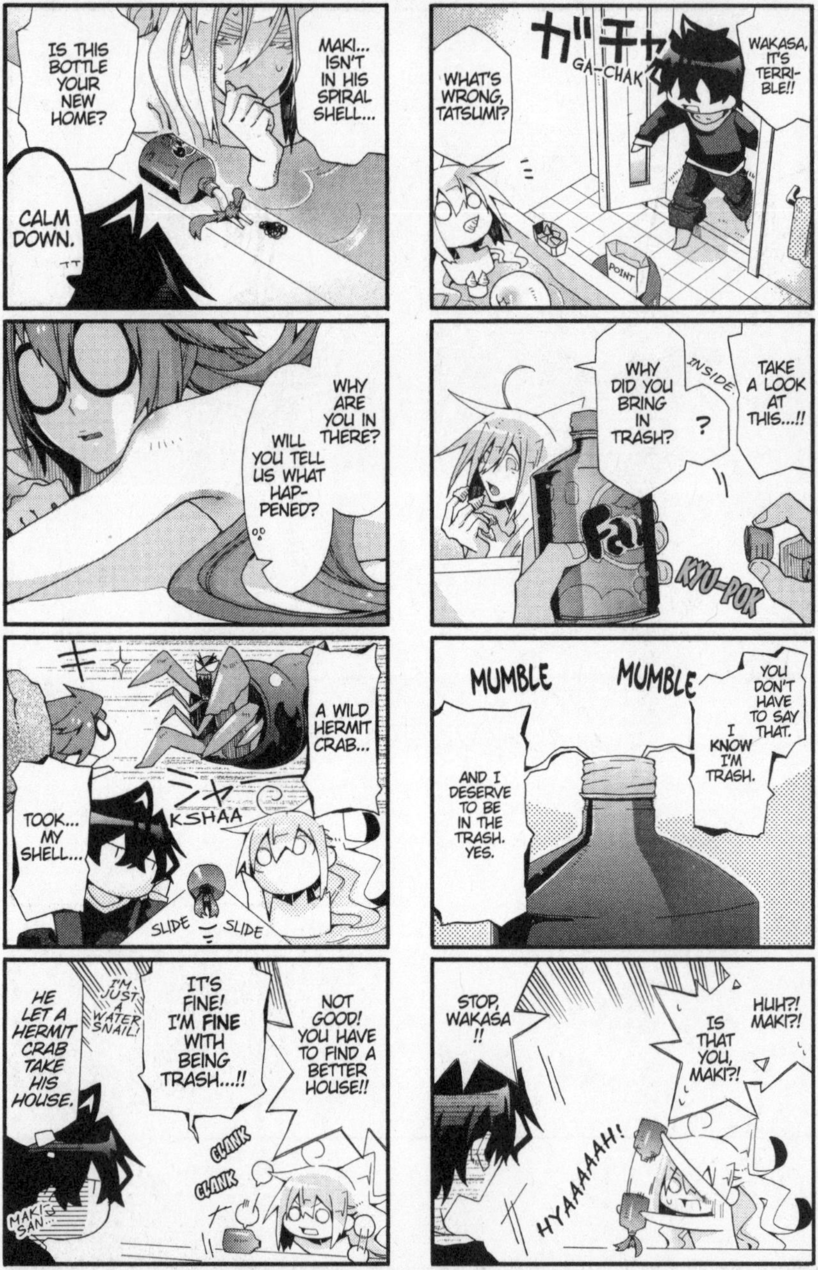
ガチャ
GA-CHAK
WAKASA, IT'S TERRIBLE!!
WHAT'S WRONG, TATSUMI?
POINT
MAKI... ISN'T IN HIS SPIRAL SHELL...
IS THIS BOTTLE YOUR NEW HOME?
CALM DOWN.
TAKE A LOOK AT THIS...!!
INSIDE.
WHY DID YOU BRING IN TRASH?
?
KYU-POK
WHY ARE YOU IN THERE?
WILL YOU TELL US WHAT HAP-PENED?
YOU DON'T HAVE TO SAY THAT.
I KNOW I'M TRASH.
MUMBLE
MUMBLE
AND I DESERVE TO BE IN THE TRASH. YES.
A WILD HERMIT CRAB...
KSHAA
TOOK... MY SHELL...
SLIDE
SLIDE
HUH?! MAKI?!
IS THAT YOU, MAKI?!
STOP, WAKASA!!
HYAAAAAH!
NOT GOOD! YOU HAVE TO FIND A BETTER HOUSE!!
IT'S FINE! I'M FINE WITH BEING TRASH...!!
I'M JUST A WATER SNAIL!
HE LET A HERMIT CRAB TAKE HIS HOUSE.
CLANK
CLANK
MAKI-SAN...

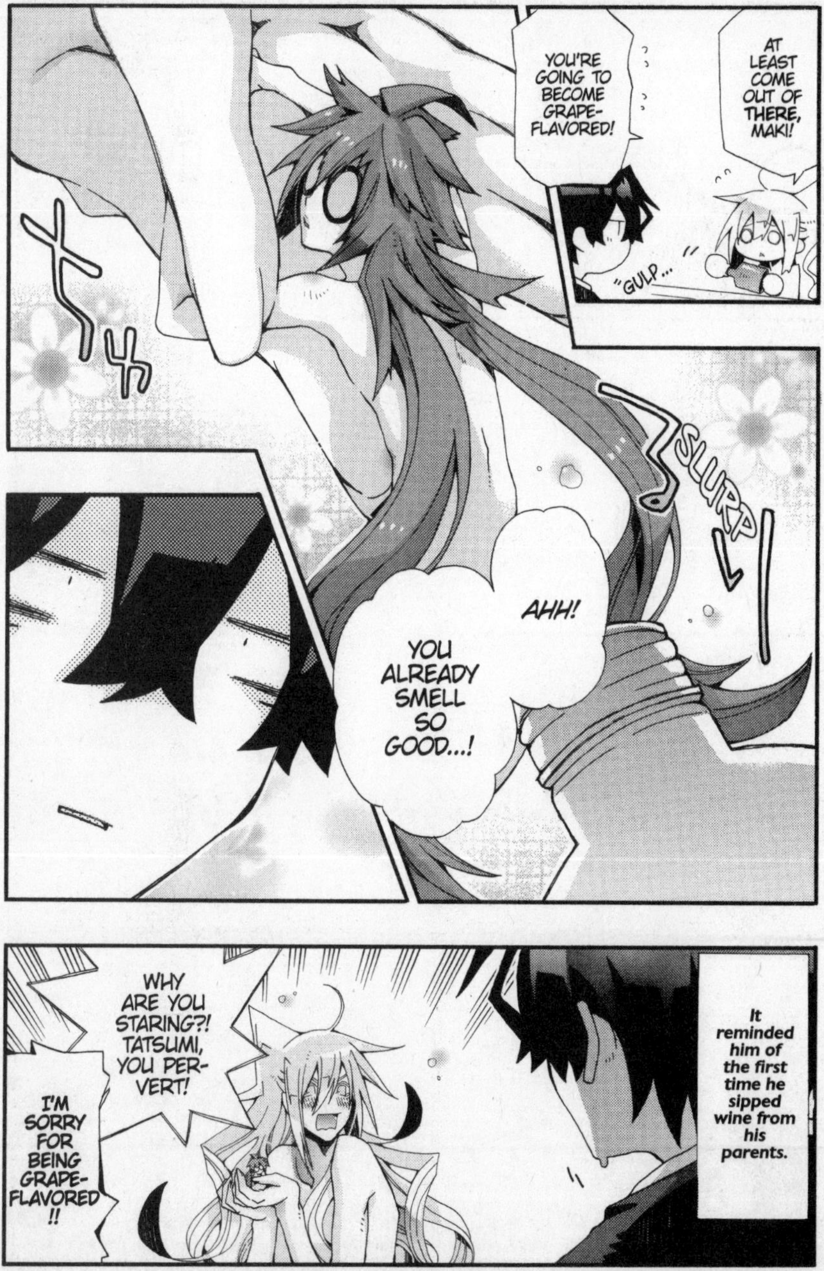
AT LEAST COME OUT OF THERE, MAKI!
YOU'RE GOING TO BECOME GRAPE-FLAVORED!
"GULP..."
SLURP
AHH!
YOU ALREADY SMELL SO GOOD...!
It reminded him of the first time he sipped wine from his parents.
WHY ARE YOU STARING?! TATSUMI, YOU PERVERT!
I'M SORRY FOR BEING GRAPE-FLAVORED!!

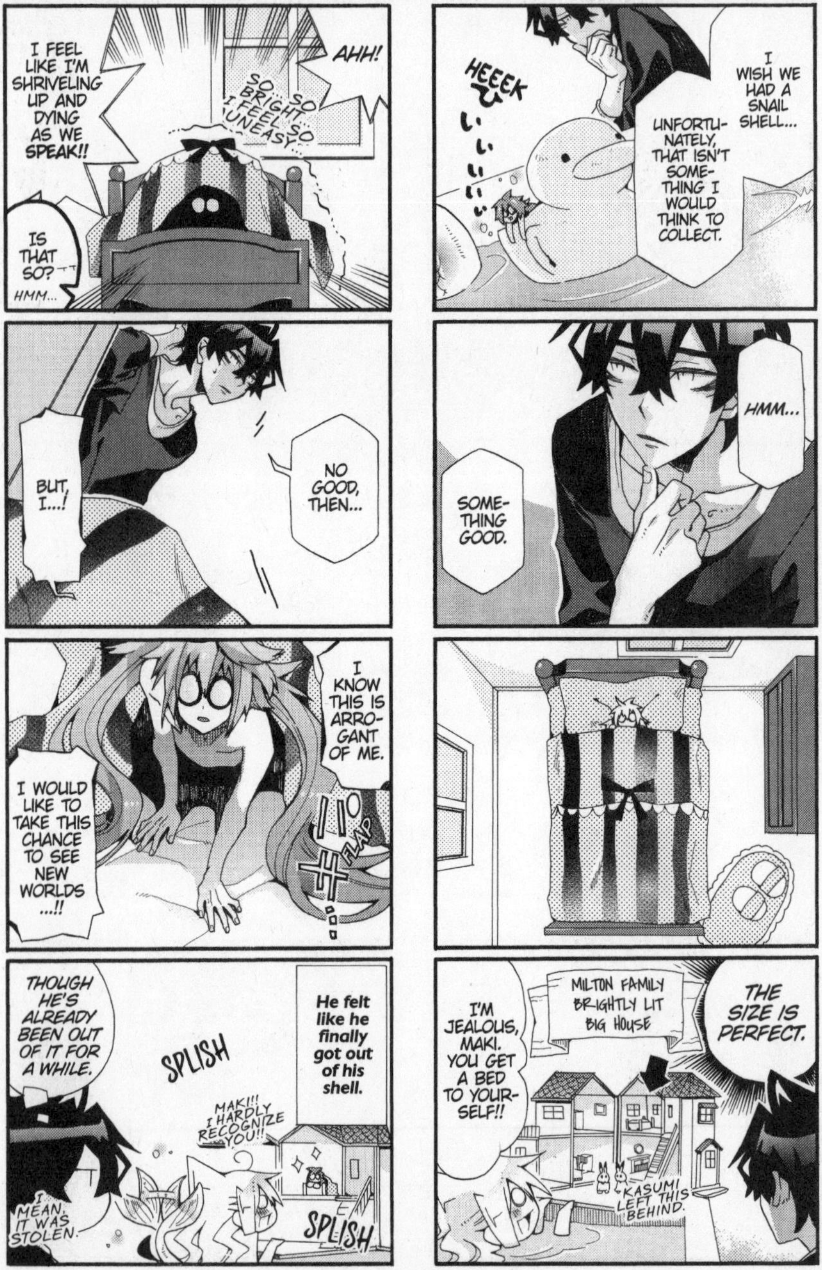
I WISH WE HAD A SNAIL SHELL...
UNFORTUNATELY, THAT ISN'T SOMETHING I WOULD THINK TO COLLECT.
HEEEK
いいいいい
HMM...
SOMETHING GOOD.
THE SIZE IS PERFECT.
MILTON FAMILY BRIGHTLY LIT BIG HOUSE
I'M JEALOUS, MAKI. YOU GET A BED TO YOURSELF!!
KASUMI LEFT THIS BEHIND.
AHH!
SO... SO BRIGHT. I FEEL SO UNEASY...
I FEEL LIKE I'M SHRIVELING UP AND DYING AS WE SPEAK!!
IS THAT SO?
HMM...
NO GOOD, THEN...
BUT, I...!
I KNOW THIS IS ARROGANT OF ME.
I WOULD LIKE TO TAKE THIS CHANCE TO SEE NEW WORLDS...!!
FLAP
He felt like he finally got out of his shell.
SPLISH
THOUGH HE'S ALREADY BEEN OUT OF IT FOR A WHILE.
MAKI!!! I HARDLY RECOGNIZE YOU!!
SPLISH
I MEAN, IT WAS STOLEN.

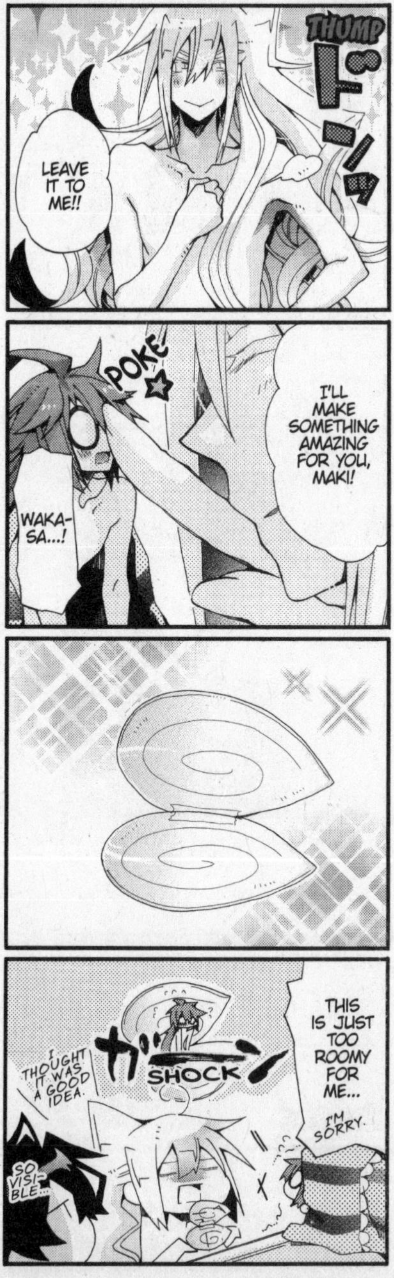
THUMP
LEAVE IT TO ME!!
POKE
I'LL MAKE SOMETHING AMAZING FOR YOU, MAKI!
WAKA-SA...!
THIS IS JUST TOO ROOMY FOR ME...
I'M SORRY.
SHOCK
I THOUGHT IT WAS A GOOD IDEA.
SO VISIBLE...
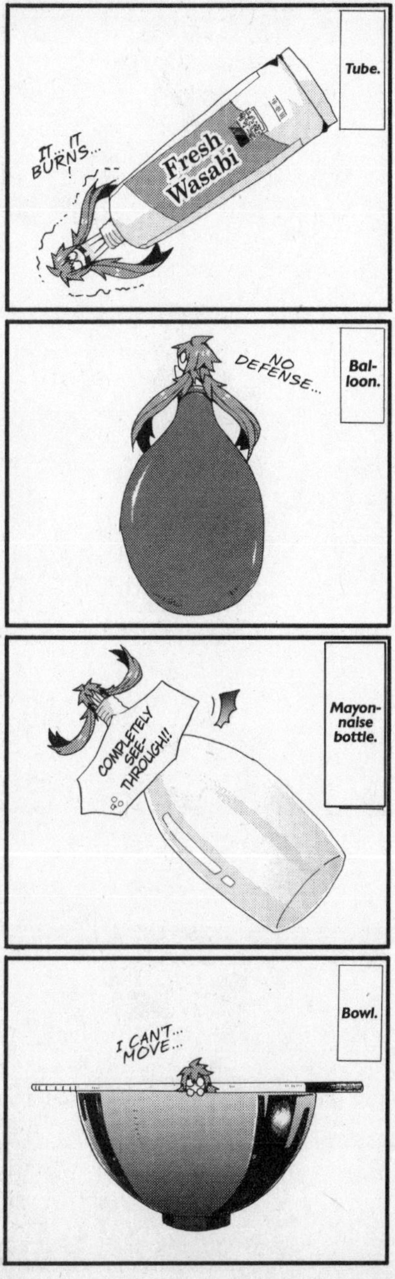
Tube.
Fresh Wasabi
IT... IT BURNS...!
Bal-loon.
NO DEFENSE...
Mayon-naise bottle.
COMPLETELY SEE-THROUGH!!
Bowl.
I CAN'T... MOVE...

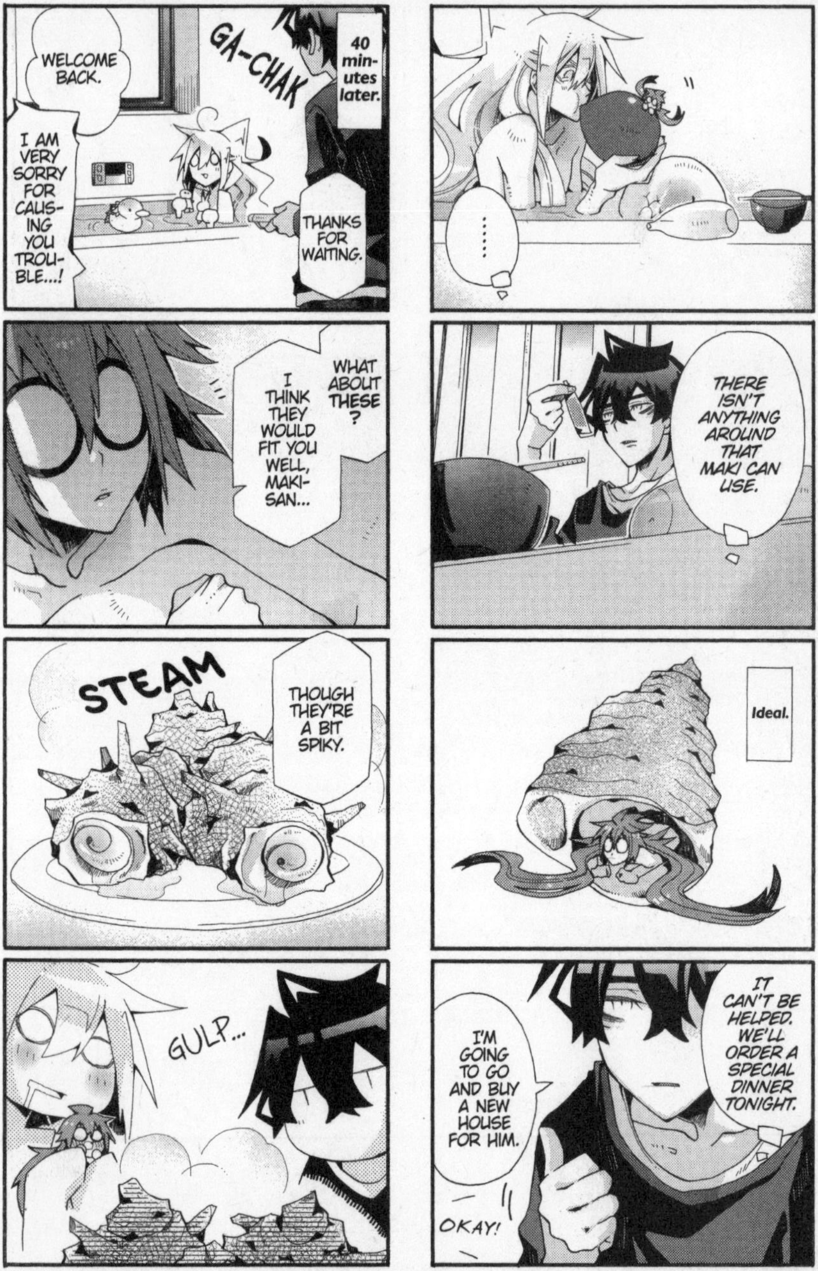
......
40 minutes later.
GA-CHAK
THANKS FOR WAITING.
WELCOME BACK.
I AM VERY SORRY FOR CAUSING YOU TROUBLE...!
THERE ISN'T ANYTHING AROUND THAT MAKI CAN USE.
WHAT ABOUT THESE?
I THINK THEY WOULD FIT YOU WELL, MAKI-SAN...
Ideal.
THOUGH THEY'RE A BIT SPIKY.
STEAM
IT CAN'T BE HELPED. WE'LL ORDER A SPECIAL DINNER TONIGHT.
I'M GOING TO GO AND BUY A NEW HOUSE FOR HIM.
OKAY!
GULP...

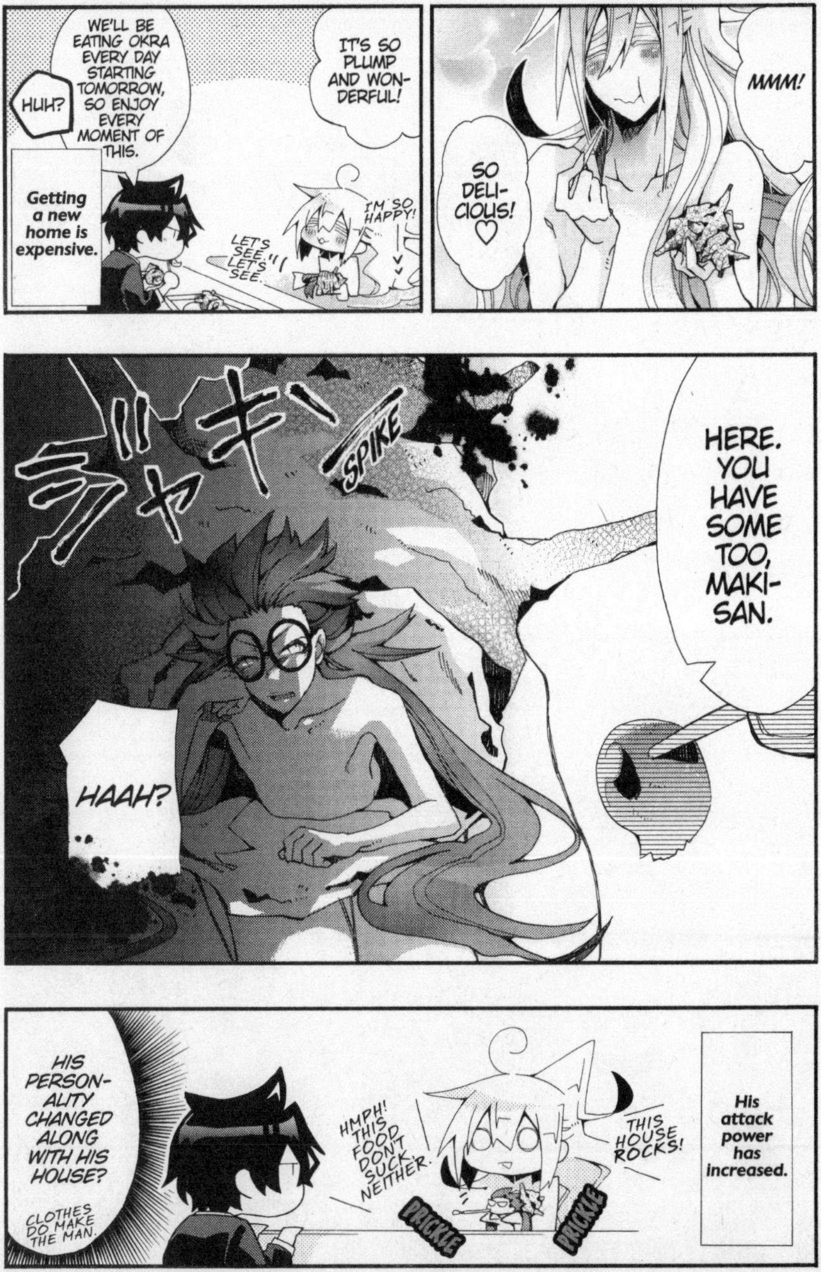
MMM!
SO DELI-CIOUS! ♡
IT'S SO PLUMP AND WON-DERFUL!
I'M SO HAPPY!
LET'S SEE, LET'S SEE.
WE'LL BE EATING OKRA EVERY DAY STARTING TOMORROW, SO ENJOY EVERY MOMENT OF THIS.
HUH?
Getting a new home is expensive.
HERE. YOU HAVE SOME TOO, MAKI-SAN.
シャキーン
SPIKE
HAAH?
His attack power has increased.
THIS HOUSE ROCKS!
HMPH! THIS FOOD DON'T SUCK NEITHER.
PRICKLE
PRICKLE
HIS PERSON-ALITY CHANGED ALONG WITH HIS HOUSE?
CLOTHES DO MAKE THE MAN.

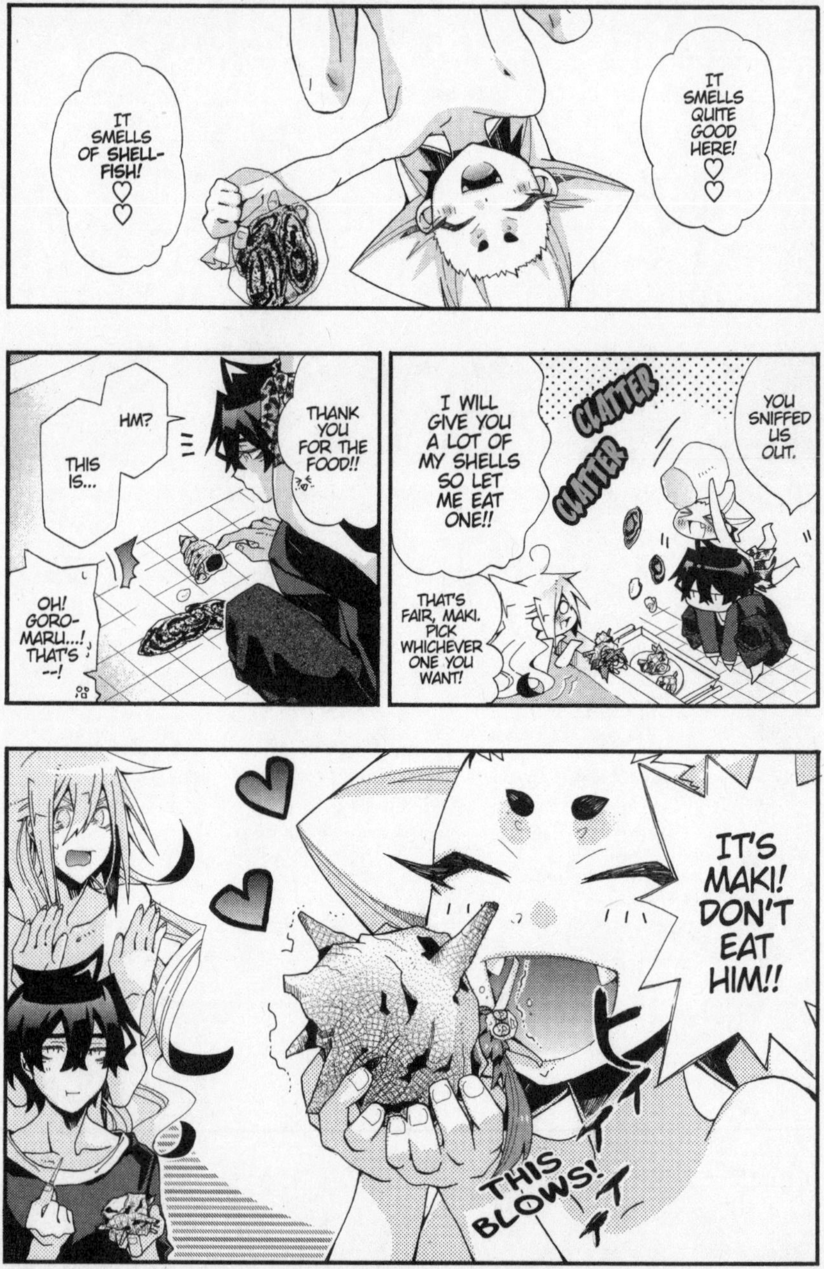
IT SMELLS QUITE GOOD HERE! ♡ ♡
IT SMELLS OF SHELL-FISH! ♡ ♡
YOU SNIFFED US OUT.
CLATTER
CLATTER
I WILL GIVE YOU A LOT OF MY SHELLS SO LET ME EAT ONE!!
THAT'S FAIR, MAKI. PICK WHICHEVER ONE YOU WANT!
THANK YOU FOR THE FOOD!!
HM?
THIS IS...
OH! GORO-MARU...! THAT'S --!
IT'S MAKI! DON'T EAT HIM!!
THIS BLOWS!

Merman in My Tub

オレん家のフロ事情

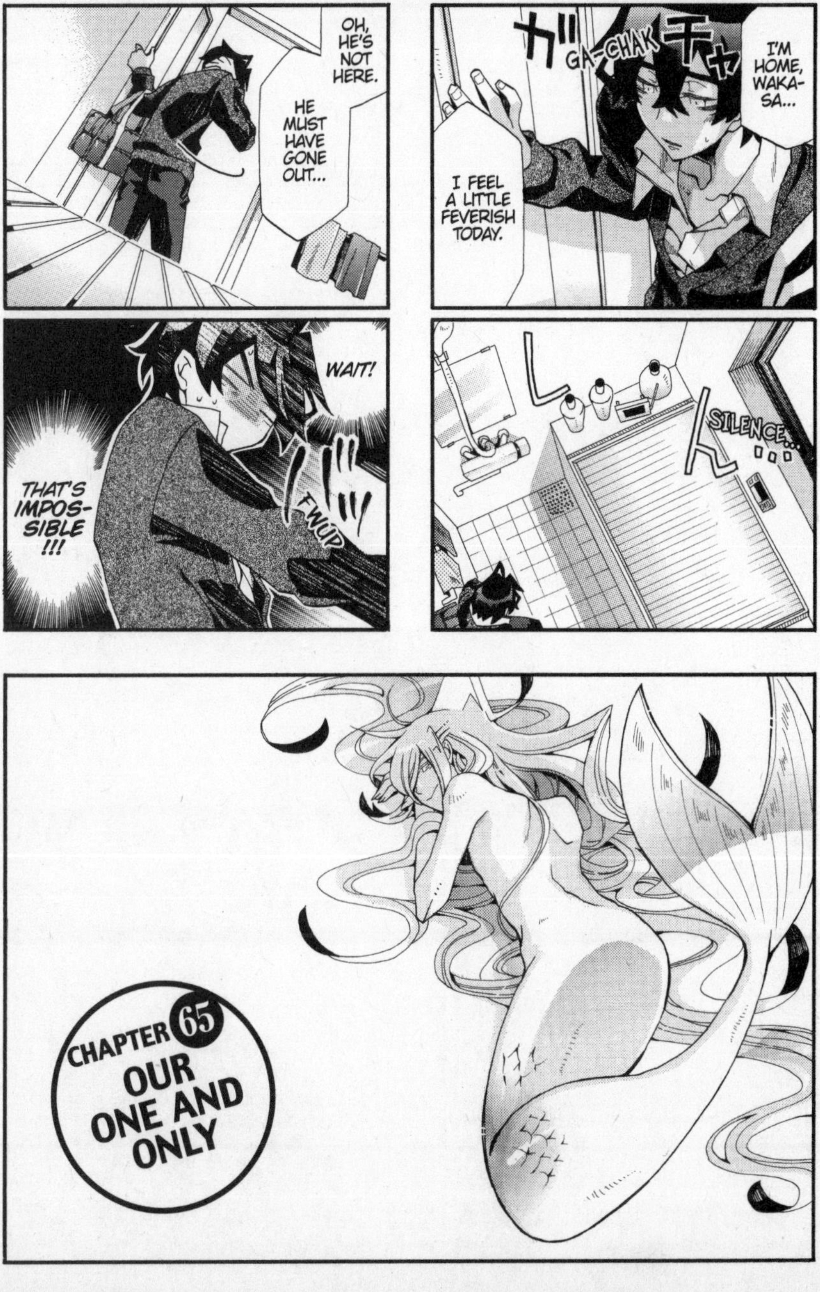
ガ GA-CHAK チャ
I'M HOME, WAKA-SA...
I FEEL A LITTLE FEVERISH TODAY.
OH, HE'S NOT HERE.
HE MUST HAVE GONE OUT...
しん SILENCE...
WAIT!
FWUP
THAT'S IMPOS-SIBLE!!!
CHAPTER 65
OUR ONE AND ONLY

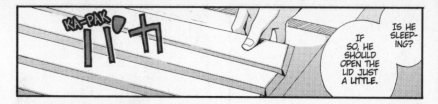

IS HE SLEEP-ING?

IF SO, HE SHOULD OPEN THE LID JUST A LITTLE.

KA-PAK

?

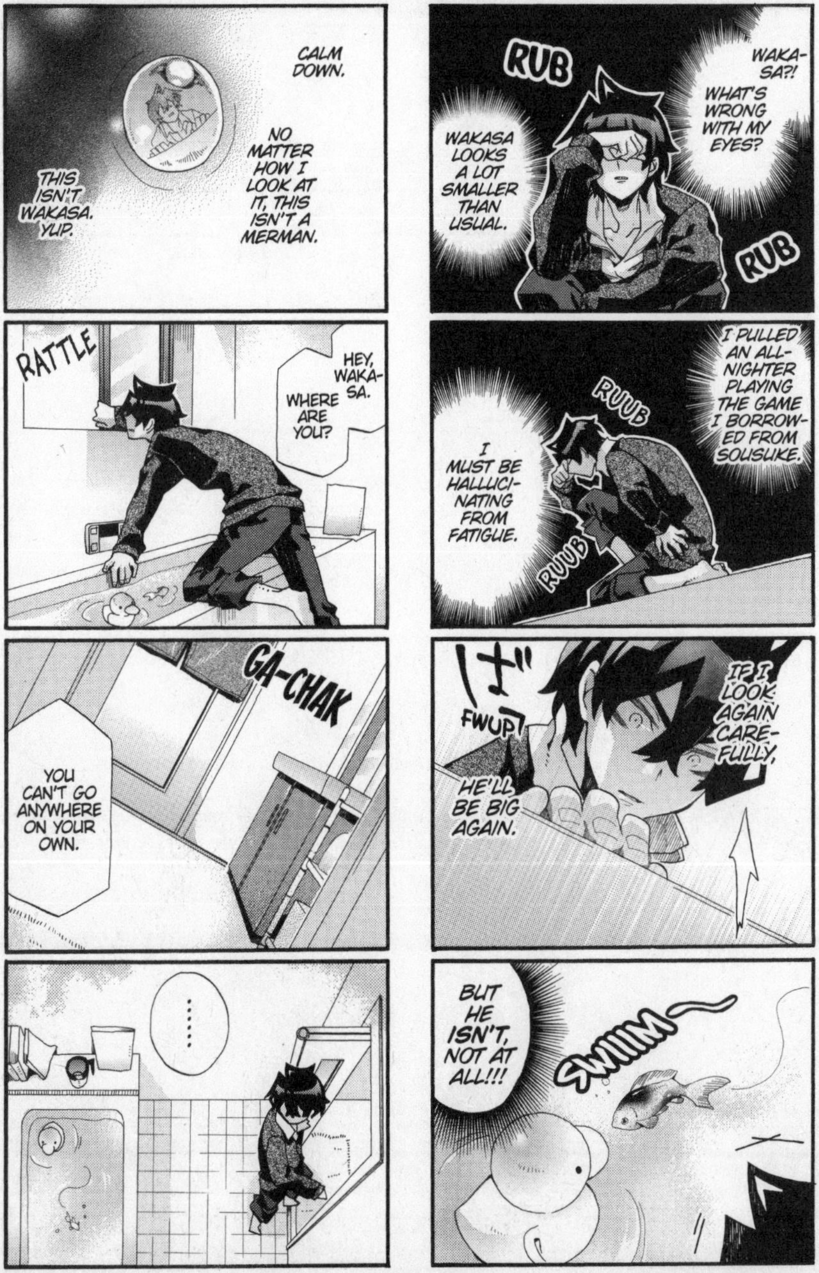
WAKA-SA?!
WHAT'S WRONG WITH MY EYES?
RUB
WAKASA LOOKS A LOT SMALLER THAN USUAL.
RUB
CALM DOWN.
NO MATTER HOW I LOOK AT IT, THIS ISN'T A MERMAN.
THIS ISN'T WAKASA. YUP.
I PULLED AN ALL-NIGHTER PLAYING THE GAME I BORROW-ED FROM SOUSUKE.
RUUB
I MUST BE HALLUCI-NATING FROM FATIGUE.
RUUB
HEY, WAKA-SA.
WHERE ARE YOU?
RATTLE
IF I LOOK AGAIN CARE-FULLY,
ば
FWUP
HE'LL BE BIG AGAIN.
GA-CHAK
YOU CAN'T GO ANYWHERE ON YOUR OWN.
BUT HE ISN'T, NOT AT ALL!!!
SWIIIM
......

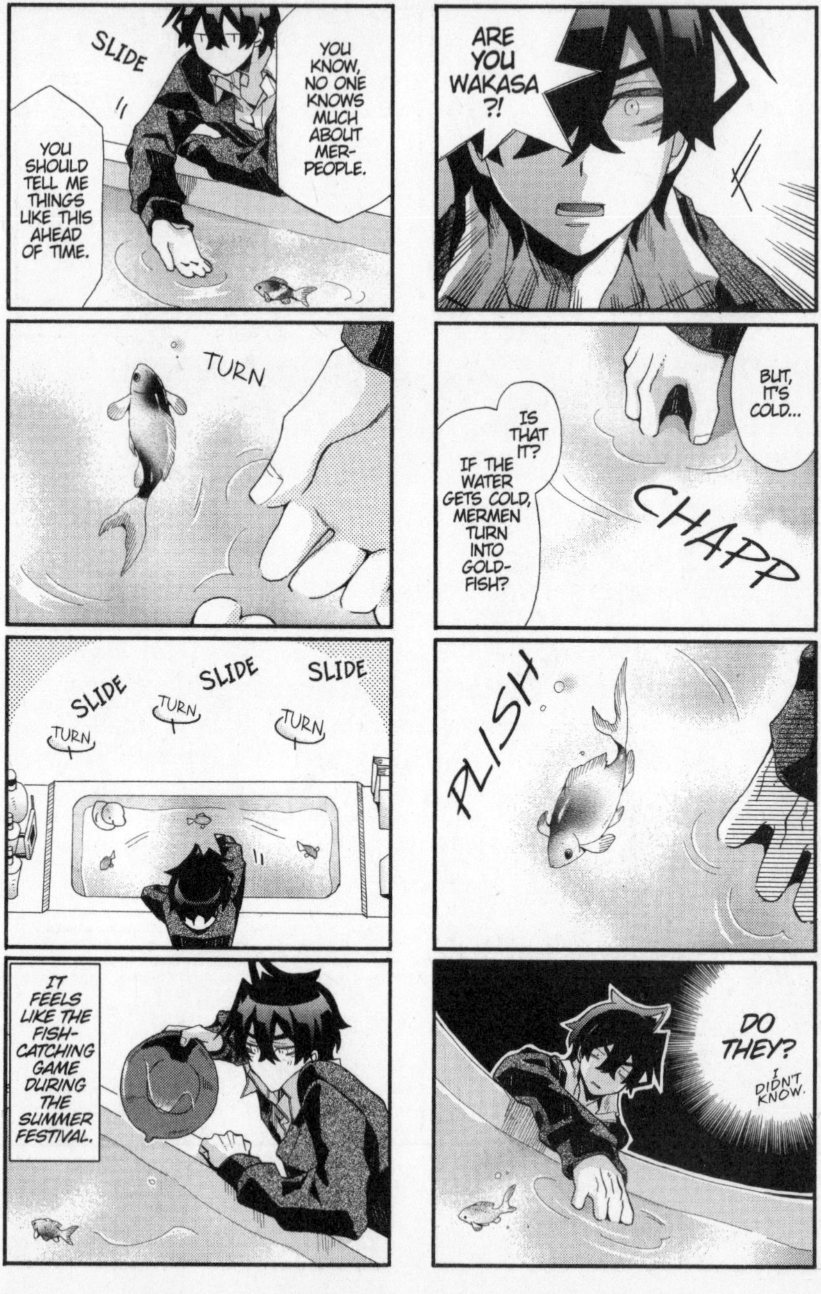
ARE YOU WAKASA?!
YOU KNOW, NO ONE KNOWS MUCH ABOUT MER-PEOPLE.
SLIDE
YOU SHOULD TELL ME THINGS LIKE THIS AHEAD OF TIME.
BUT, IT'S COLD...
IS THAT IT? IF THE WATER GETS COLD, MERMEN TURN INTO GOLD-FISH?
CHAPP
TURN
PLISH
SLIDE
SLIDE
SLIDE
TURN
TURN
TURN
DO THEY?
I DIDN'T KNOW.
IT FEELS LIKE THE FISH-CATCHING GAME DURING THE SUMMER FESTIVAL.

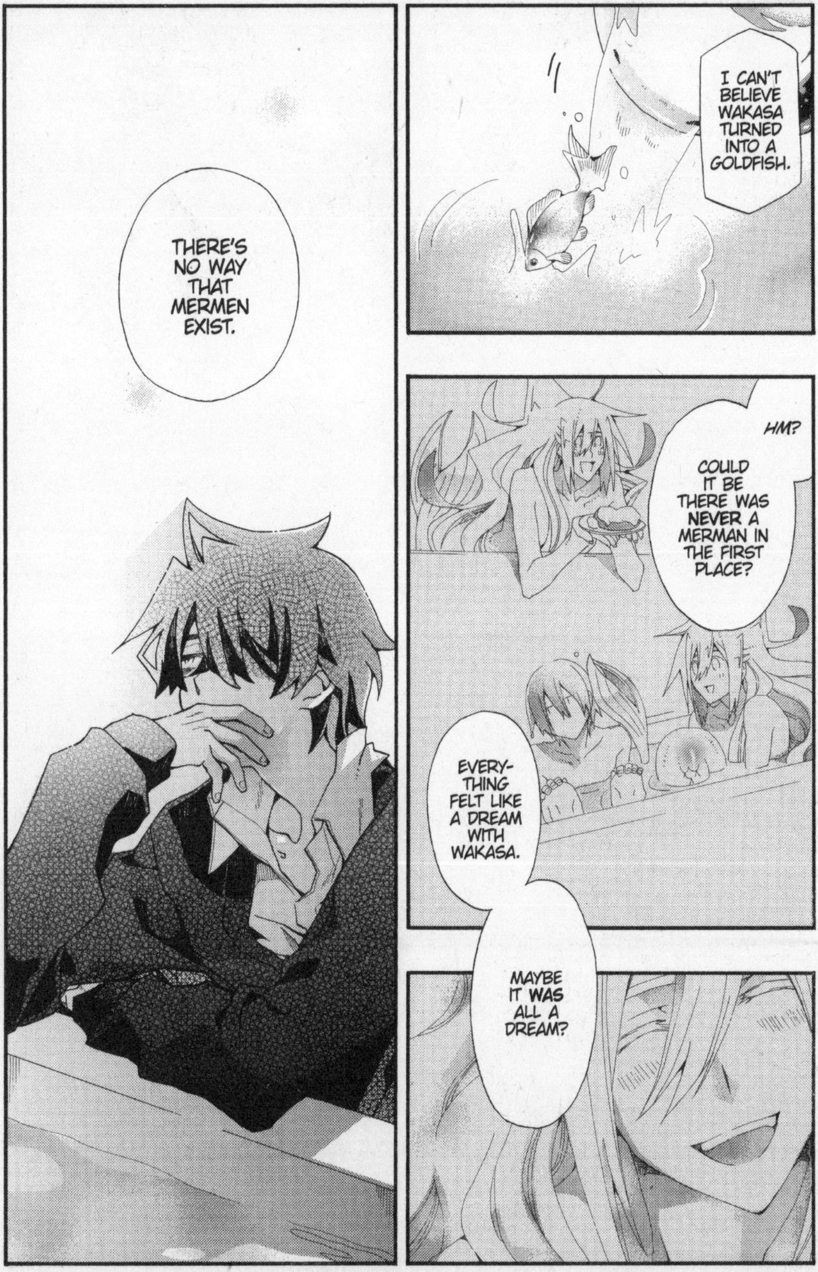
I CAN'T BELIEVE WAKASA TURNED INTO A GOLDFISH.
HM?
COULD IT BE THERE WAS NEVER A MERMAN IN THE FIRST PLACE?
EVERYTHING FELT LIKE A DREAM WITH WAKASA.
MAYBE IT WAS ALL A DREAM?
THERE'S NO WAY THAT MERMEN EXIST.

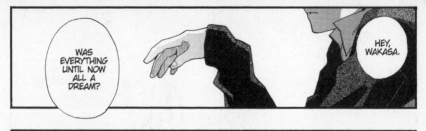

HEY, WAKASA.
WAS EVERYTHING UNTIL NOW ALL A DREAM?
YOU WON'T SPEAK WITH ME...
OR PLAY WITH ME...
EAT WITH ME...
ANYMORE?
PLISH
HEY.
SAY SOME-THING...
WAKASA.

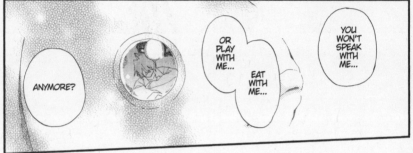

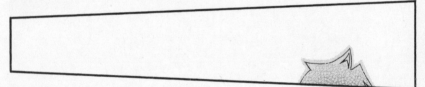

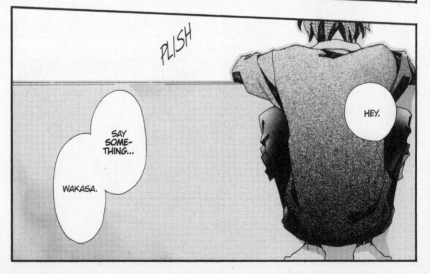

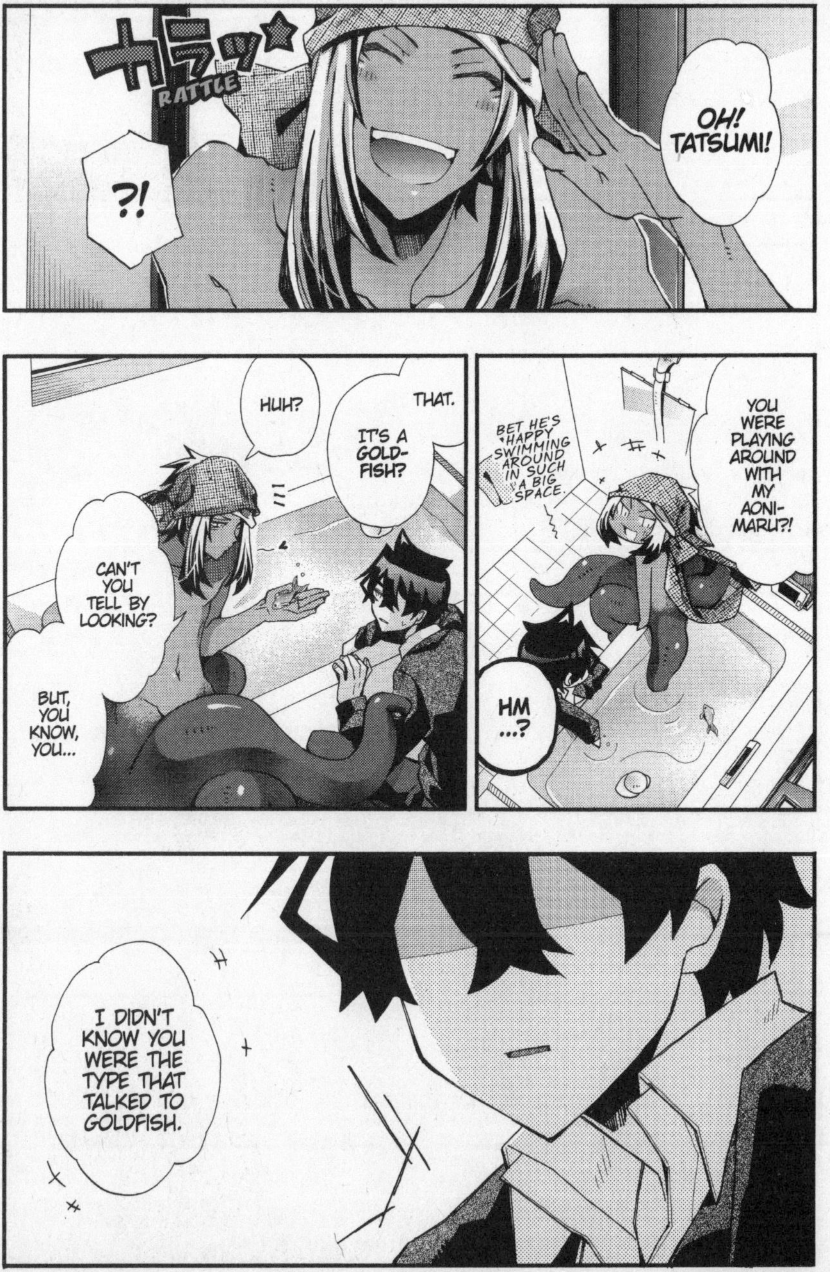
OH! TATSUMI!
カラッ☆
RATTLE
?!
YOU WERE PLAYING AROUND WITH MY AONI-MARU?!
BET HE'S HAPPY SWIMMING AROUND IN SUCH A BIG SPACE.
HM ...?
THAT.
IT'S A GOLD-FISH?
HUH?
CAN'T YOU TELL BY LOOKING?
BUT, YOU KNOW, YOU...
I DIDN'T KNOW YOU WERE THE TYPE THAT TALKED TO GOLDFISH.

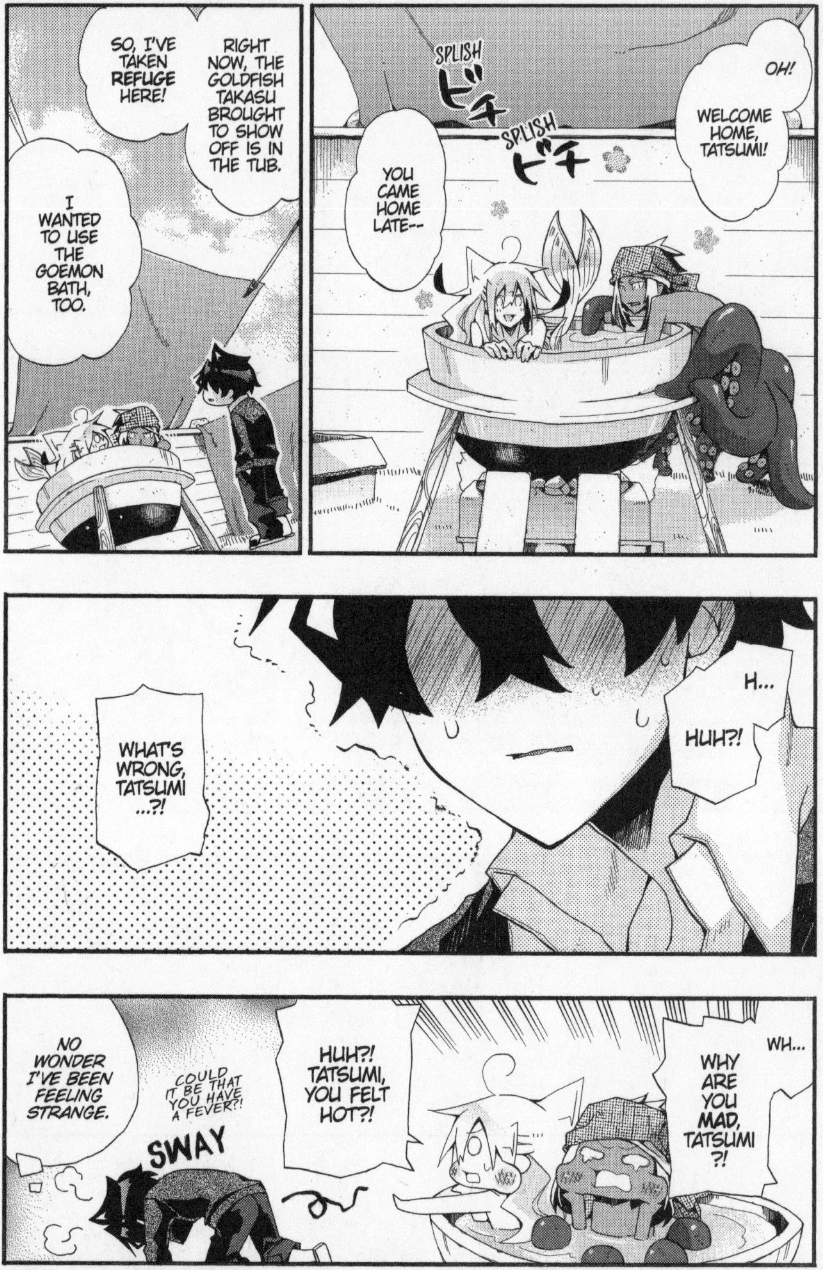
OH!
WELCOME HOME, TATSUMI!
SPLISH ビチ
SPLISH ビチ
YOU CAME HOME LATE--
RIGHT NOW, THE GOLDFISH TAKASU BROUGHT TO SHOW OFF IS IN THE TUB.
SO, I'VE TAKEN REFUGE HERE!
I WANTED TO USE THE GOEMON BATH, TOO.
H...
HUH?!
WHAT'S WRONG, TATSUMI ...?!
WH...
WHY ARE YOU MAD, TATSUMI?!
HUH?! TATSUMI, YOU FELT HOT?!
COULD IT BE THAT YOU HAVE A FEVER?!
NO WONDER I'VE BEEN FEELING STRANGE.
SWAY

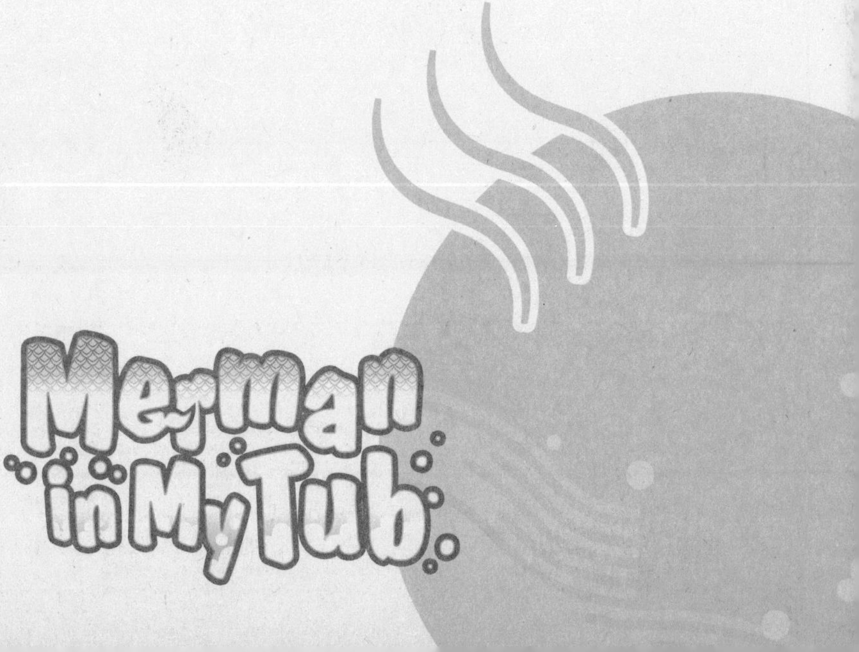

Merman in My Tub

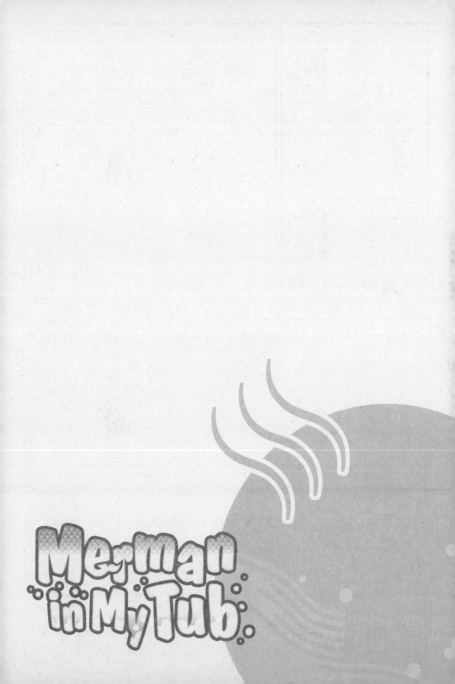

オレん家のフロ事情

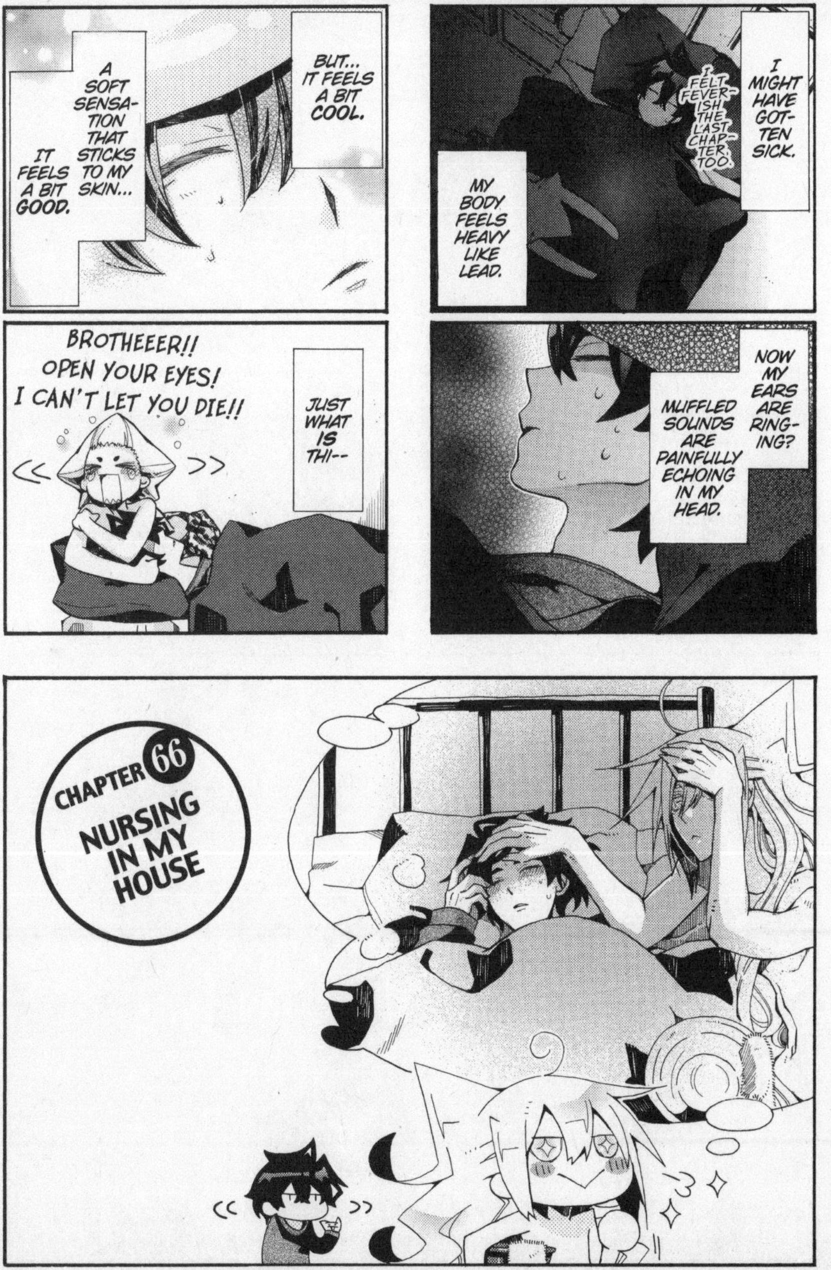
I MIGHT HAVE GOTTEN SICK.
I FELT FEVERISH THE LAST CHAPTER, TOO.
MY BODY FEELS HEAVY LIKE LEAD.
BUT... IT FEELS A BIT COOL.
A SOFT SENSATION THAT STICKS TO MY SKIN...
IT FEELS A BIT GOOD.
NOW MY EARS ARE RINGING?
MUFFLED SOUNDS ARE PAINFULLY ECHOING IN MY HEAD.
JUST WHAT IS THI--
BROTHEEER!! OPEN YOUR EYES! I CAN'T LET YOU DIE!!
CHAPTER 66
NURSING IN MY HOUSE

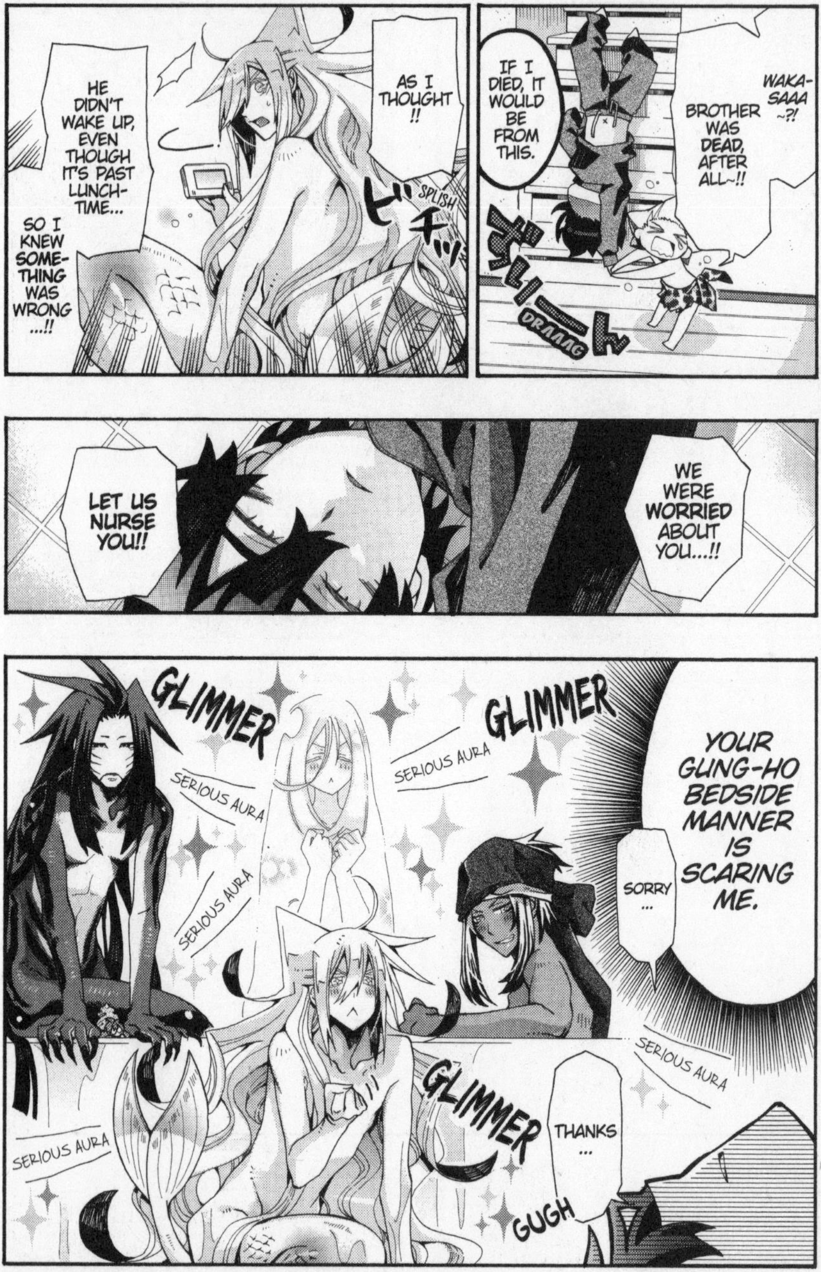
WAKA-SAAAA ~?!
BROTHER WAS DEAD, AFTER ALL~!!
IF I DIED, IT WOULD BE FROM THIS.
DRAAAG
AS I THOUGHT !!
SPLISH
HE DIDN'T WAKE UP, EVEN THOUGH IT'S PAST LUNCH-TIME...
SO I KNEW SOME-THING WAS WRONG ...!!
WE WERE WORRIED ABOUT YOU...!!
LET US NURSE YOU!!
YOUR GUNG-HO BEDSIDE MANNER IS SCARING ME.
SORRY ...
GLIMMER
SERIOUS AURA
GLIMMER
SERIOUS AURA
SERIOUS AURA
SERIOUS AURA
SERIOUS AURA
GLIMMER
THANKS ...
GUGH

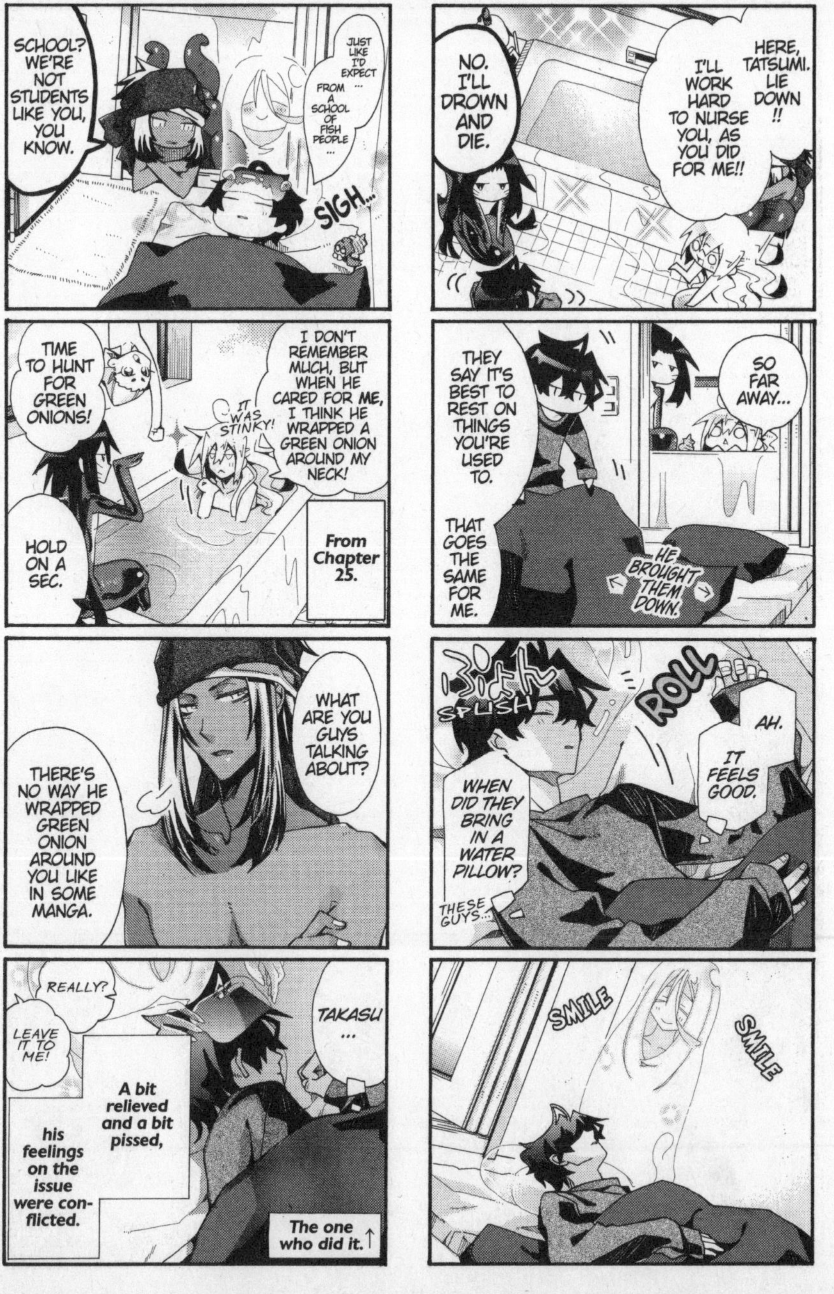
HERE, TATSUMI. LIE DOWN!!
I'LL WORK HARD TO NURSE YOU, AS YOU DID FOR ME!!
NO. I'LL DROWN AND DIE.
SO FAR AWAY...
THEY SAY IT'S BEST TO REST ON THINGS YOU'RE USED TO.
THAT GOES THE SAME FOR ME.
HE BROUGHT THEM DOWN.
ROLL
AH.
IT FEELS GOOD.
SPLISH
WHEN DID THEY BRING IN A WATER PILLOW?
THESE GUYS...
SMILE
SMILE
JUST LIKE I'D EXPECT ... FROM A SCHOOL OF FISH PEOPLE ...
SCHOOL? WE'RE NOT STUDENTS LIKE YOU, YOU KNOW.
SIGH...
I DON'T REMEMBER MUCH, BUT WHEN HE CARED FOR ME, I THINK HE WRAPPED A GREEN ONION AROUND MY NECK!
IT WAS STINKY!
TIME TO HUNT FOR GREEN ONIONS!
HOLD ON A SEC.
From Chapter 25.
WHAT ARE YOU GUYS TALKING ABOUT?
THERE'S NO WAY HE WRAPPED GREEN ONION AROUND YOU LIKE IN SOME MANGA.
TAKASU ...
REALLY?
LEAVE IT TO ME!
A bit relieved and a bit pissed,
his feelings on the issue were conflicted.
The one who did it.↑

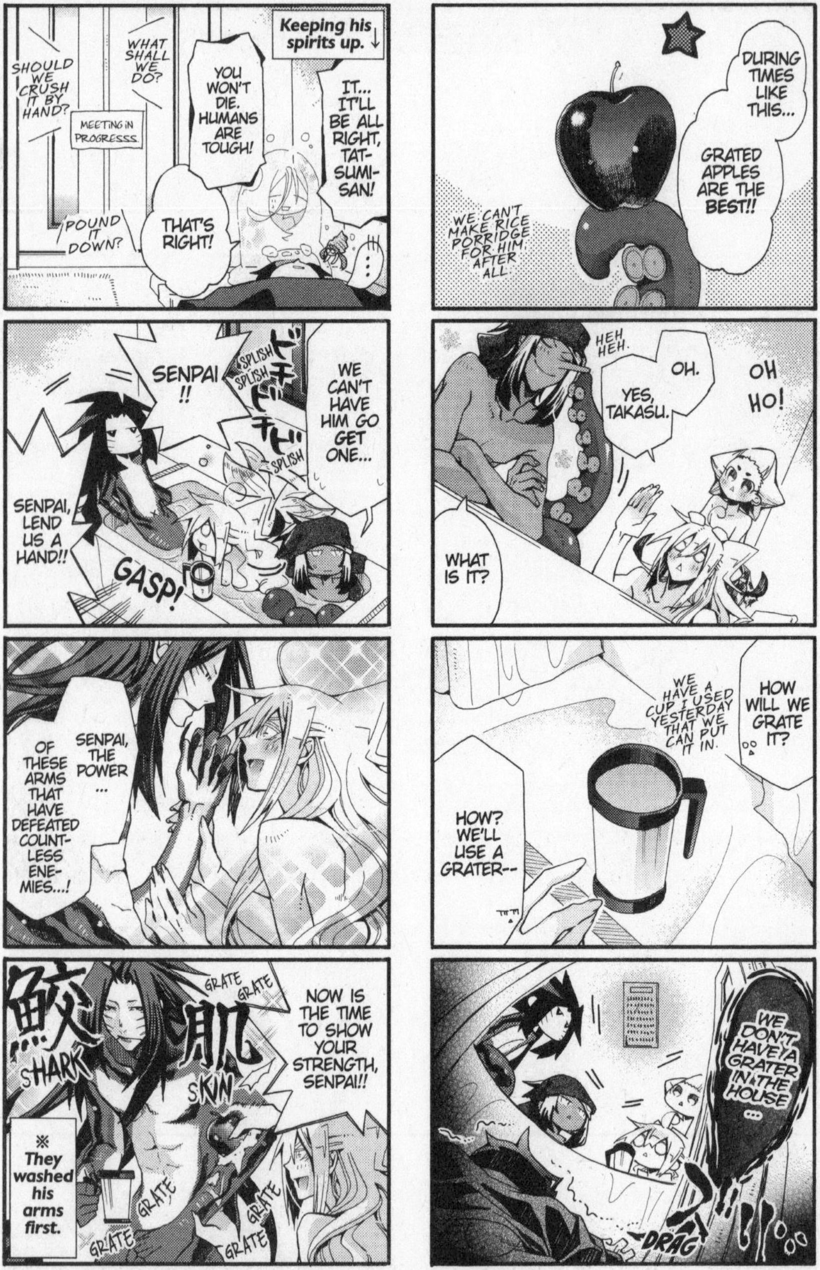
DURING TIMES LIKE THIS...
GRATED APPLES ARE THE BEST!!
WE CAN'T MAKE RICE PORRIDGE FOR HIM AFTER ALL.
OH HO!
HEH HEH.
OH.
YES, TAKASU.
WHAT IS IT?
HOW WILL WE GRATE IT?
WE HAVE A CUP I USED YESTERDAY THAT WE CAN PUT IT IN.
HOW? WE'LL USE A GRATER--
WE DON'T HAVE A GRATER IN THE HOUSE...
DRAG
Keeping his spirits up. ↓
IT... IT'LL BE ALL RIGHT, TATSUMI-SAN!
YOU WON'T DIE. HUMANS ARE TOUGH!
WHAT SHALL WE DO?
SHOULD WE CRUSH IT BY HAND?
MEETING IN PROGRESSS.
THAT'S RIGHT!
POUND IT DOWN?
WE CAN'T HAVE HIM GO GET ONE...
SPLISH SPLISH
SPLISH
SENPAI!!
SENPAI, LEND US A HAND!!
GASP!
SENPAI, THE POWER...
OF THESE ARMS THAT HAVE DEFEATED COUNTLESS ENEMIES...!
NOW IS THE TIME TO SHOW YOUR STRENGTH, SENPAI!!
GRATE GRATE
鮫 SHARK
肌 SKIN
※ They washed his arms first.
GRATE
GRATE
GRATE
GRATE

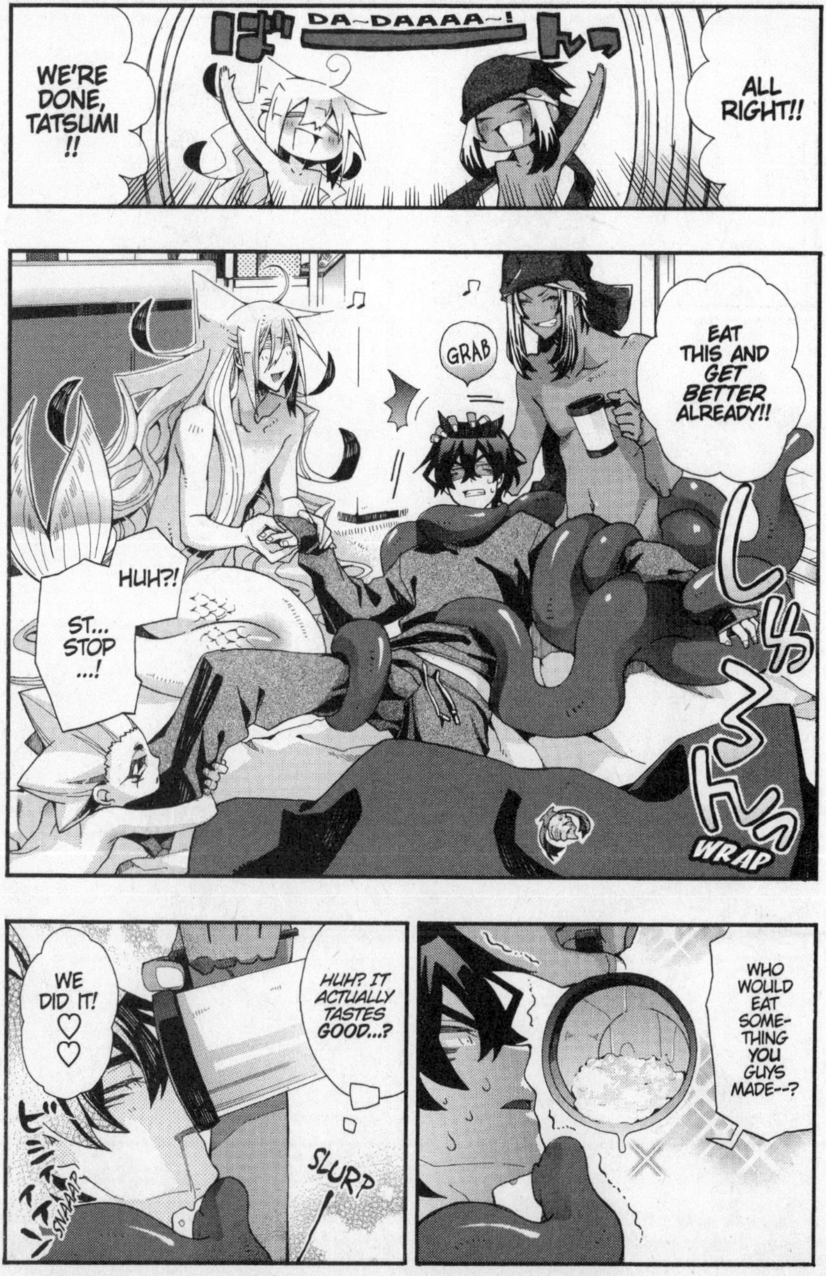
ALL RIGHT!!
DA~DAAAA~!
WE'RE DONE, TATSUMI!!
EAT THIS AND GET BETTER ALREADY!!
GRAB
HUH?!
ST... STOP ...!
WRAP
WHO WOULD EAT SOME-THING YOU GUYS MADE--?
HUH? IT ACTUALLY TASTES GOOD...?
WE DID IT! ♡ ♡
SLURP

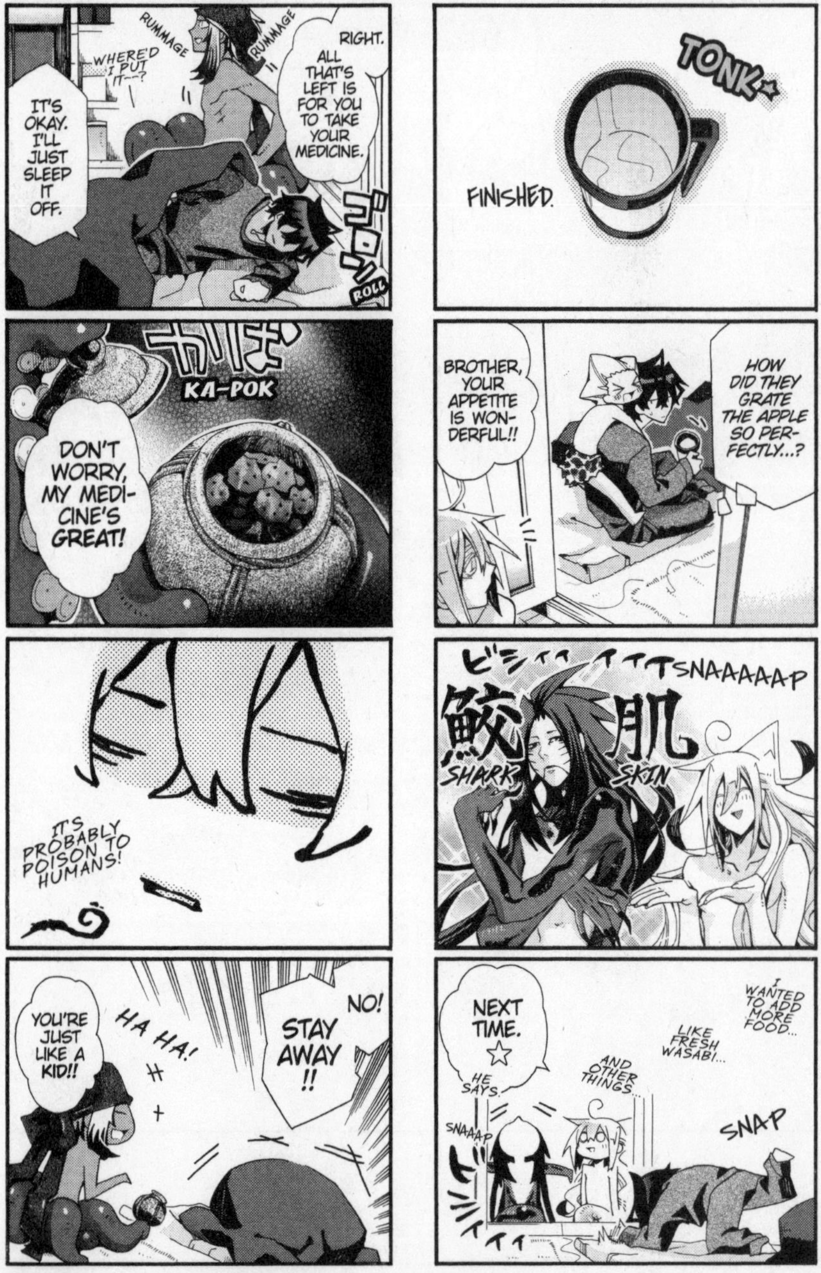
TONK
FINISHED.
HOW DID THEY GRATE THE APPLE SO PERFECTLY...?
BROTHER, YOUR APPETITE IS WONDERFUL!!
ビシィィイイ SNAAAAAAP
鮫 SHARK
肌 SKIN
I WANTED TO ADD MORE FOOD...
LIKE FRESH WASABI...
AND OTHER THINGS...
SNAP
NEXT TIME. ☆
HE SAYS.
SNAAAP
RIGHT. ALL THAT'S LEFT IS FOR YOU TO TAKE YOUR MEDICINE.
RUMMAGE
RUMMAGE
WHERE'D I PUT IT--?
IT'S OKAY. I'LL JUST SLEEP IT OFF.
ゴロン ROLL
かぽ KA-POK
DON'T WORRY, MY MEDI-CINE'S GREAT!
IT'S PROBABLY POISON TO HUMANS!
NO!
STAY AWAY!!
HA HA!
YOU'RE JUST LIKE A KID!!

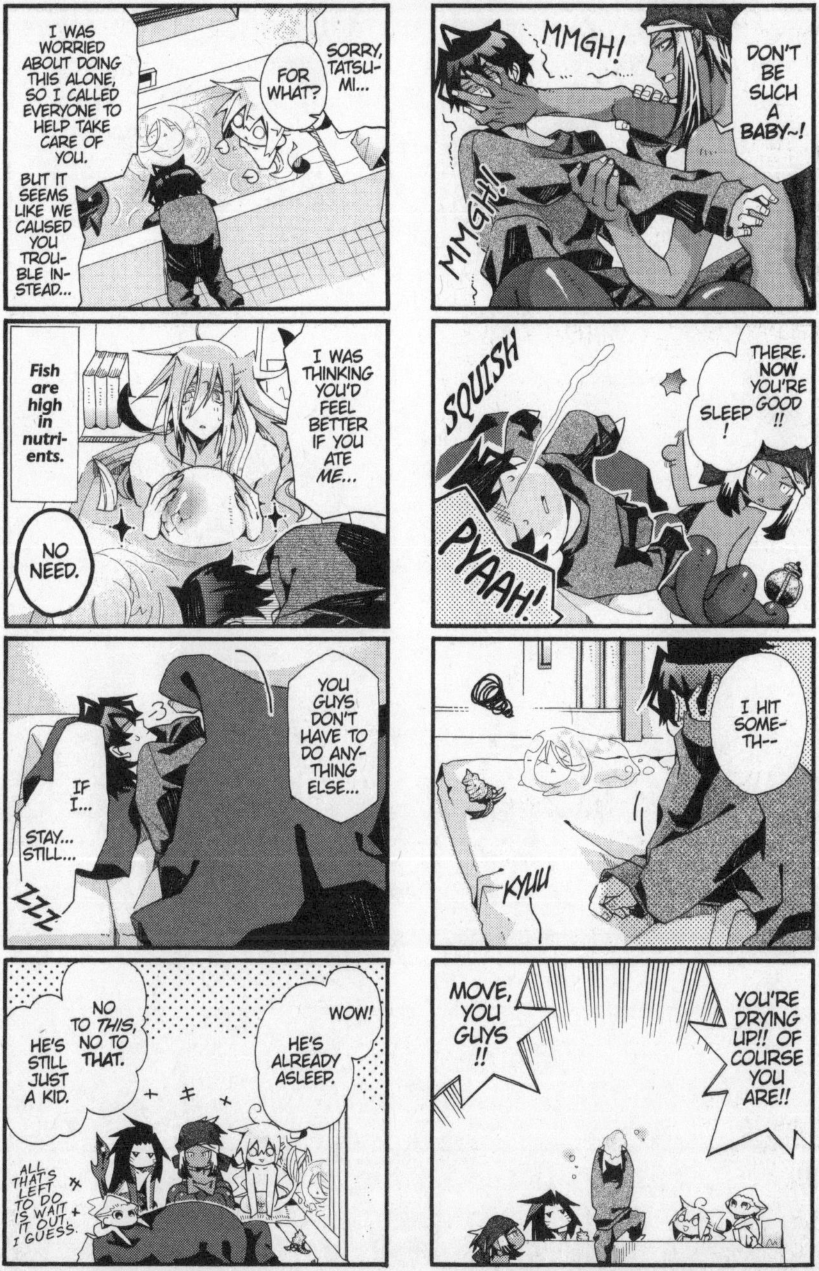
DON'T BE SUCH A BABY~!
MMGH!
MMGH!
THERE. NOW YOU'RE GOOD!!
SLEEP!
SQUISH
PYAAH!
I HIT SOMETH--
KYUU
YOU'RE DRYING UP!! OF COURSE YOU ARE!!
MOVE, YOU GUYS!!
SORRY, TATSUMI...
FOR WHAT?
I WAS WORRIED ABOUT DOING THIS ALONE, SO I CALLED EVERYONE TO HELP TAKE CARE OF YOU.
BUT IT SEEMS LIKE WE CAUSED YOU TROUBLE INSTEAD...
I WAS THINKING YOU'D FEEL BETTER IF YOU ATE ME...
Fish are high in nutrients.
NO NEED.
YOU GUYS DON'T HAVE TO DO ANYTHING ELSE...
IF I...
STAY... STILL...
ZZZ
WOW!
HE'S ALREADY ASLEEP.
NO TO THIS, NO TO THAT.
HE'S STILL JUST A KID.
ALL THAT'S LEFT TO DO IS WAIT IT OUT, I GUESS.

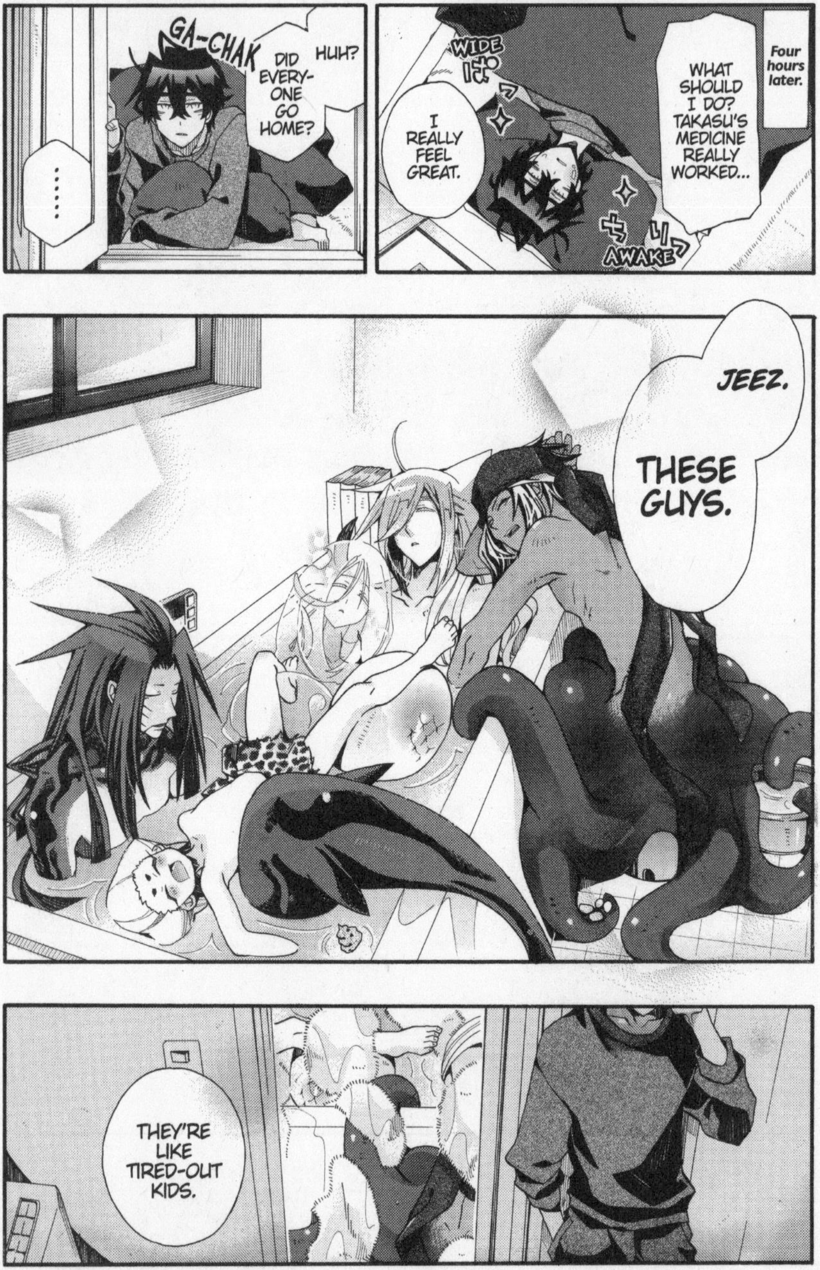
Four hours later.
WHAT SHOULD I DO? TAKASU'S MEDICINE REALLY WORKED...
WIDE
I REALLY FEEL GREAT.
AWAKE
GA-CHAK
HUH?
DID EVERY-ONE GO HOME?
......
JEEZ.
THESE GUYS.
THEY'RE LIKE TIRED-OUT KIDS.

Merman in My Tub

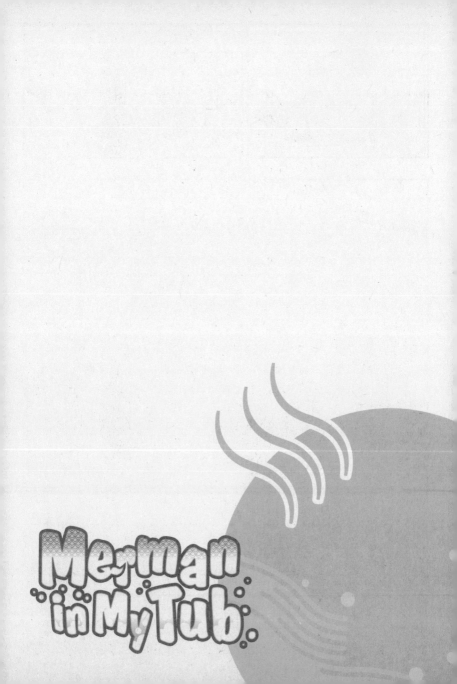

オレん家のフロ事情

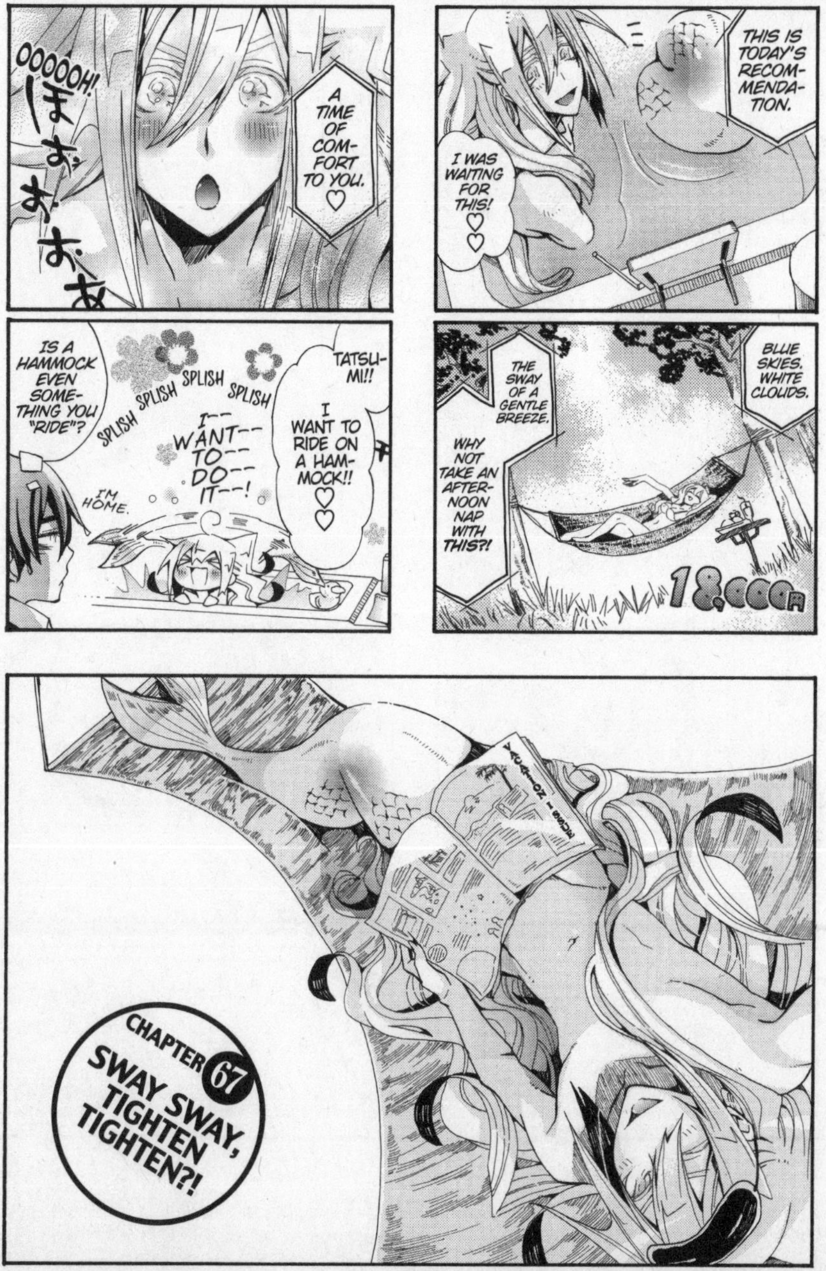
THIS IS TODAY'S RECOMMENDATION.
I WAS WAITING FOR THIS! ♡ ♡
A TIME OF COMFORT TO YOU. ♡
OOOOOH!
BLUE SKIES. WHITE CLOUDS.
THE SWAY OF A GENTLE BREEZE.
WHY NOT TAKE AN AFTERNOON NAP WITH THIS?!
TATSUMI!!
I WANT TO RIDE ON A HAMMOCK!! ♡ ♡
I-- WANT-- TO-- DO IT--!
SPLISH SPLISH SPLISH SPLISH
I'M HOME.
IS A HAMMOCK EVEN SOMETHING YOU "RIDE"?
CHAPTER 67
SWAY SWAY, TIGHTEN TIGHTEN?!

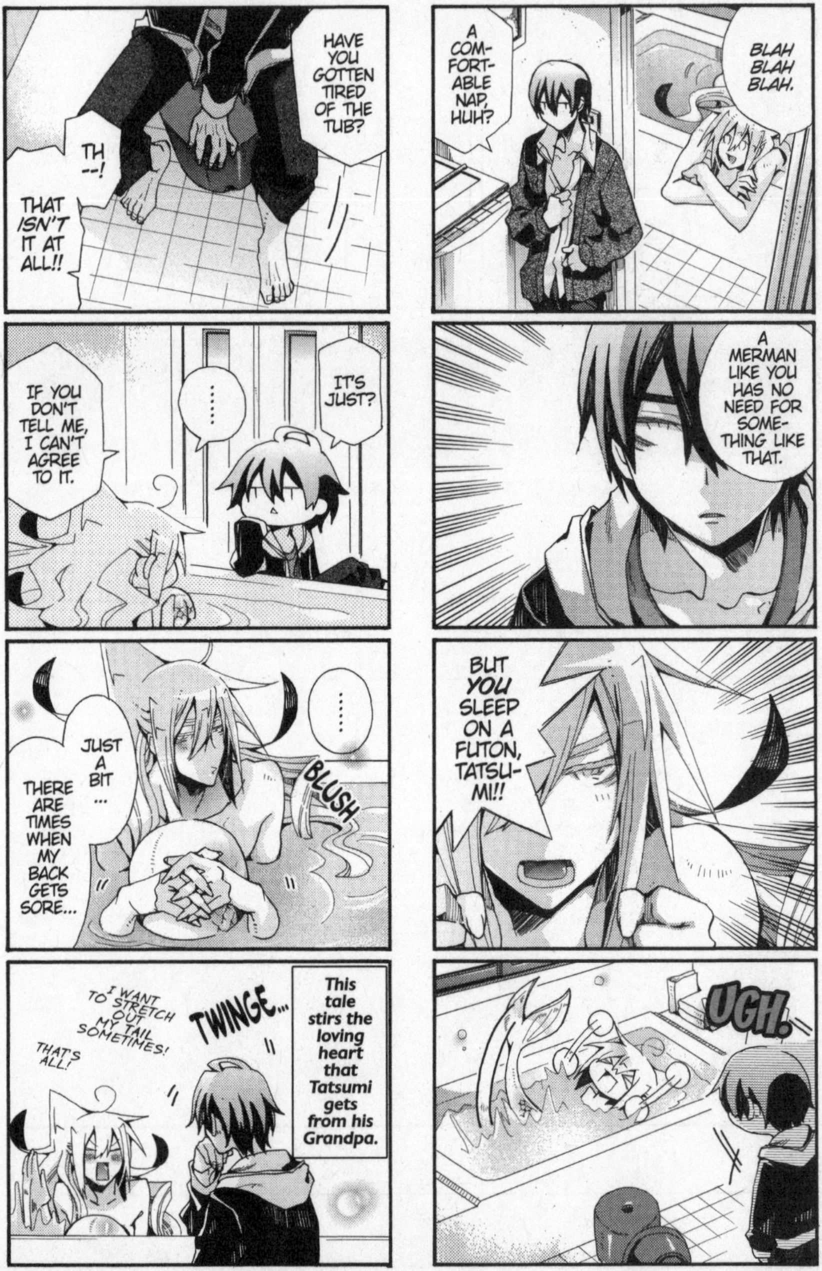
BLAH BLAH BLAH.
A COM-FORT-ABLE NAP, HUH?
HAVE YOU GOTTEN TIRED OF THE TUB?
TH--!
THAT ISN'T IT AT ALL!!
A MERMAN LIKE YOU HAS NO NEED FOR SOME-THING LIKE THAT.
IT'S JUST?
......
IF YOU DON'T TELL ME, I CAN'T AGREE TO IT.
BUT YOU SLEEP ON A FUTON, TATSU-MI!!
......
BLUSH
JUST A BIT ...
THERE ARE TIMES WHEN MY BACK GETS SORE...
UGH.
This tale stirs the loving heart that Tatsumi gets from his Grandpa.
TWINGE...
I WANT TO STRETCH OUT MY TAIL SOMETIMES!
THAT'S ALL!

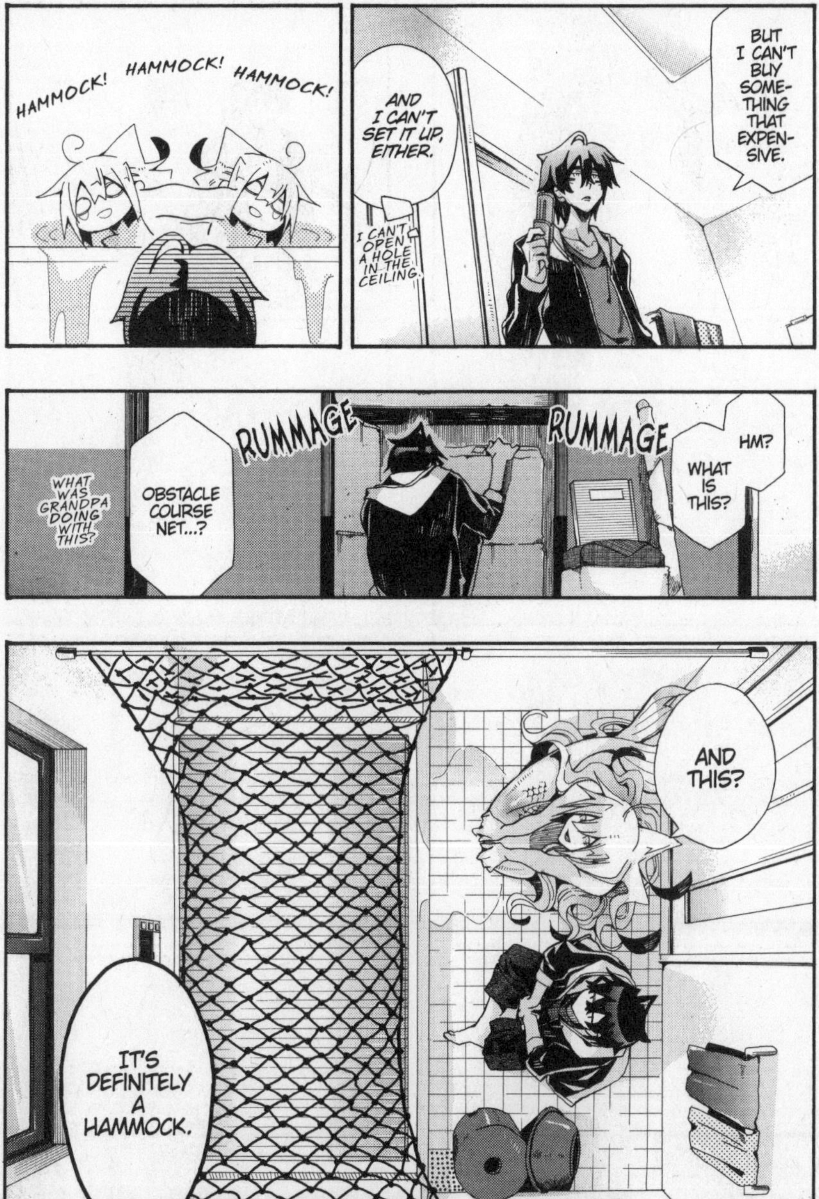
BUT I CAN'T BUY SOMETHING THAT EXPENSIVE.
AND I CAN'T SET IT UP, EITHER.
I CAN'T OPEN A HOLE IN THE CEILING.
HAMMOCK!
HAMMOCK!
HAMMOCK!
HM? WHAT IS THIS?
RUMMAGE
RUMMAGE
OBSTACLE COURSE NET...?
WHAT WAS GRANDPA DOING WITH THIS?
AND THIS?
IT'S DEFINITELY A HAMMOCK.

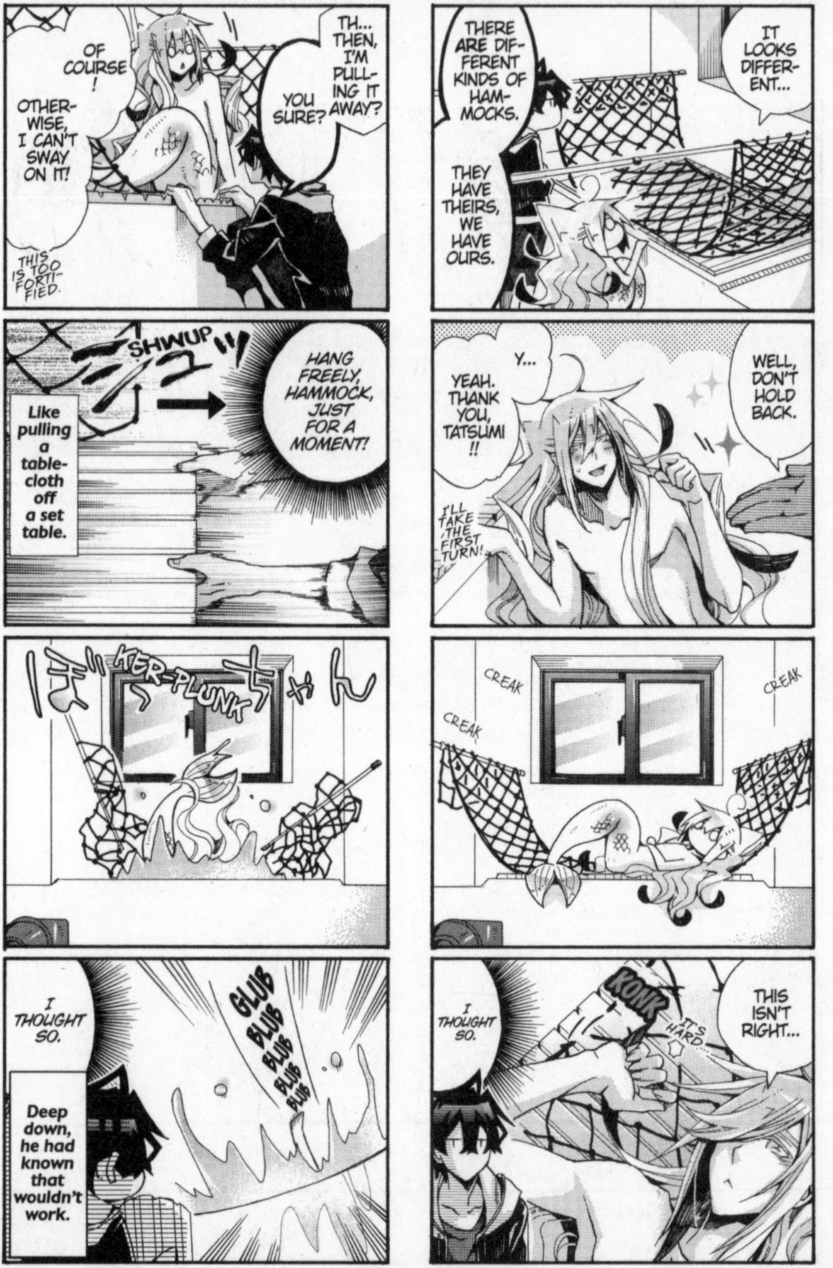
IT LOOKS DIFFERENT...
THERE ARE DIFFERENT KINDS OF HAMMOCKS.
THEY HAVE THEIRS, WE HAVE OURS.
WELL, DON'T HOLD BACK.
Y...
YEAH. THANK YOU, TATSUMI!!
I'LL TAKE THE FIRST TURN!
CREAK
CREAK
CREAK
THIS ISN'T RIGHT...
KONK
IT'S HARD...
I THOUGHT SO.
TH... THEN, I'M PULLING IT AWAY?
YOU SURE?
OF COURSE! OTHERWISE, I CAN'T SWAY ON IT!
THIS IS TOO FORTIFIED.
HANG FREELY, HAMMOCK, JUST FOR A MOMENT!
SHWUP
Like pulling a tablecloth off a set table.
KER-PLUNK
GLUB BLUB BLUB BLUB BLUB
I THOUGHT SO.
Deep down, he had known that wouldn't work.

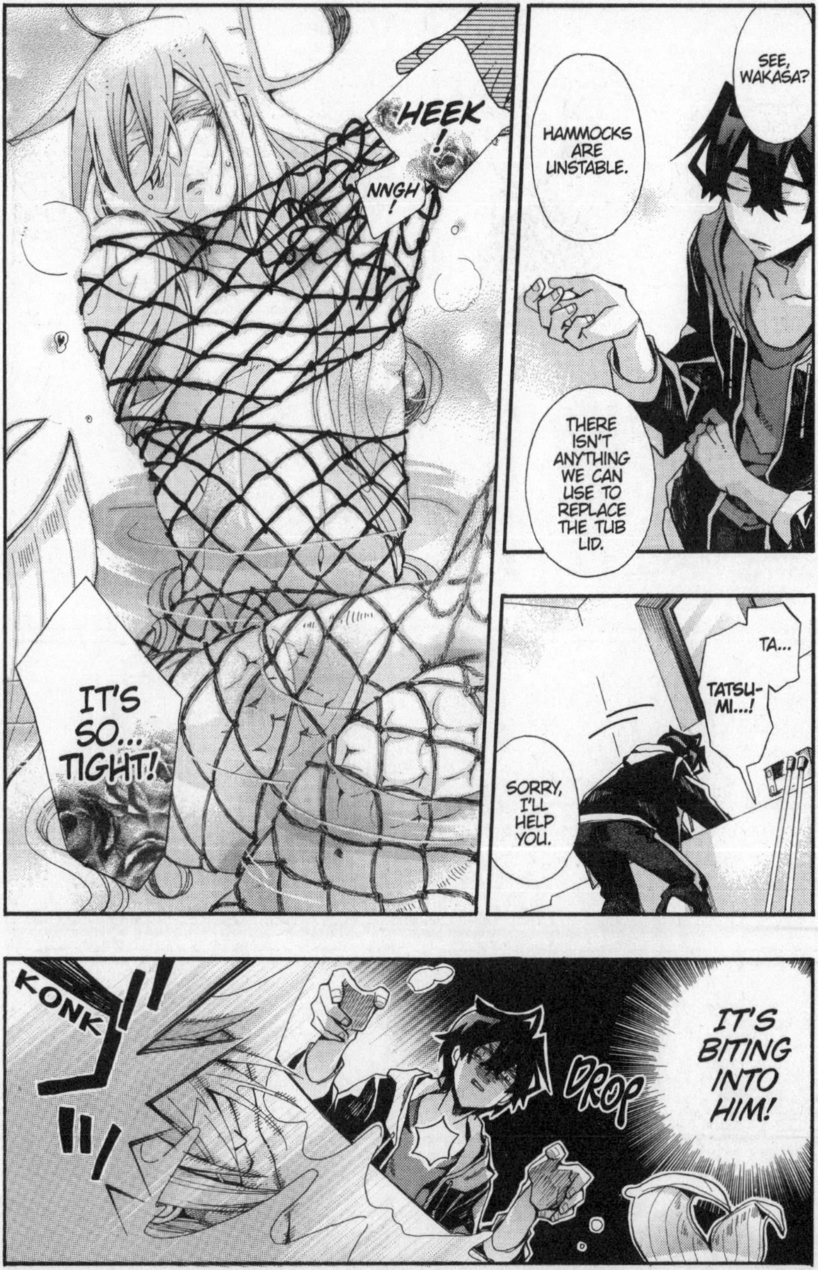
SEE, WAKASA?
HAMMOCKS ARE UNSTABLE.
THERE ISN'T ANYTHING WE CAN USE TO REPLACE THE TUB LID.
TA... TATSUMI...!
SORRY, I'LL HELP YOU.
HEEK!
NNGH!
IT'S SO... TIGHT!
IT'S BITING INTO HIM!
DROP
KONK

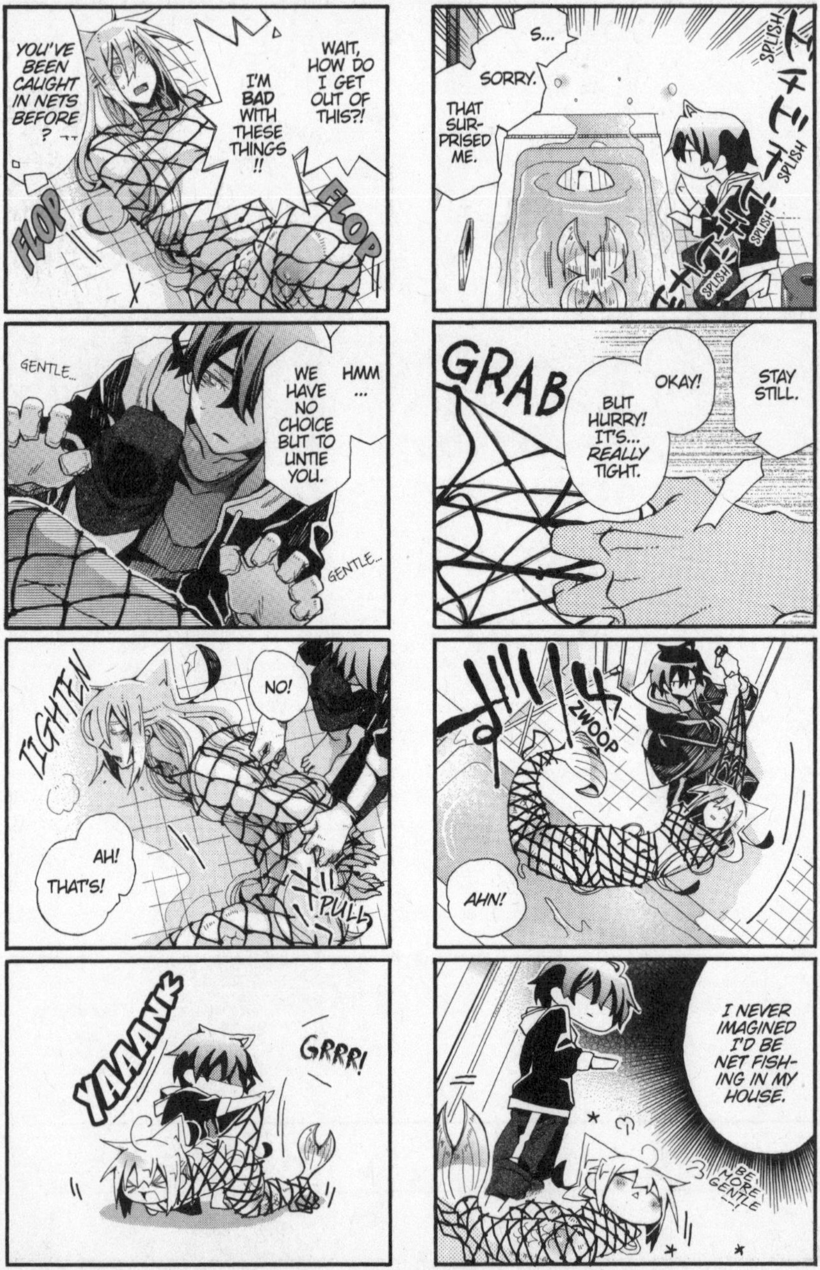
S...
SORRY.
THAT SUR-PRISED ME.
SPLISH
SPLISH
SPLISH
SPLISH
SPLISH
WAIT, HOW DO I GET OUT OF THIS?!
I'M BAD WITH THESE THINGS !!
YOU'VE BEEN CAUGHT IN NETS BEFORE ?
FLOP
FLOP
STAY STILL.
OKAY!
BUT HURRY! IT'S... REALLY TIGHT.
GRAB
HMM ...
WE HAVE NO CHOICE BUT TO UNTIE YOU.
GENTLE...
GENTLE...
ZWOOP
AHN!
NO!
TIGHTEN
AH! THAT'S!
PULL
I NEVER IMAGINED I'D BE NET FISH-ING IN MY HOUSE.
BE MORE GENTLE—!
GRRR!
YAAAANK

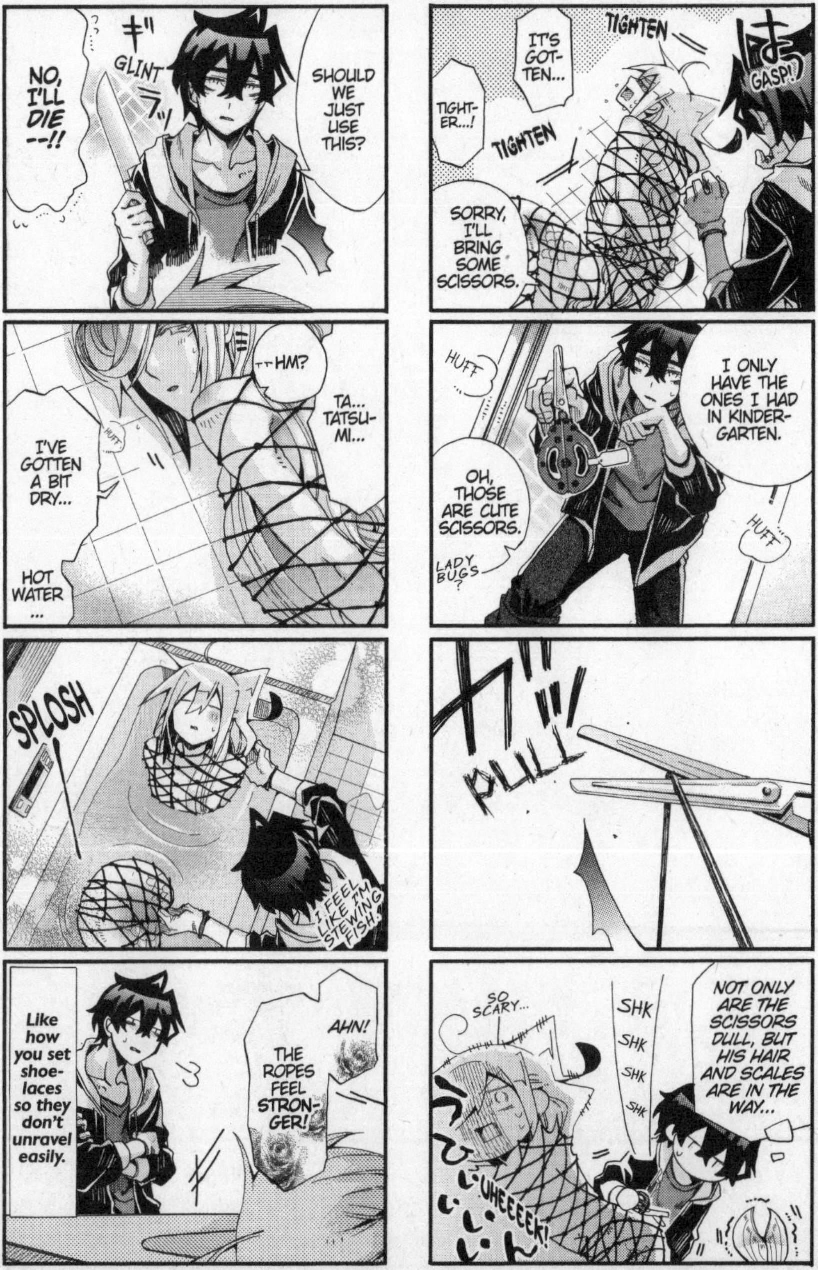
GASP!
TIGHTEN
IT'S GOTTEN...
TIGHTER...!
TIGHTEN
SORRY, I'LL BRING SOME SCISSORS.
I ONLY HAVE THE ONES I HAD IN KINDERGARTEN.
HUFF
HUFF
OH, THOSE ARE CUTE SCISSORS.
LADY BUGS?
PULL
NOT ONLY ARE THE SCISSORS DULL, BUT HIS HAIR AND SCALES ARE IN THE WAY...
SHK
SHK
SHK
SHK
SO SCARY...
UHEEEEK!
SHOULD WE JUST USE THIS?
GLINT
NO, I'LL DIE--!!
HM?
TA... TATSUMI...
HUFF
I'VE GOTTEN A BIT DRY...
HOT WATER...
I FEEL LIKE I'M STEWING FISH.
SPLOSH
AHN!
THE ROPES FEEL STRONGER!
Like how you set shoe-laces so they don't unravel easily.

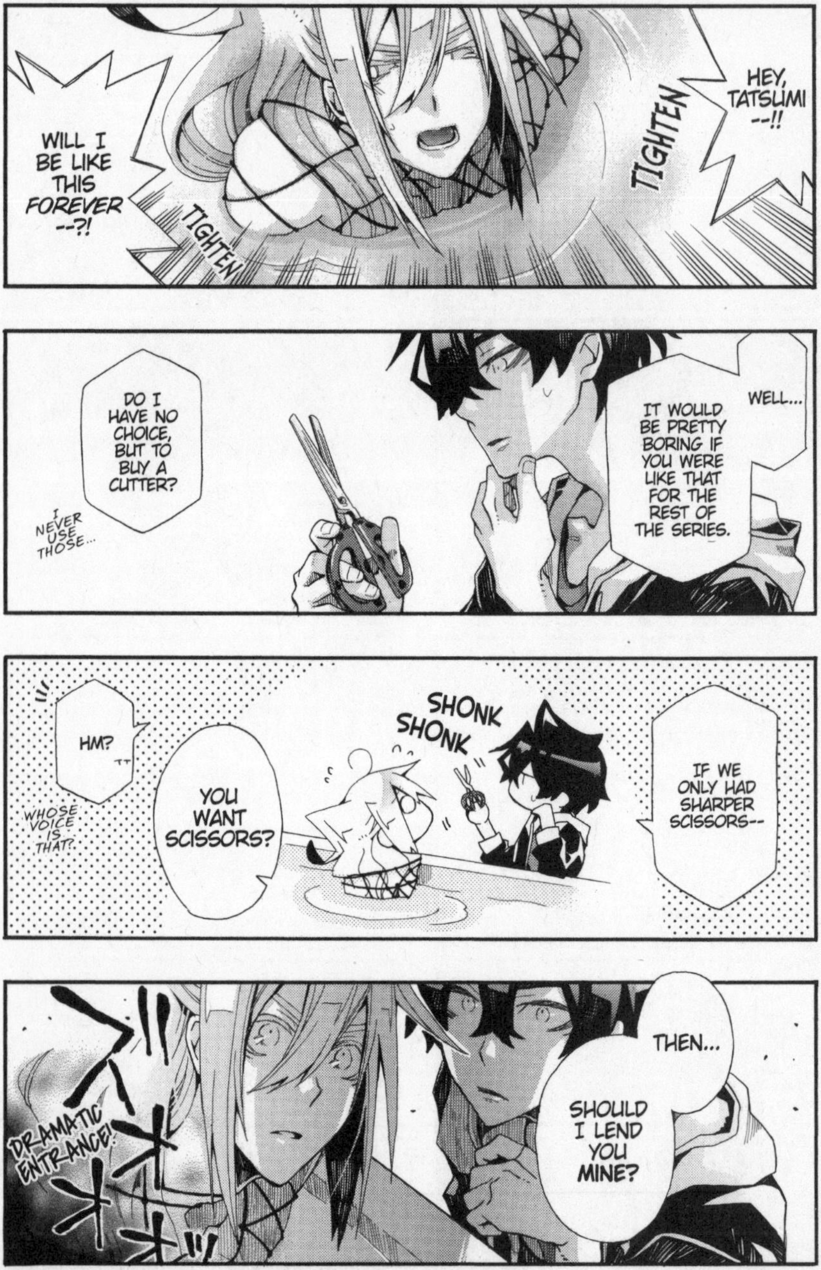
HEY, TATSUMI --!!
TIGHTEN
WILL I BE LIKE THIS FOREVER --?!
TIGHTEN
WELL...
IT WOULD BE PRETTY BORING IF YOU WERE LIKE THAT FOR THE REST OF THE SERIES.
DO I HAVE NO CHOICE, BUT TO BUY A CUTTER?
I NEVER USE THOSE...
IF WE ONLY HAD SHARPER SCISSORS--
SHONK SHONK
YOU WANT SCISSORS?
HM?
WHOSE VOICE IS THAT?
THEN...
SHOULD I LEND YOU MINE?
DRAMATIC ENTRANCE!

Merman in My Tub

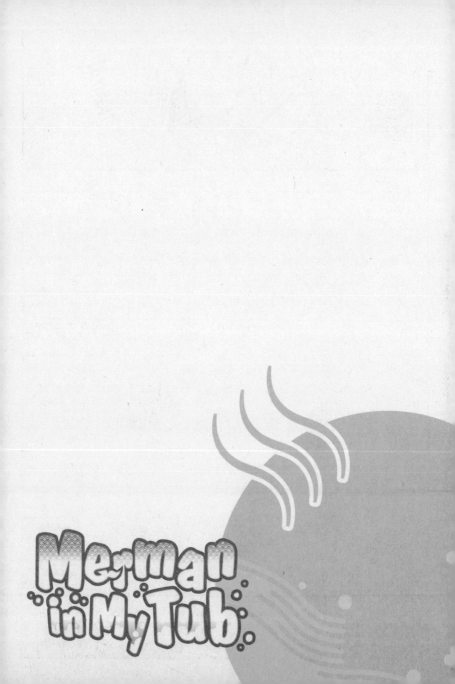

オレん家のフロ事情

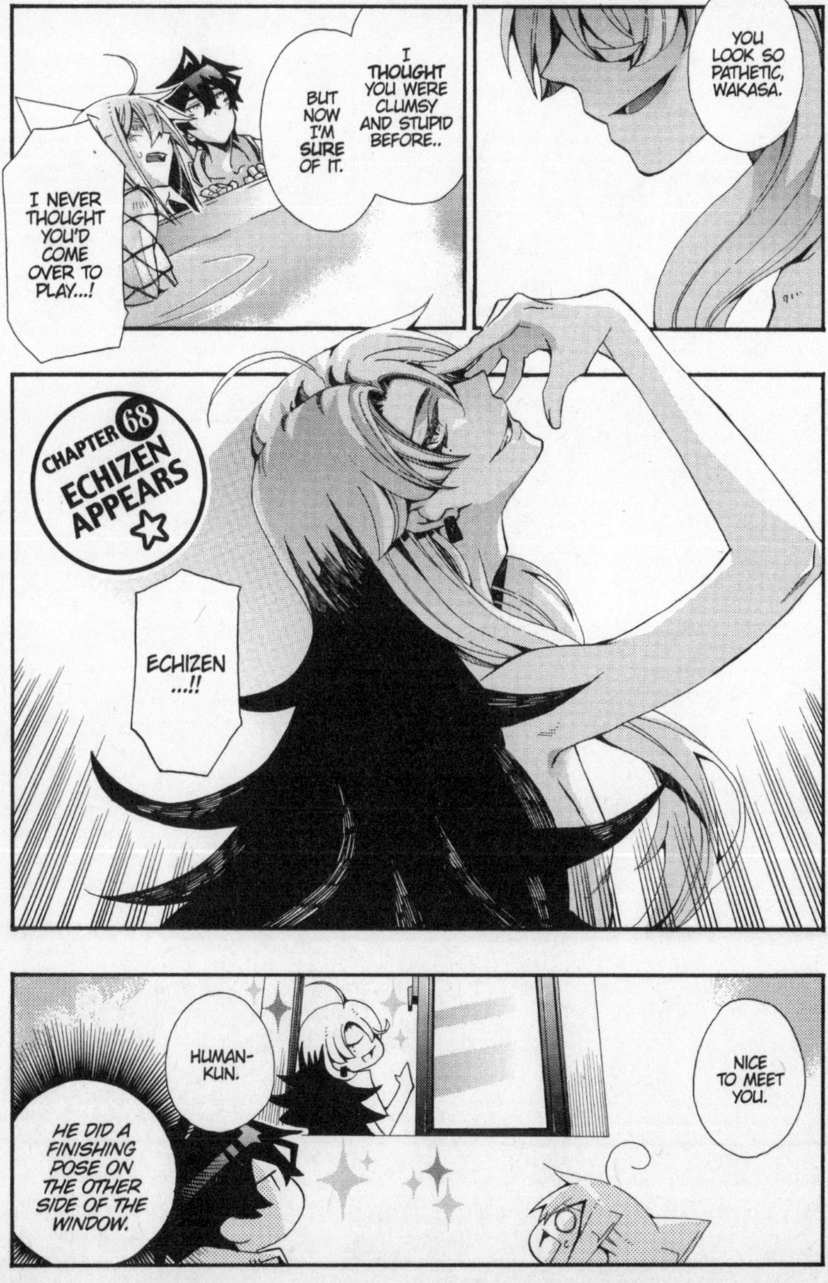
YOU LOOK SO PATHETIC, WAKASA.
I THOUGHT YOU WERE CLUMSY AND STUPID BEFORE..
BUT NOW I'M SURE OF IT.
I NEVER THOUGHT YOU'D COME OVER TO PLAY...!
CHAPTER 68
ECHIZEN APPEARS ☆
ECHIZEN ...!!
NICE TO MEET YOU.
HUMAN-KUN.
HE DID A FINISHING POSE ON THE OTHER SIDE OF THE WINDOW.

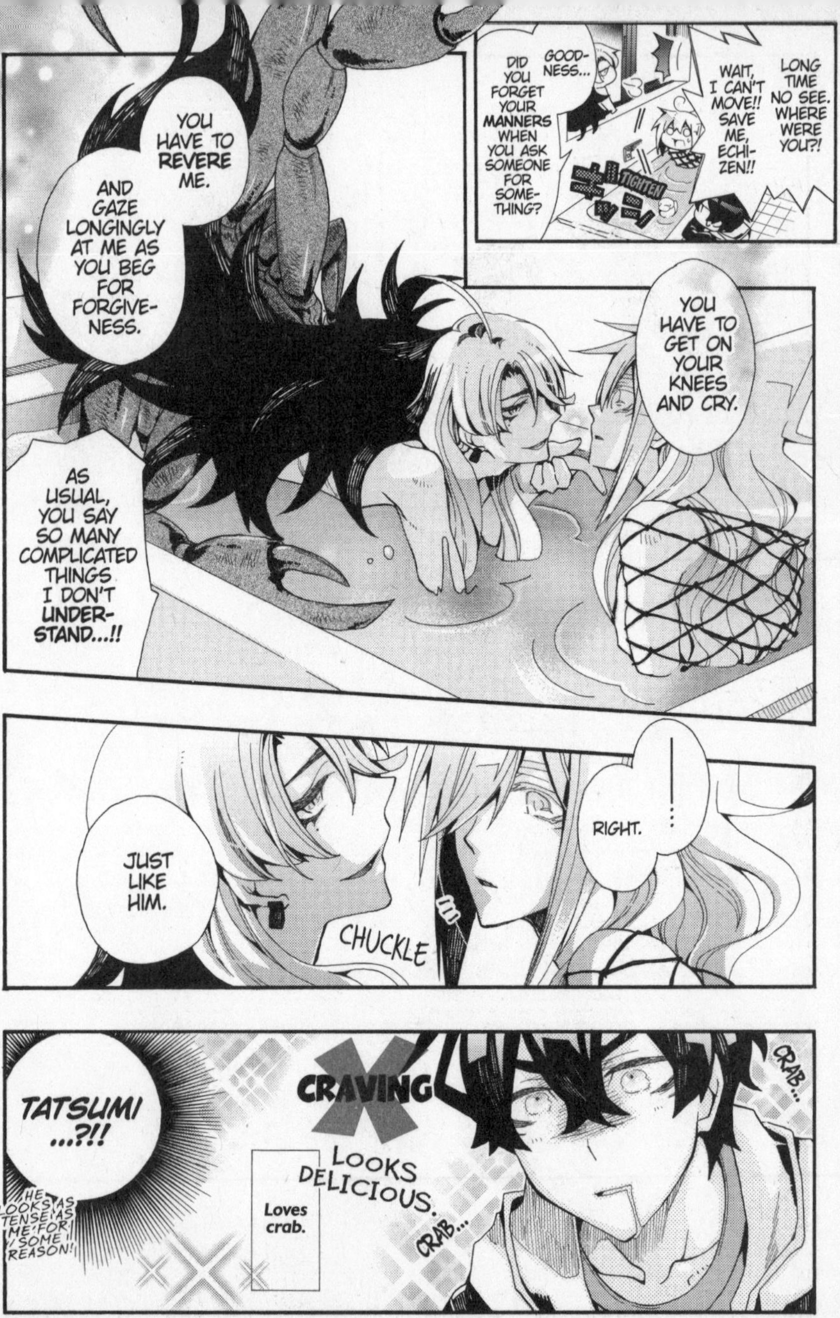
LONG TIME NO SEE. WHERE WERE YOU?!
WAIT, I CAN'T MOVE!! SAVE ME, ECHIZEN!!
TIGHTEN
GOODNESS...
DID YOU FORGET YOUR MANNERS WHEN YOU ASK SOMEONE FOR SOMETHING?
YOU HAVE TO GET ON YOUR KNEES AND CRY.
YOU HAVE TO REVERE ME.
AND GAZE LONGINGLY AT ME AS YOU BEG FOR FORGIVENESS.
AS USUAL, YOU SAY SO MANY COMPLICATED THINGS I DON'T UNDERSTAND...!!
—...
RIGHT.
JUST LIKE HIM.
CHUCKLE
CRAB...
CRAVING X LOOKS DELICIOUS.
CRAB...
Loves crab.
TATSUMI...?!!
HE LOOKS AS TENSE AS ME FOR SOME REASON!

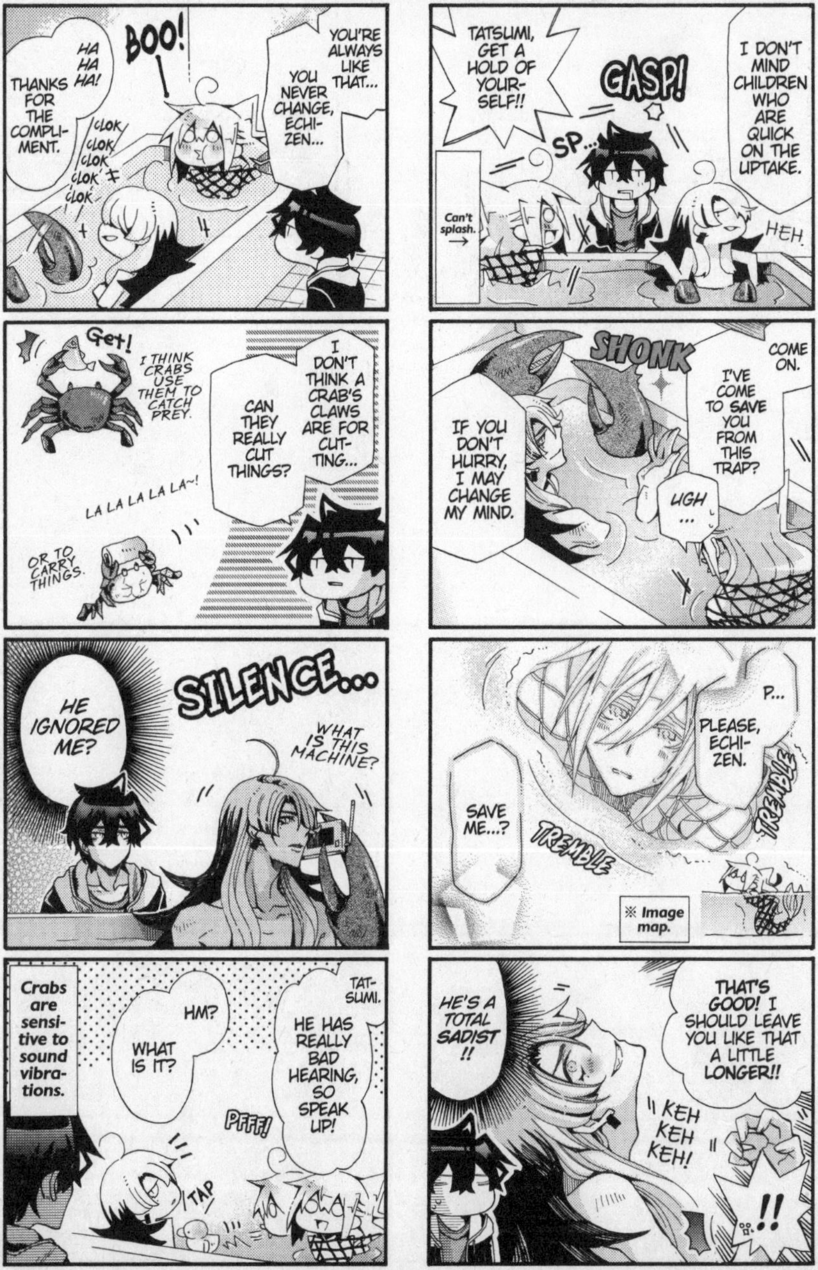
I DON'T MIND CHILDREN WHO ARE QUICK ON THE UPTAKE.
GASP!
TATSUMI, GET A HOLD OF YOURSELF!!
SP...
HEH
Can't splash.
COME ON.
I'VE COME TO SAVE YOU FROM THIS TRAP?
SHONK
IF YOU DON'T HURRY, I MAY CHANGE MY MIND.
UGH ...
P... PLEASE, ECHIZEN.
TREMBLE
SAVE ME...?
TREMBLE
※ Image map.
THAT'S GOOD! I SHOULD LEAVE YOU LIKE THAT A LITTLE LONGER!!
HE'S A TOTAL SADIST !!
KEH KEH KEH!
!!
YOU'RE ALWAYS LIKE THAT...
YOU NEVER CHANGE, ECHIZEN...
BOO!
HA HA HA!
THANKS FOR THE COMPLIMENT.
CLOK CLOK CLOK CLOK CLOK
I DON'T THINK A CRAB'S CLAWS ARE FOR CUTTING...
CAN THEY REALLY CUT THINGS?
I THINK CRABS USE THEM TO CATCH PREY.
Get!
LA LA LA LA LA~!
OR TO CARRY THINGS.
SILENCE...
WHAT IS THIS MACHINE?
HE IGNORED ME?
TAT-SUMI.
HE HAS REALLY BAD HEARING, SO SPEAK UP!
HM?
WHAT IS IT?
Crabs are sensitive to sound vibrations.
PFFF!
TAP

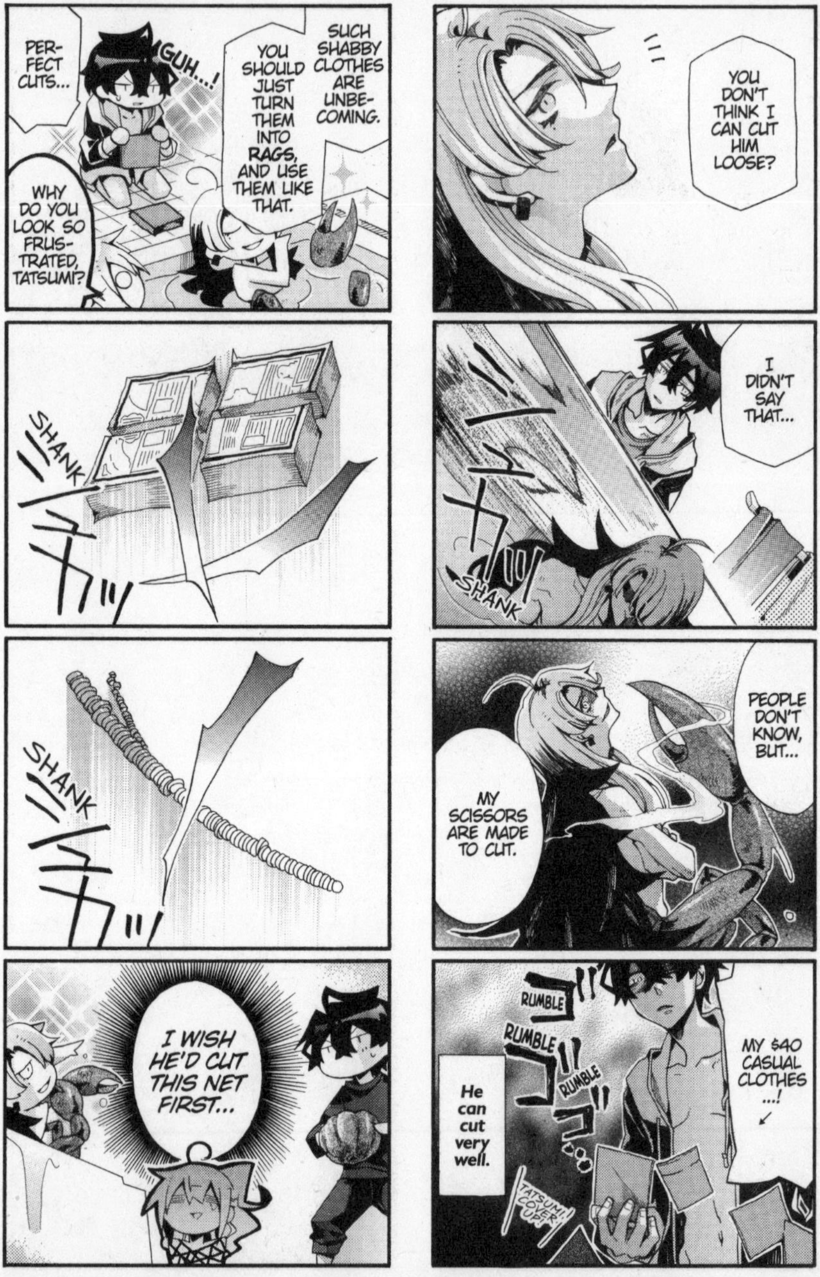
YOU DON'T THINK I CAN CUT HIM LOOSE?
I DIDN'T SAY THAT...
SHANK
PEOPLE DON'T KNOW, BUT...
MY SCISSORS ARE MADE TO CUT.
RUMBLE
RUMBLE
RUMBLE
MY $40 CASUAL CLOTHES ...!
He can cut very well.
TATSUMI, COVER UP!
SUCH SHABBY CLOTHES ARE UNBE-COMING.
YOU SHOULD JUST TURN THEM INTO RAGS, AND USE THEM LIKE THAT.
GUH...!
PER-FECT CUTS...
WHY DO YOU LOOK SO FRUS-TRATED, TATSUMI?
SHANK
SHANK
I WISH HE'D CUT THIS NET FIRST...

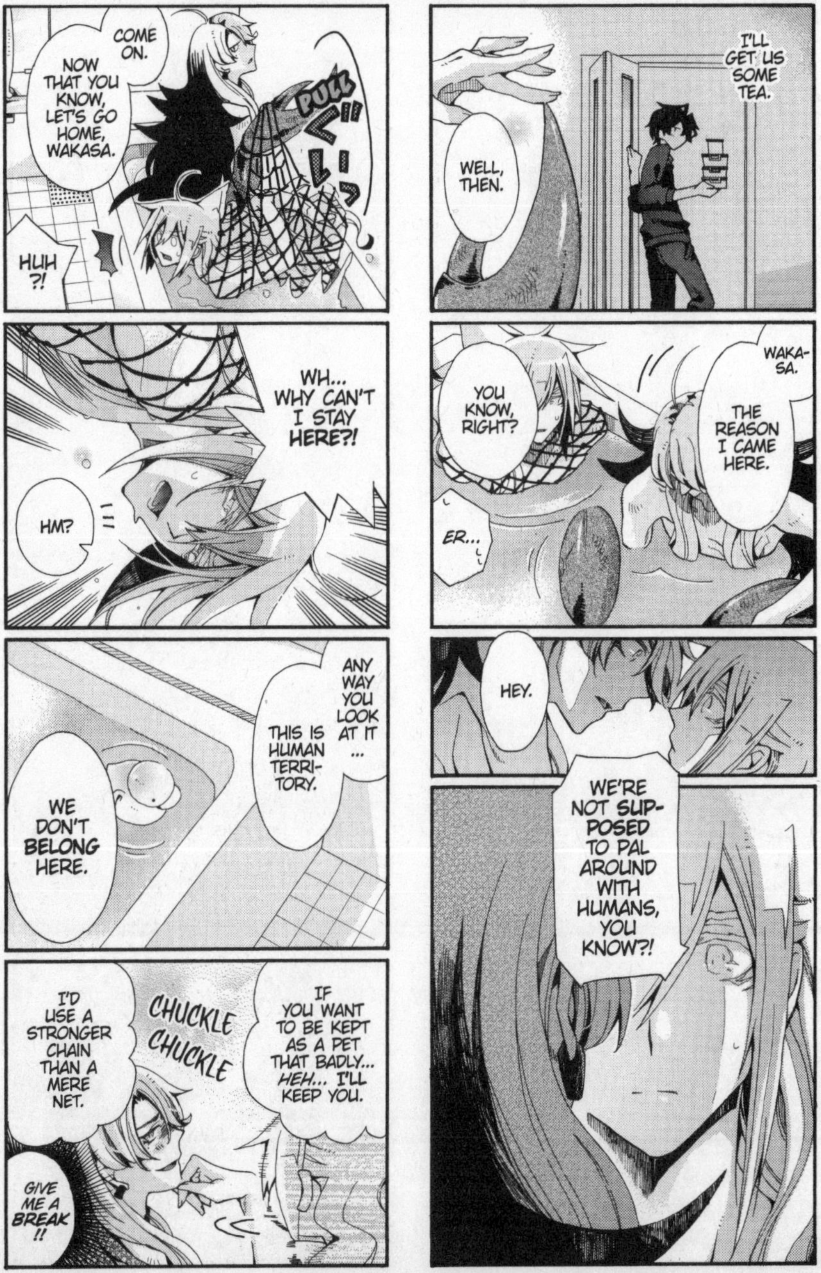
I'LL GET US SOME TEA.
WELL, THEN.
WAKA-SA.
THE REASON I CAME HERE.
YOU KNOW, RIGHT?
ER...
HEY.
WE'RE NOT SUP-POSED TO PAL AROUND WITH HUMANS, YOU KNOW?!
COME ON.
NOW THAT YOU KNOW, LET'S GO HOME, WAKASA.
PULL
HUH?!
WH... WHY CAN'T I STAY HERE?!
HM?
ANY WAY YOU LOOK AT IT...
THIS IS HUMAN TERRI-TORY.
WE DON'T BELONG HERE.
IF YOU WANT TO BE KEPT AS A PET THAT BADLY... HEH... I'LL KEEP YOU.
CHUCKLE CHUCKLE
I'D USE A STRONGER CHAIN THAN A MERE NET.
GIVE ME A BREAK!!

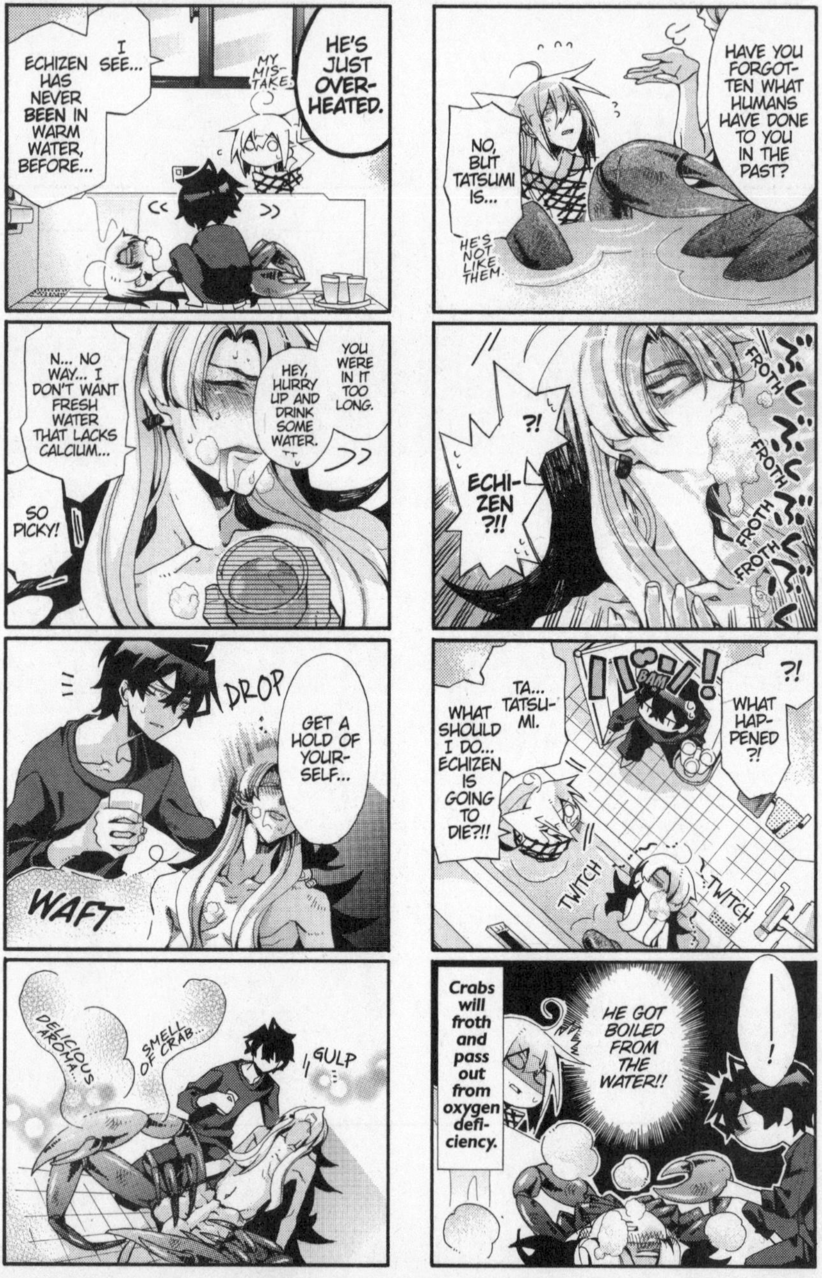

HAVE YOU FORGOTTEN WHAT HUMANS HAVE DONE TO YOU IN THE PAST?
NO, BUT TATSUMI IS...
HE'S NOT LIKE THEM.
HE'S JUST OVER-HEATED.
MY MIS-TAKE.
I SEE... ECHIZEN HAS NEVER BEEN IN WARM WATER, BEFORE...
FROTH
FROTH
FROTH
FROTH
?!
ECHI-ZEN ?!!
YOU WERE IN IT TOO LONG.
HEY, HURRY UP AND DRINK SOME WATER.
N... NO WAY... I DON'T WANT FRESH WATER THAT LACKS CALCIUM...
SO PICKY!
?!
WHAT HAP-PENED ?!
BAM
TA... TATSU-MI.
WHAT SHOULD I DO... ECHIZEN IS GOING TO DIE?!!
TWITCH
TWITCH
DROP
GET A HOLD OF YOUR-SELF...
WAFT
!
HE GOT BOILED FROM THE WATER!!
Crabs will froth and pass out from oxygen defi-ciency.
GULP
SMELL OF CRAB...
DELICIOUS AROMA...

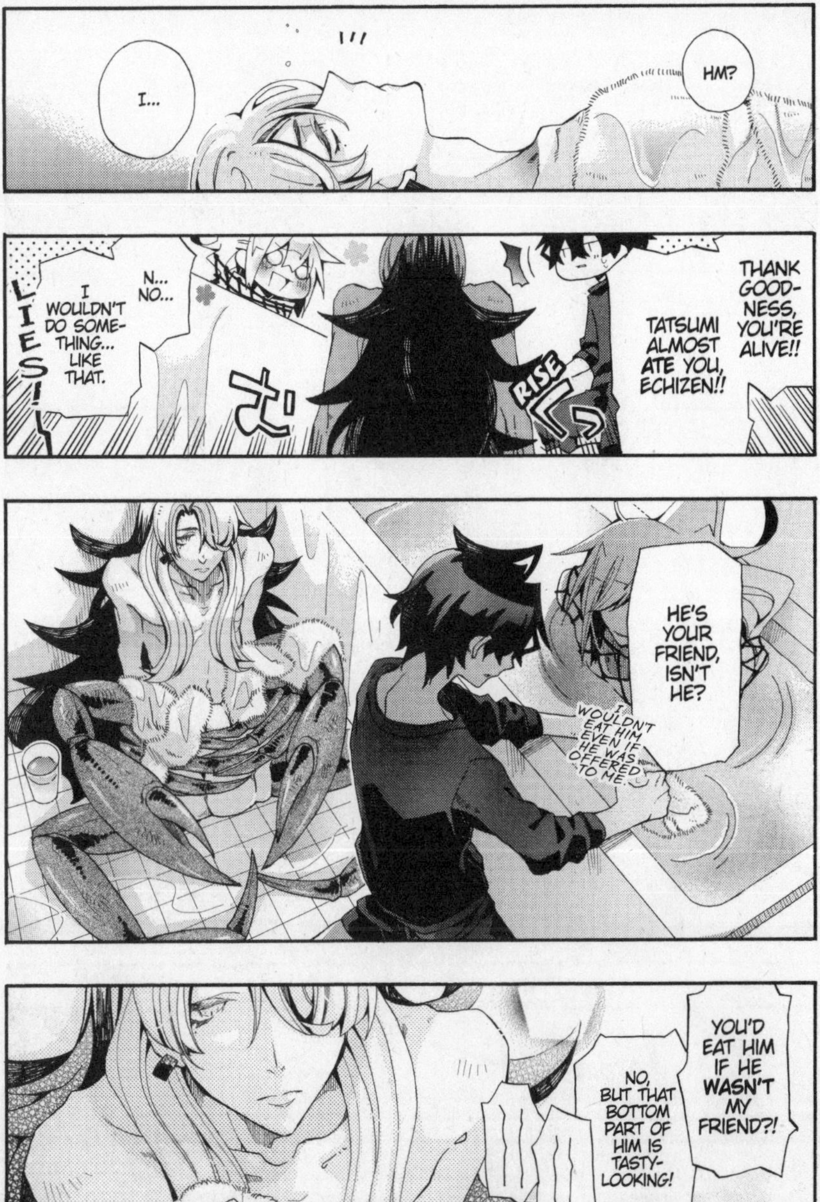
HM?
I...
THANK GOODNESS, YOU'RE ALIVE!!
TATSUMI ALMOST ATE YOU, ECHIZEN!!
RISE
N... NO...
I WOULDN'T DO SOMETHING... LIKE THAT.
LIES!
HE'S YOUR FRIEND, ISN'T HE?
I WOULDN'T EAT HIM EVEN IF HE WAS OFFERED TO ME.
YOU'D EAT HIM IF HE WASN'T MY FRIEND?!
NO, BUT THAT BOTTOM PART OF HIM IS TASTY-LOOKING!

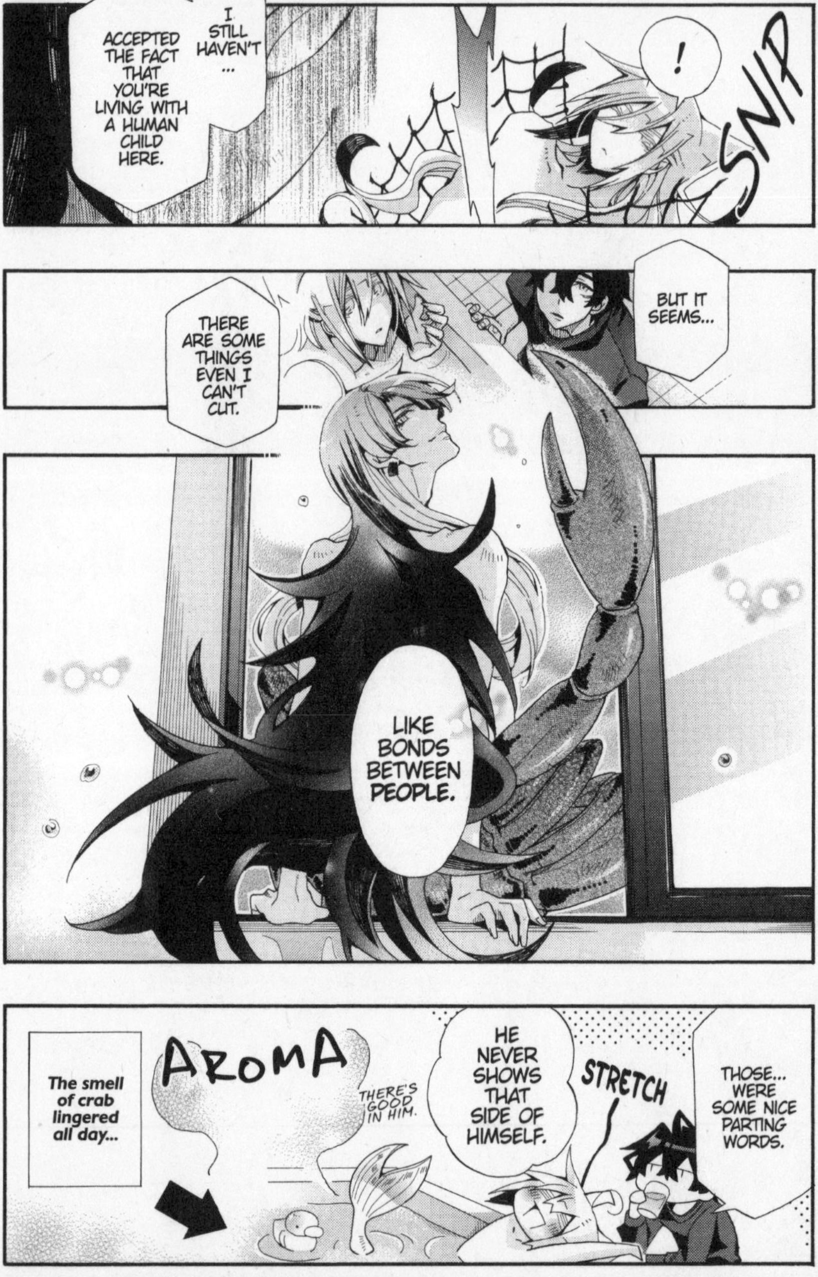
!
SNIP
I STILL HAVEN'T...
ACCEPTED THE FACT THAT YOU'RE LIVING WITH A HUMAN CHILD HERE.
BUT IT SEEMS...
THERE ARE SOME THINGS EVEN I CAN'T CUT.
LIKE BONDS BETWEEN PEOPLE.
THOSE... WERE SOME NICE PARTING WORDS.
STRETCH
HE NEVER SHOWS THAT SIDE OF HIMSELF.
THERE'S GOOD IN HIM.
AROMA
The smell of crab lingered all day...

Merman in My Tub

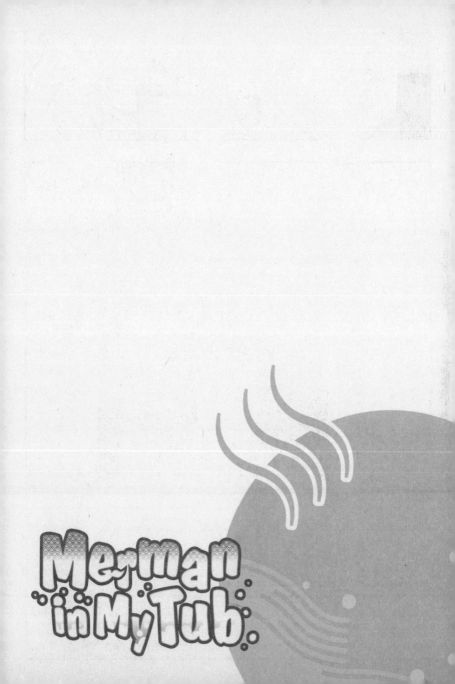

オレん家のフロ事情

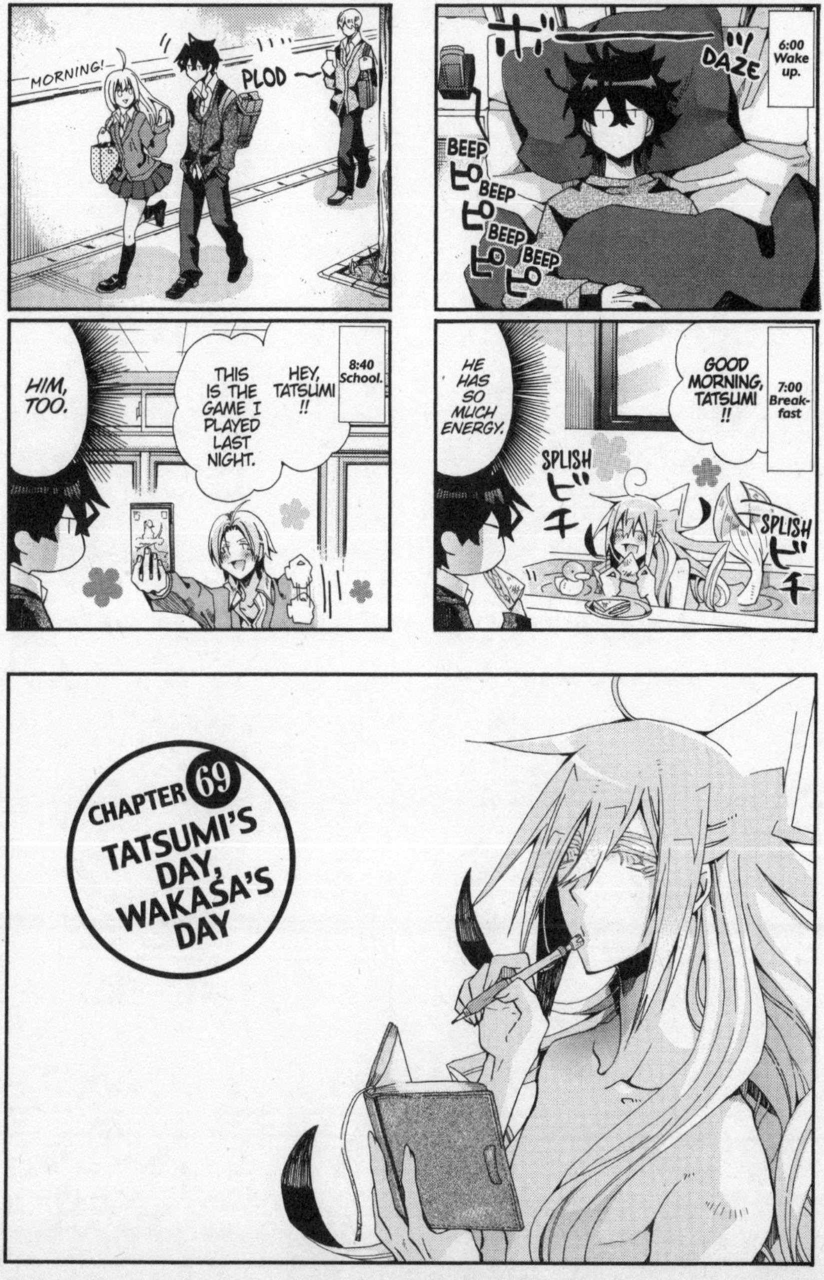

6:00 Wake up.
DAZE
BEEP
BEEP
BEEP
BEEP
MORNING!
PLOD
7:00 Breakfast
GOOD MORNING, TATSUMI!!
HE HAS SO MUCH ENERGY.
SPLISH
SPLISH
8:40 School.
HEY, TATSUMI!!
THIS IS THE GAME I PLAYED LAST NIGHT.
HIM, TOO.
CHAPTER 69
TATSUMI'S DAY, WAKASA'S DAY

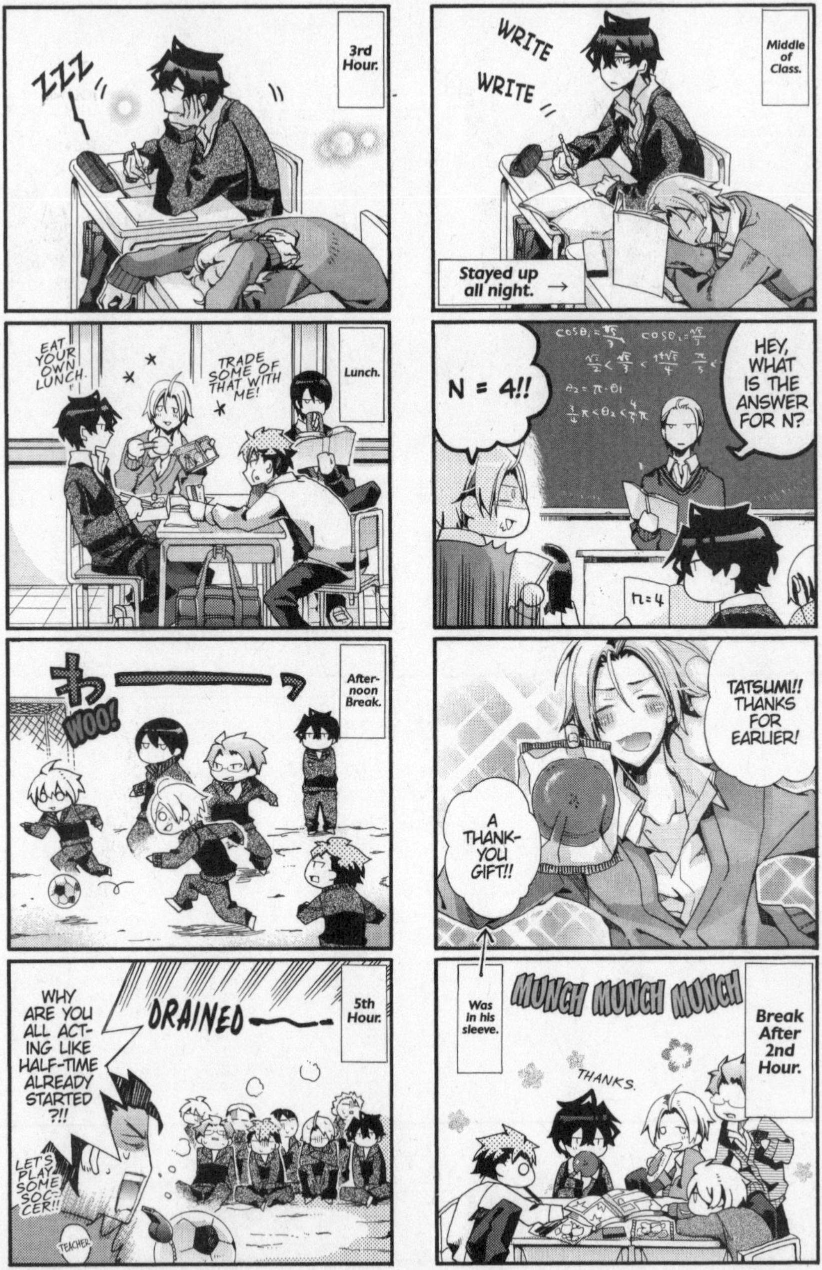

Middle of Class.
WRITE
WRITE
Stayed up all night. →
HEY, WHAT IS THE ANSWER FOR N?
N = 4!!
n=4
TATSUMI!! THANKS FOR EARLIER!
A THANK-YOU GIFT!!
Break After 2nd Hour.
Was in his sleeve.
MUNCH MUNCH MUNCH
THANKS.
3rd Hour.
ZZZ
Lunch.
TRADE SOME OF THAT WITH ME!
EAT YOUR OWN LUNCH.
After-noon Break.
わーーーっ
WOO!
5th Hour.
DRAINED
WHY ARE YOU ALL ACT-ING LIKE HALF-TIME ALREADY STARTED?!!
LET'S PLAY SOME SOC-CER!!
TEACHER

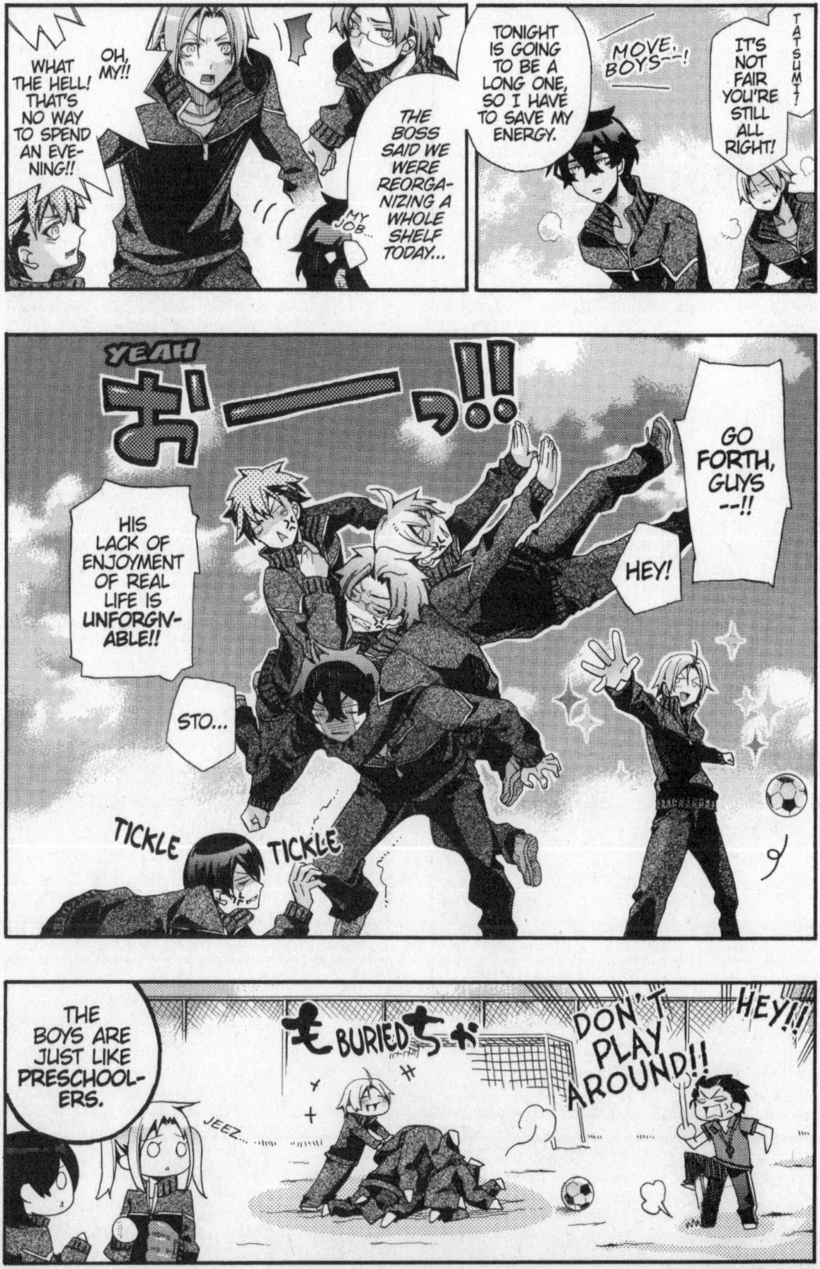
TATSUMI!
IT'S NOT FAIR YOU'RE STILL ALL RIGHT!
MOVE, BOYS--!
TONIGHT IS GOING TO BE A LONG ONE, SO I HAVE TO SAVE MY ENERGY.
THE BOSS SAID WE WERE REORGANIZING A WHOLE SHELF TODAY...
MY JOB...
OH, MY!!
WHAT THE HELL! THAT'S NO WAY TO SPEND AN EVENING!!
GO FORTH, GUYS--!!
HEY!
YEAH
おーーっ!!
HIS LACK OF ENJOYMENT OF REAL LIFE IS UNFORGIVABLE!!
STO...
TICKLE
TICKLE
HEY!!
DON'T PLAY AROUND!!
もちゃ BURIED
THE BOYS ARE JUST LIKE PRESCHOOLERS.
JEEZ...

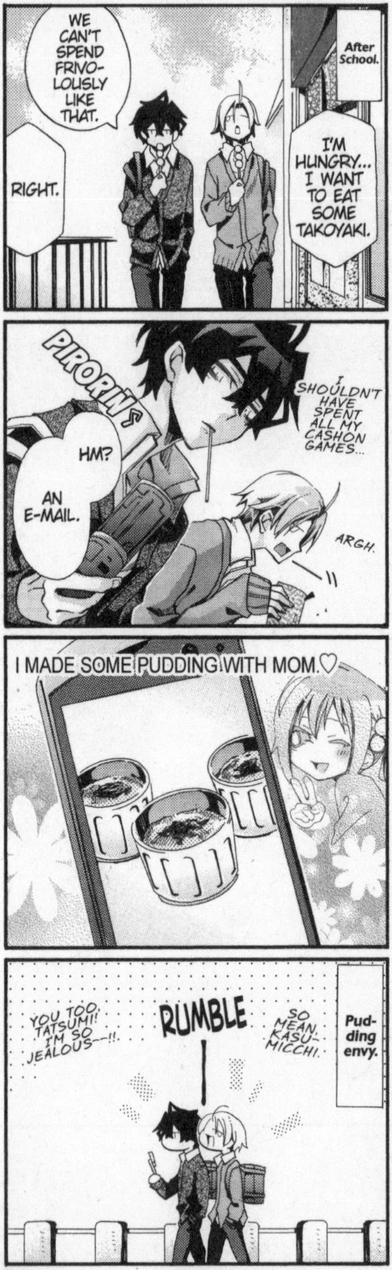
After School.
I'M HUNGRY... I WANT TO EAT SOME TAKOYAKI.
WE CAN'T SPEND FRIVOLOUSLY LIKE THAT.
RIGHT.
I SHOULDN'T HAVE SPENT ALL MY CASHON GAMES...
PIRORIN♪
ARGH.
HM?
AN E-MAIL.
I MADE SOME PUDDING WITH MOM.♡
Pudding envy.
SO MEAN, KASUMICCHI.
RUMBLE
YOU TOO, TATSUMI! I'M SO JEALOUS--!!
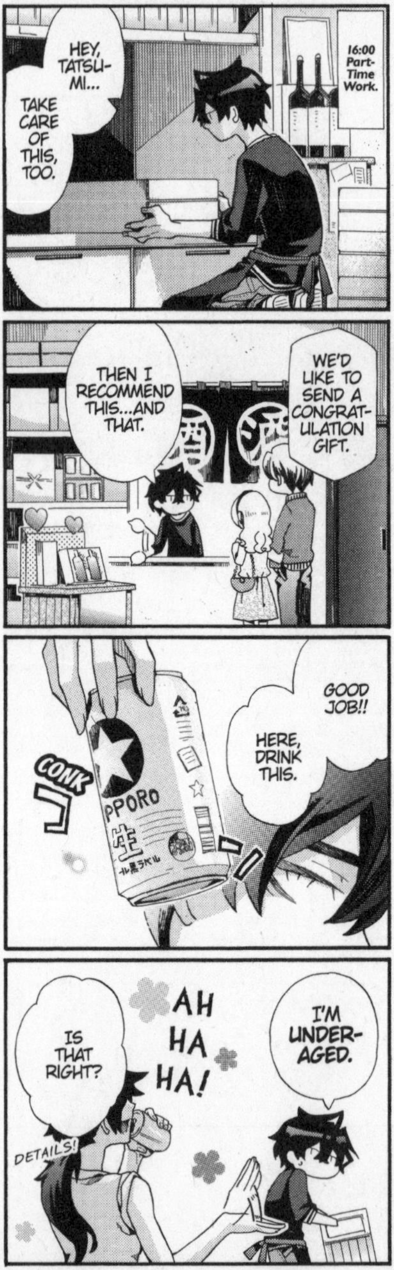
16:00 Part-Time Work.
HEY, TATSUMI...
TAKE CARE OF THIS, TOO.
WE'D LIKE TO SEND A CONGRATULATION GIFT.
THEN I RECOMMEND THIS...AND THAT.
GOOD JOB!!
HERE, DRINK THIS.
CONK
I'M UNDERAGED.
AH HA HA!
IS THAT RIGHT?
DETAILS!

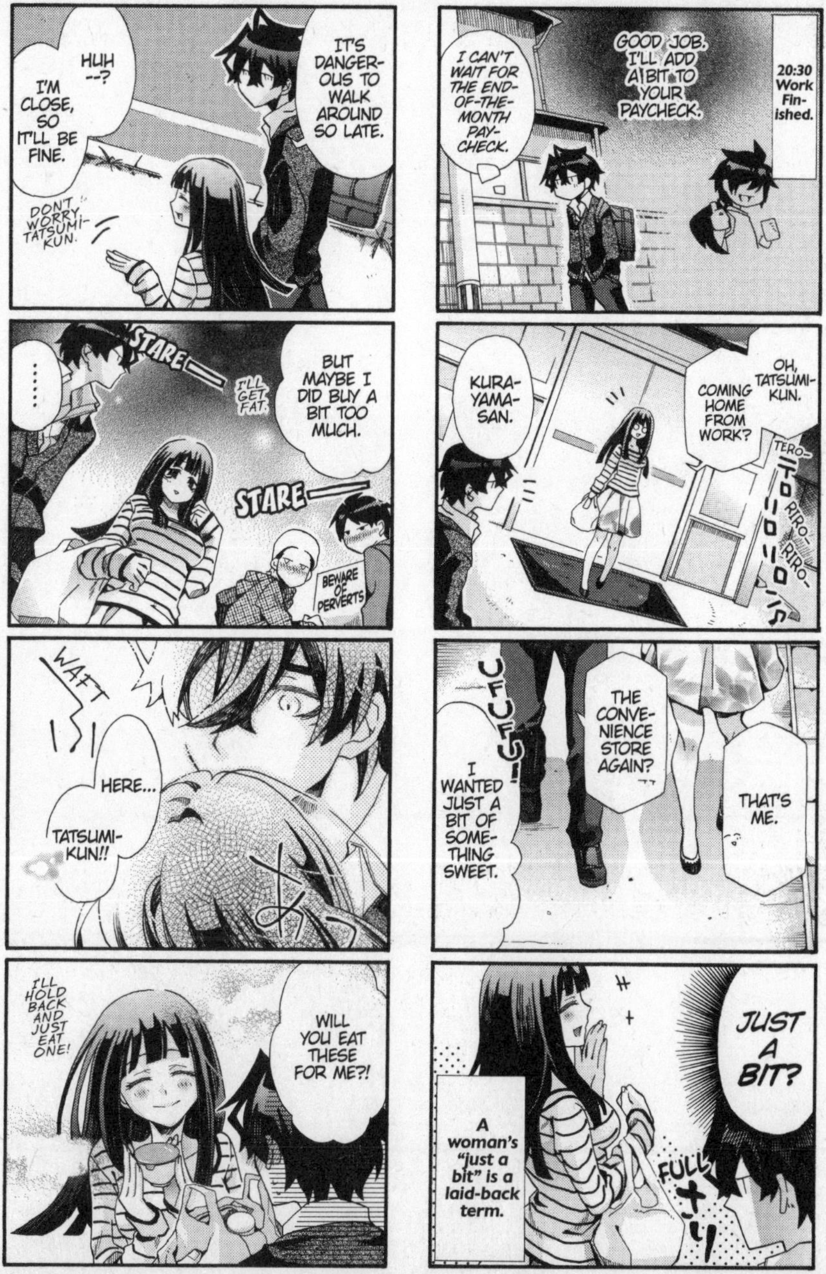
20:30 Work Finished.
GOOD JOB. I'LL ADD A BIT TO YOUR PAYCHECK.
I CAN'T WAIT FOR THE END-OF-THE-MONTH PAYCHECK.
TERO-RIRO-RIRO-
OH, TATSUMI-KUN.
COMING HOME FROM WORK?
KURAYAMA-SAN.
THAT'S ME.
THE CONVENIENCE STORE AGAIN?
I WANTED JUST A BIT OF SOMETHING SWEET.
UFUFU!
JUST A BIT?
FULL
A woman's "just a bit" is a laid-back term.
IT'S DANGEROUS TO WALK AROUND SO LATE.
HUH--?
I'M CLOSE, SO IT'LL BE FINE.
DON'T WORRY TATSUMI-KUN.
BUT MAYBE I DID BUY A BIT TOO MUCH.
I'LL GET FAT.
STARE—
STARE—
BEWARE OF PERVERTS
......
WAFT
HERE...
TATSUMI-KUN!!
WILL YOU EAT THESE FOR ME?!
I'LL HOLD BACK AND JUST EAT ONE!

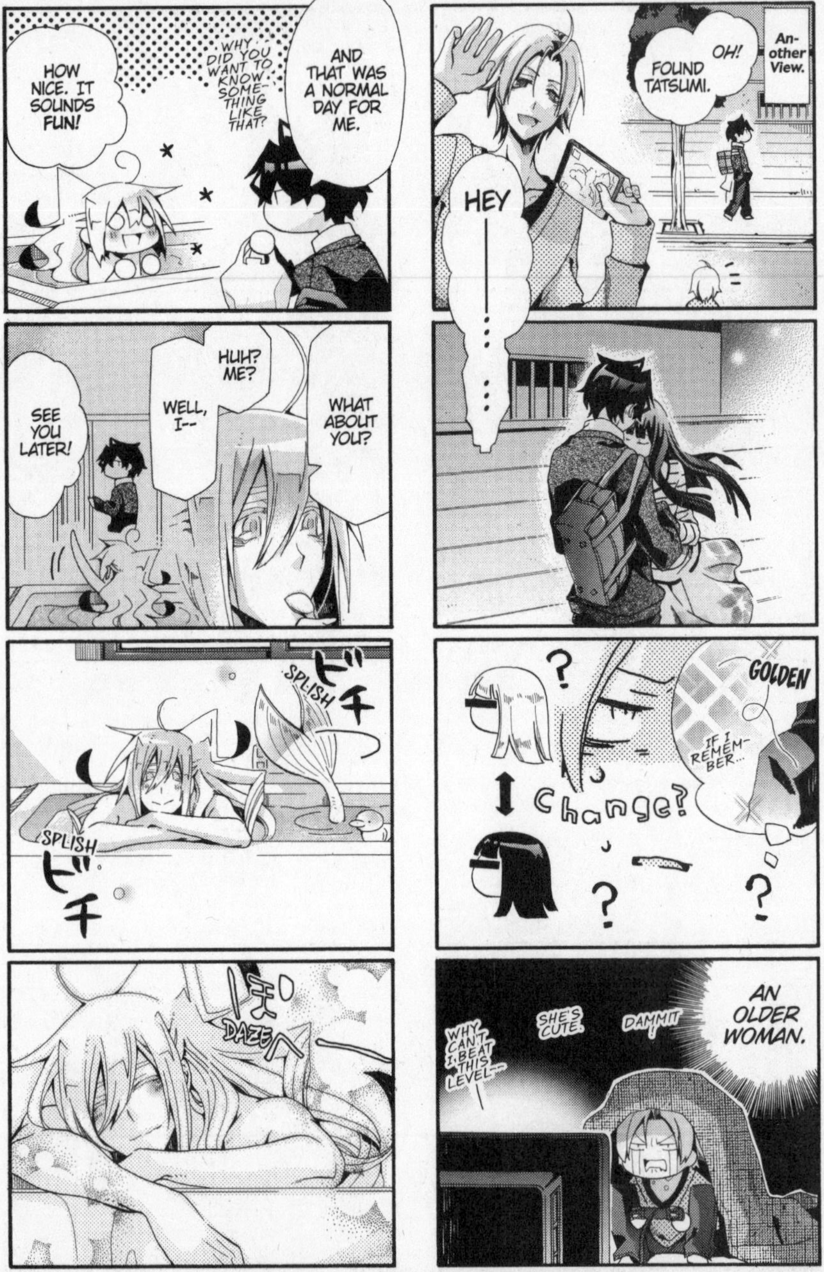
An-other View.
OH!
FOUND TATSUMI.
HEY —....
GOLDEN
IF I REMEMBER...
Change?
AN OLDER WOMAN.
DAMMIT!
SHE'S CUTE.
WHY CAN'T I BEAT THIS LEVEL---
AND THAT WAS A NORMAL DAY FOR ME.
WHY DID YOU WANT TO KNOW SOMETHING LIKE THAT?
HOW NICE. IT SOUNDS FUN!
WHAT ABOUT YOU?
HUH? ME?
WELL, I--
SEE YOU LATER!
SPLISH
ビチ
SPLISH
ビチ
DAZE

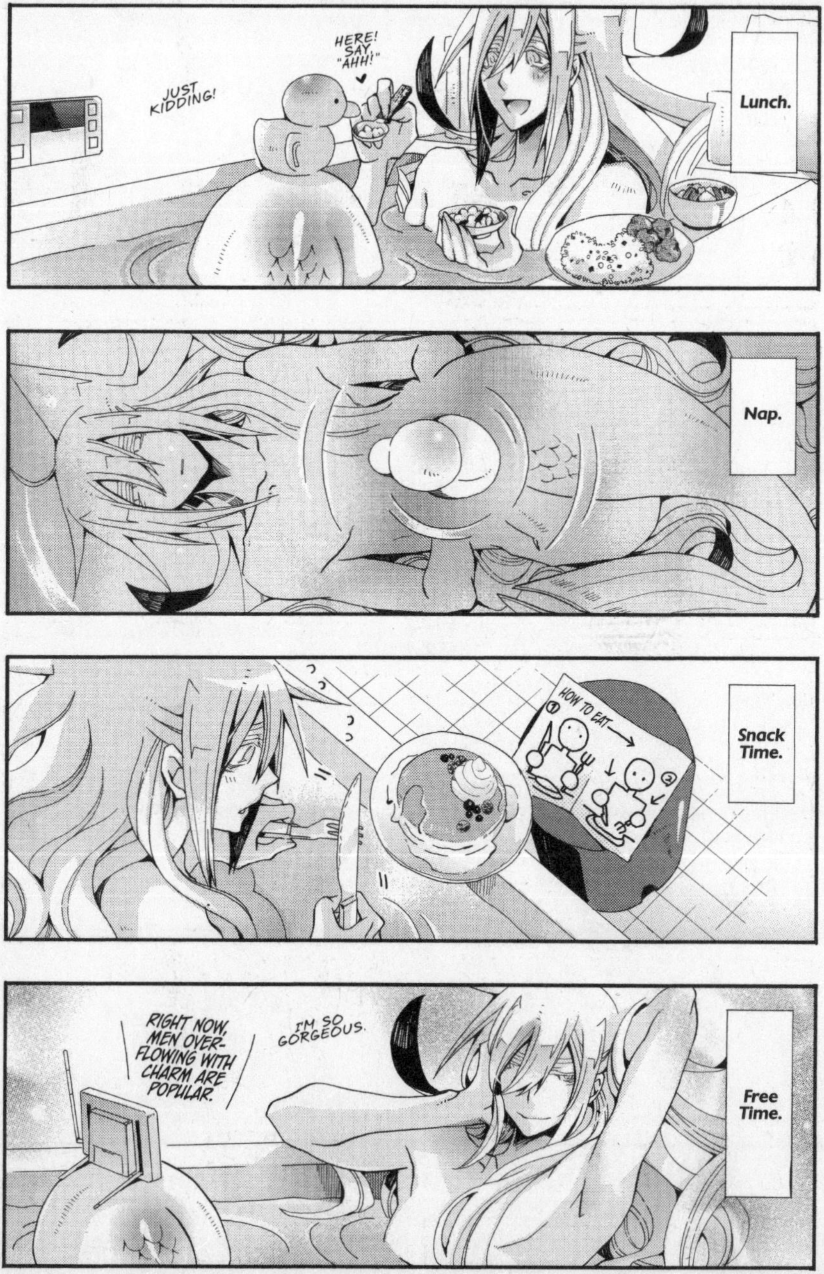
Lunch.
HERE! SAY "AHH!"
JUST KIDDING!
Nap.
Snack Time.
HOW TO EAT
Free Time.
I'M SO GORGEOUS.
RIGHT NOW, MEN OVER-FLOWING WITH CHARM ARE POPULAR.

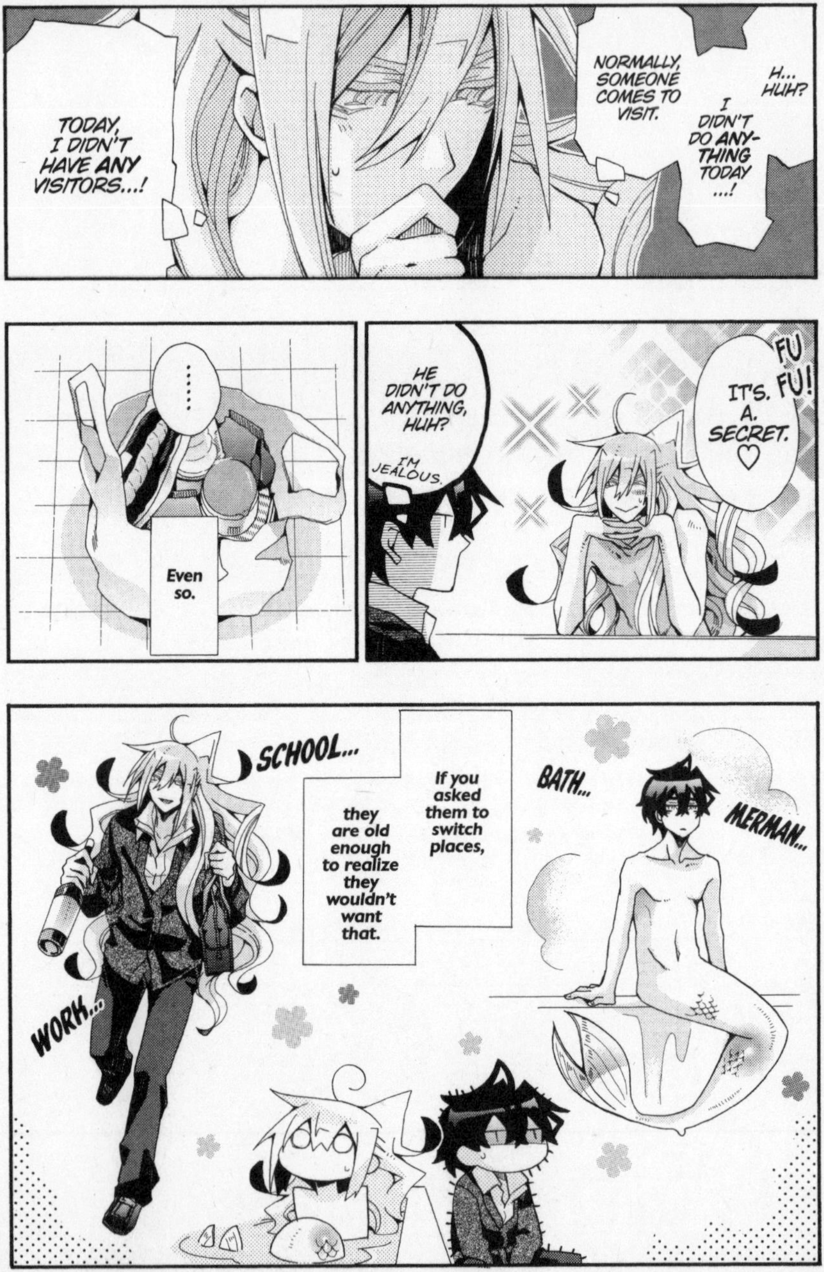
H... HUH?
I DIDN'T DO ANYTHING TODAY ...!
NORMALLY, SOMEONE COMES TO VISIT.
TODAY, I DIDN'T HAVE ANY VISITORS...!
FU FU!
IT'S. A. SECRET. ♡
HE DIDN'T DO ANYTHING, HUH?
I'M JEALOUS.
......
Even so.
MERMAN...
BATH...
If you asked them to switch places,
they are old enough to realize they wouldn't want that.
SCHOOL...
WORK...

Merman in My Tub

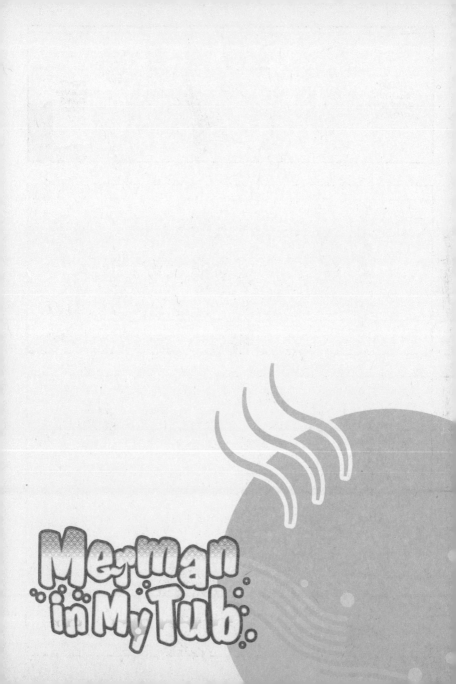

オレん家のフロ事情

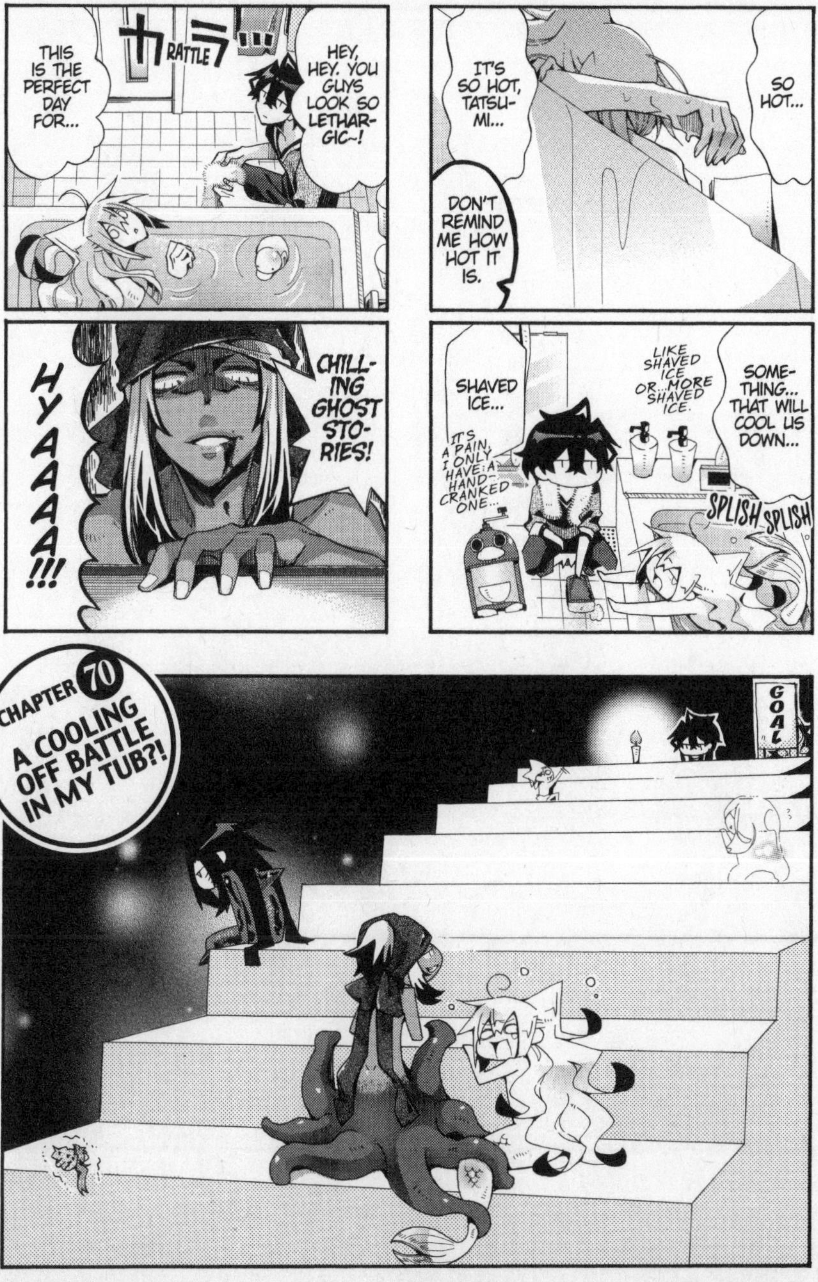
SO HOT...
IT'S SO HOT, TATSUMI...
DON'T REMIND ME HOW HOT IT IS.
HEY, HEY. YOU GUYS LOOK SO LETHARGIC~!
RATTLE
THIS IS THE PERFECT DAY FOR...
SOMETHING... THAT WILL COOL US DOWN...
LIKE SHAVED ICE OR...MORE SHAVED ICE.
SHAVED ICE...
IT'S A PAIN, I ONLY HAVE A HAND-CRANKED ONE...
SPLISH SPLISH
CHILLING GHOST STORIES!
HYAAAAAA!!!
CHAPTER 70
A COOLING OFF BATTLE IN MY TUB?!
GOAL

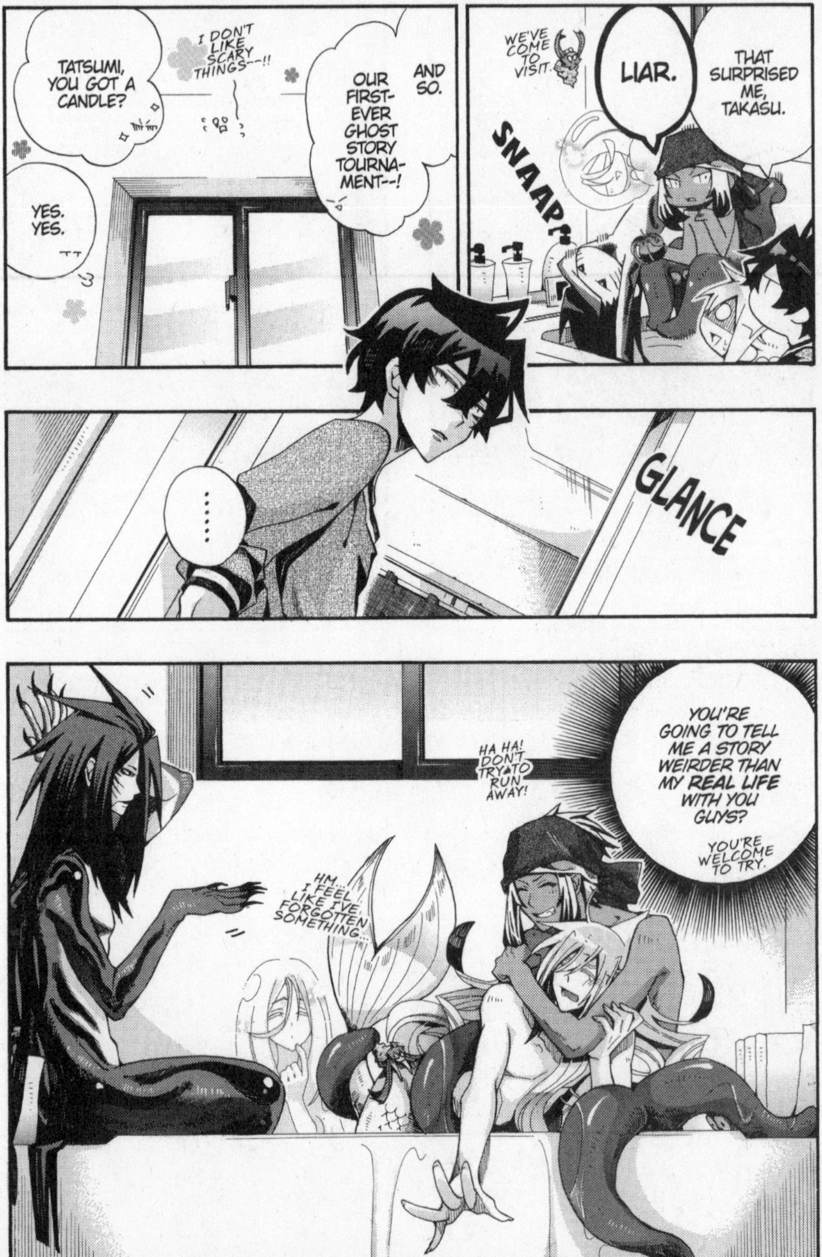
THAT SURPRISED ME, TAKASU.
LIAR.
WE'VE COME TO VISIT.
SNAAP!
AND SO.
OUR FIRST-EVER GHOST STORY TOURNAMENT--!
I DON'T LIKE SCARY THINGS--!!
TATSUMI, YOU GOT A CANDLE?
YES. YES.
GLANCE
......
YOU'RE GOING TO TELL ME A STORY WEIRDER THAN MY REAL LIFE WITH YOU GUYS?
YOU'RE WELCOME TO TRY.
HA HA! DON'T TRY TO RUN AWAY!
HM... I FEEL LIKE I'VE FORGOTTEN SOMETHING...

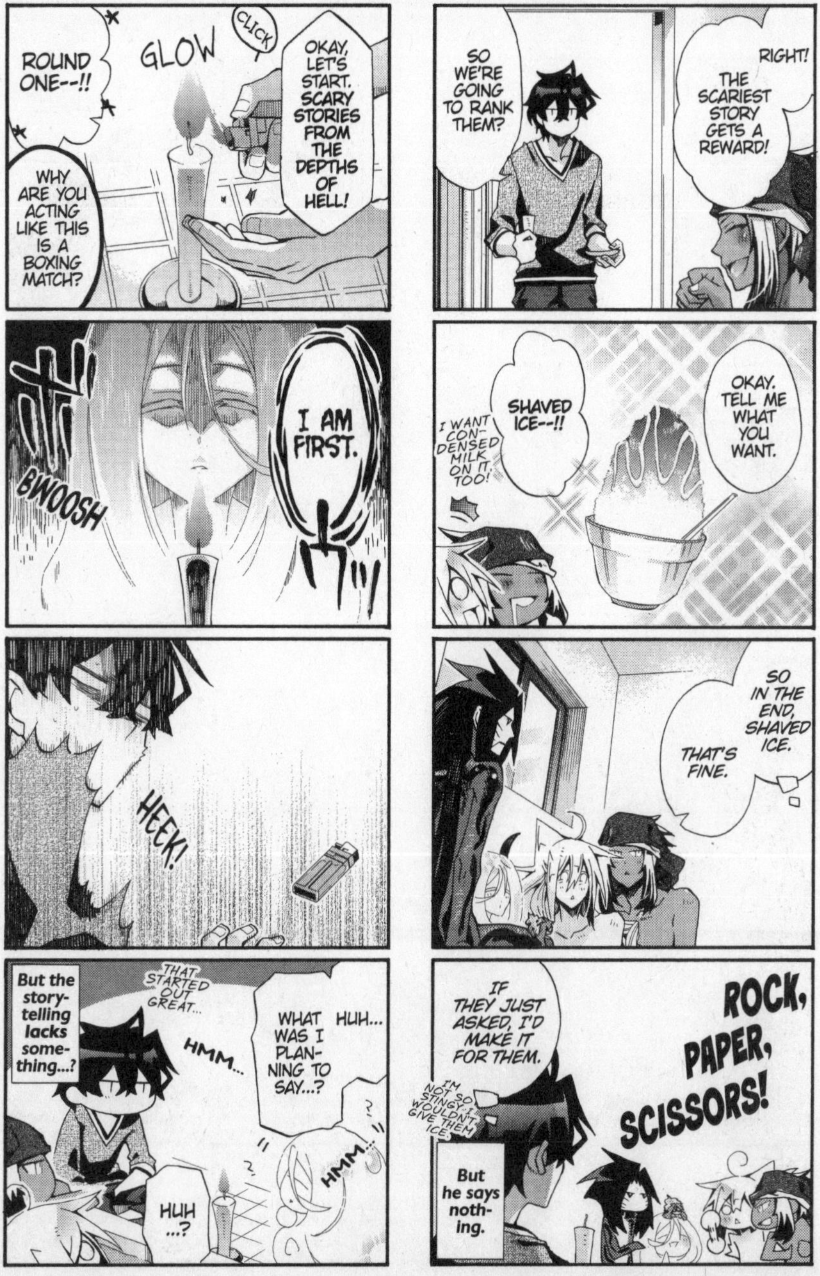
RIGHT! THE SCARIEST STORY GETS A REWARD!
SO WE'RE GOING TO RANK THEM?
OKAY. TELL ME WHAT YOU WANT.
SHAVED ICE--!!
I WANT CONDENSED MILK ON IT, TOO!
SO IN THE END, SHAVED ICE.
THAT'S FINE.
ROCK, PAPER, SCISSORS!
IF THEY JUST ASKED, I'D MAKE IT FOR THEM.
I'M NOT SO STINGY I WOULDN'T GIVE THEM ICE.
But he says nothing.
OKAY, LET'S START. SCARY STORIES FROM THE DEPTHS OF HELL!
CLICK
GLOW
ROUND ONE--!!
WHY ARE YOU ACTING LIKE THIS IS A BOXING MATCH?
I AM FIRST.
BWOOSH
HEEK!
HUH...
WHAT WAS I PLANNING TO SAY...?
HMM...
THAT STARTED OUT GREAT...
HMM...
But the storytelling lacks something...?
HUH...?

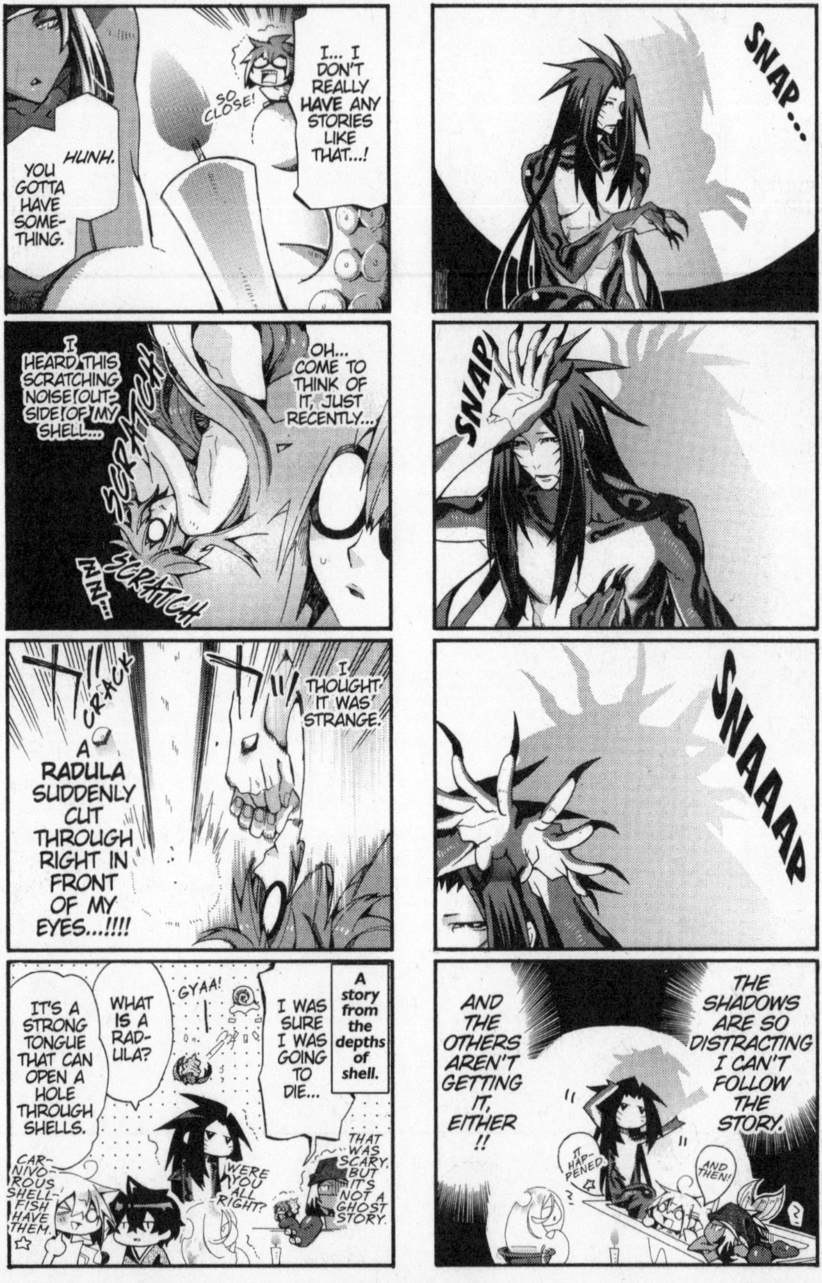
SNAP...
SNAP!
SNAAAAP
THE SHADOWS ARE SO DISTRACTING I CAN'T FOLLOW THE STORY.
AND THE OTHERS AREN'T GETTING IT, EITHER !!
AND THEN!
IT HAPPENED.
I... I DON'T REALLY HAVE ANY STORIES LIKE THAT...!
SO CLOSE!
HUNH. YOU GOTTA HAVE SOME-THING.
OH... COME TO THINK OF IT, JUST RECENTLY...
I HEARD THIS SCRATCHING NOISE OUT-SIDE OF MY SHELL...
SCRATCH
SCRATCH
NN...
I THOUGHT IT WAS STRANGE.
CRACK
A RADULA SUDDENLY CUT THROUGH RIGHT IN FRONT OF MY EYES...!!!!
A story from the depths of shell.
I WAS SURE I WAS GOING TO DIE...
GYAA!
WHAT IS A RAD-ULA?
IT'S A STRONG TONGUE THAT CAN OPEN A HOLE THROUGH SHELLS.
THAT WAS SCARY, BUT IT'S NOT A GHOST STORY.
WERE YOU ALL RIGHT?
CAR-NIVO-ROUS SHELL-FISH HAVE THEM.

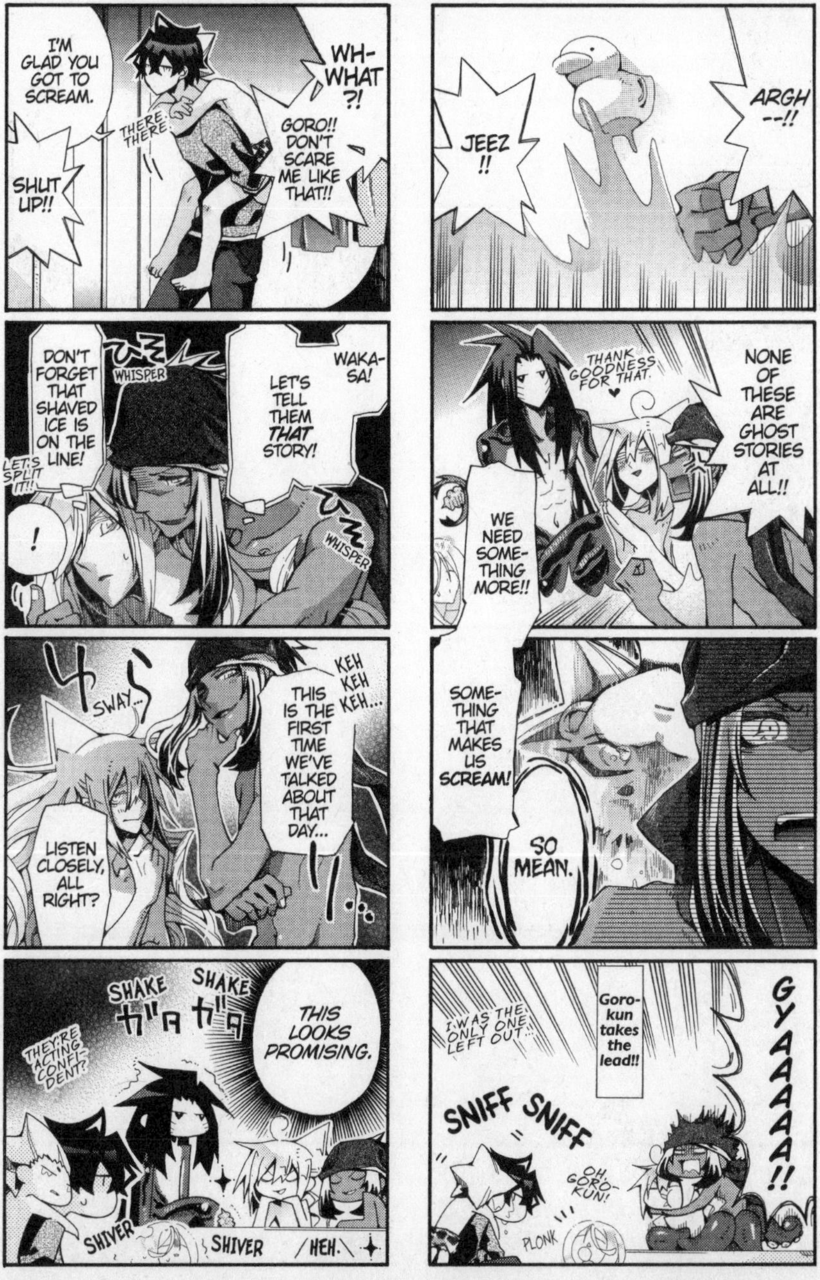
ARGH--!!
JEEZ!!
NONE OF THESE ARE GHOST STORIES AT ALL!!
THANK GOODNESS FOR THAT.
WE NEED SOMETHING MORE!!
SOMETHING THAT MAKES US SCREAM!
SO MEAN.
GYAAAAAA!!
Goro-kun takes the lead!!
I WAS THE ONLY ONE LEFT OUT...
SNIFF SNIFF
OH, GORO-KUN!
PLONK
WH-WHAT?!
GORO!! DON'T SCARE ME LIKE THAT!!
I'M GLAD YOU GOT TO SCREAM.
THERE, THERE.
SHUT UP!!
WAKASA!
LET'S TELL THEM *THAT* STORY!
DON'T FORGET THAT SHAVED ICE IS ON THE LINE!
ひそ WHISPER
ひそ WHISPER
LET'S SPLIT IT!!
!
KEH KEH KEH...
THIS IS THE FIRST TIME WE'VE TALKED ABOUT THAT DAY...
ゆら SWAY...
LISTEN CLOSELY, ALL RIGHT?
THIS LOOKS PROMISING.
SHAKE SHAKE
ガタガタ
THEY'RE ACTING CONFIDENT?
SHIVER
SHIVER
HEH.

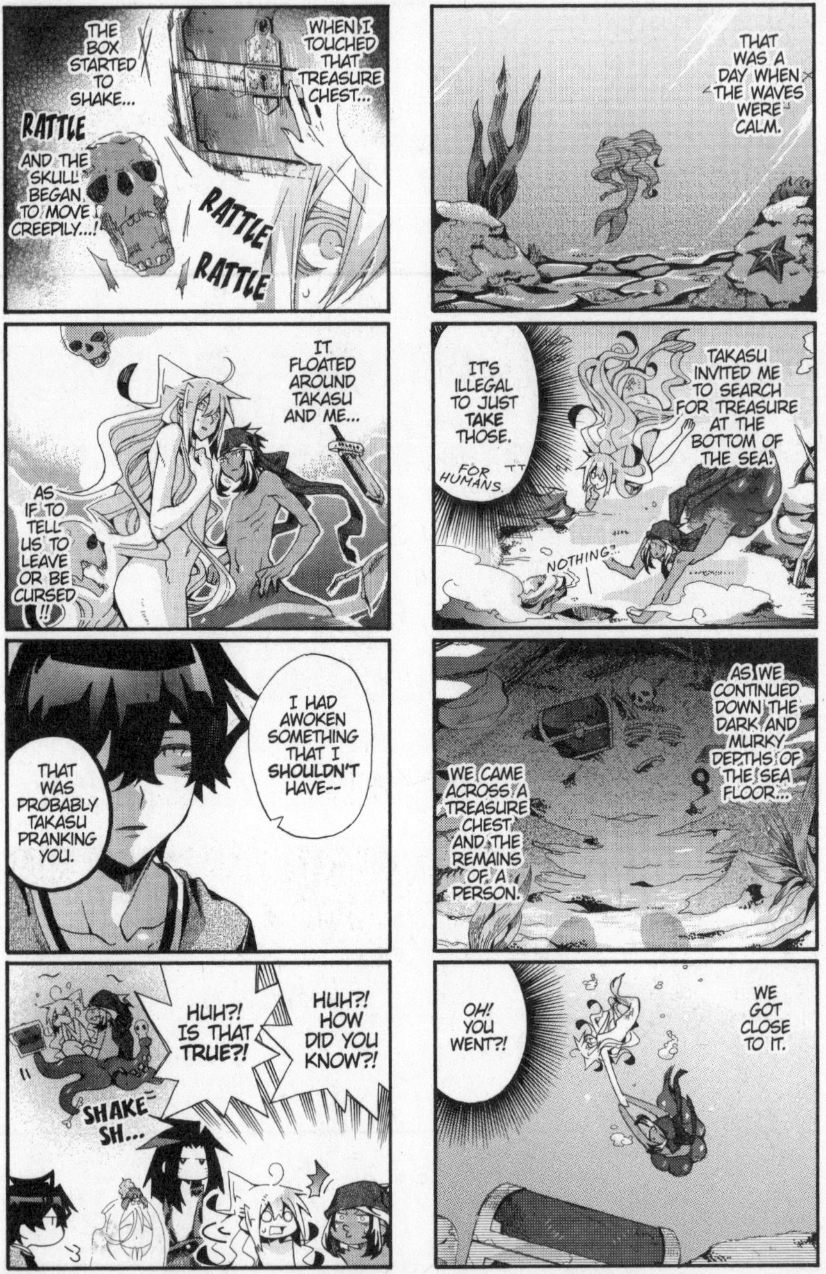
THAT WAS A DAY WHEN THE WAVES WERE CALM.
TAKASU INVITED ME TO SEARCH FOR TREASURE AT THE BOTTOM OF THE SEA.
IT'S ILLEGAL TO JUST TAKE THOSE.
FOR HUMANS.
NOTHING?..
AS WE CONTINUED DOWN THE DARK AND MURKY DEPTHS OF THE SEA FLOOR...
WE CAME ACROSS A TREASURE CHEST AND THE REMAINS OF A PERSON.
WE GOT CLOSE TO IT.
OH! YOU WENT?!
WHEN I TOUCHED THAT TREASURE CHEST...
THE BOX STARTED TO SHAKE...
RATTLE
AND THE SKULL BEGAN TO MOVE CREEPILY...!
RATTLE
RATTLE
IT FLOATED AROUND TAKASU AND ME...
AS IF TO TELL US TO LEAVE OR BE CURSED!!
I HAD AWOKEN SOMETHING THAT I SHOULDN'T HAVE--
THAT WAS PROBABLY TAKASU PRANKING YOU.
HUH?! HOW DID YOU KNOW?!
HUH?! IS THAT TRUE?!
SHAKE
SH...

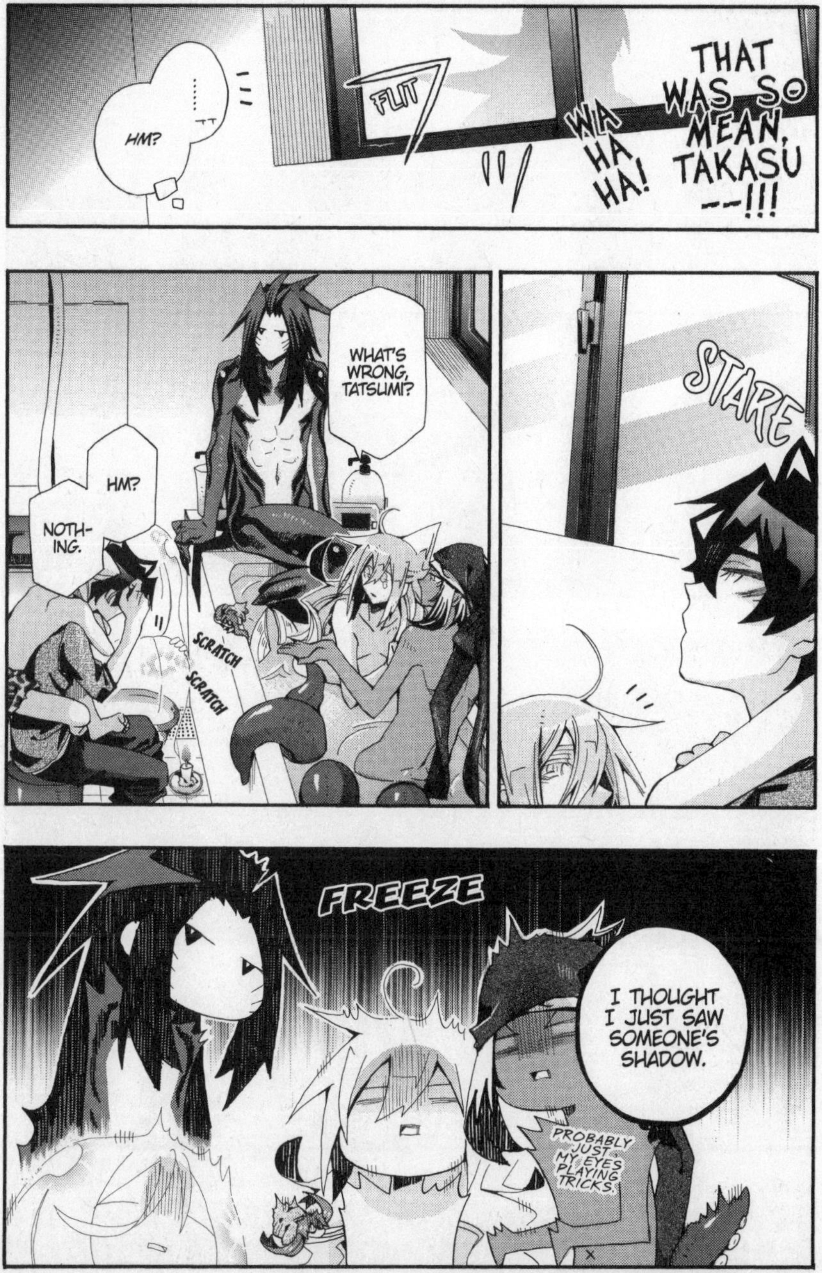
THAT WAS SO MEAN, TAKASU--!!!
WA HA HA!
FLIT
HM?
STARE
WHAT'S WRONG, TATSUMI?
HM?
NOTH-ING.
SCRATCH
SCRATCH
FREEZE
I THOUGHT I JUST SAW SOMEONE'S SHADOW.
PROBABLY JUST MY EYES PLAYING TRICKS.

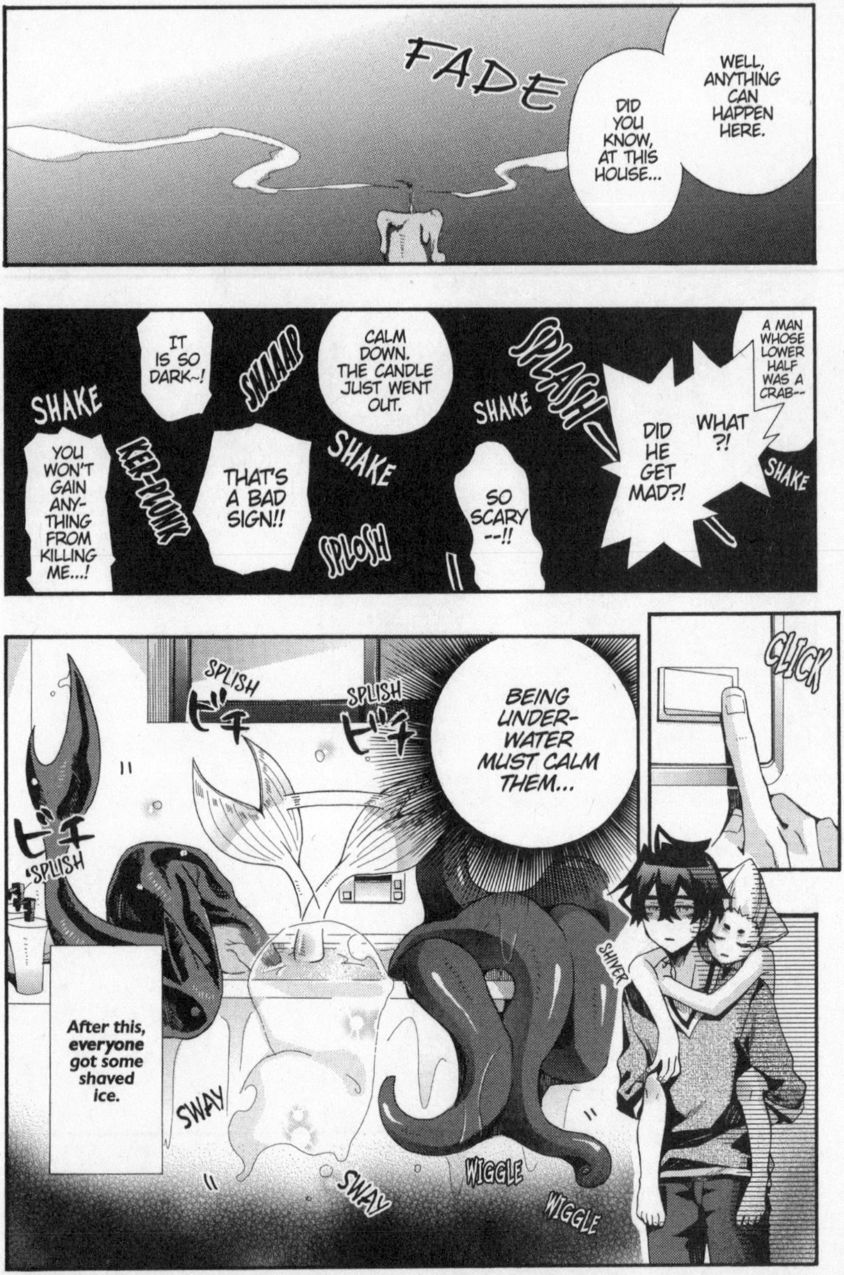
FADE
WELL, ANYTHING CAN HAPPEN HERE.
DID YOU KNOW, AT THIS HOUSE...
A MAN WHOSE LOWER HALF WAS A CRAB--
WHAT?!
DID HE GET MAD?!
SHAKE
SPLASH
SHAKE
SO SCARY--!!
CALM DOWN. THE CANDLE JUST WENT OUT.
SHAKE
SPLOSH
SNAAAP
IT IS SO DARK~!
THAT'S A BAD SIGN!!
KER-PLUNK
SHAKE
YOU WON'T GAIN ANYTHING FROM KILLING ME...!
CLICK
BEING UNDERWATER MUST CALM THEM...
SPLISH ピチ
SPLISH ピチ
SHIVER
ピチ SPLISH
SWAY
WIGGLE
WIGGLE
SWAY
After this, everyone got some shaved ice.

Merman in My Tub

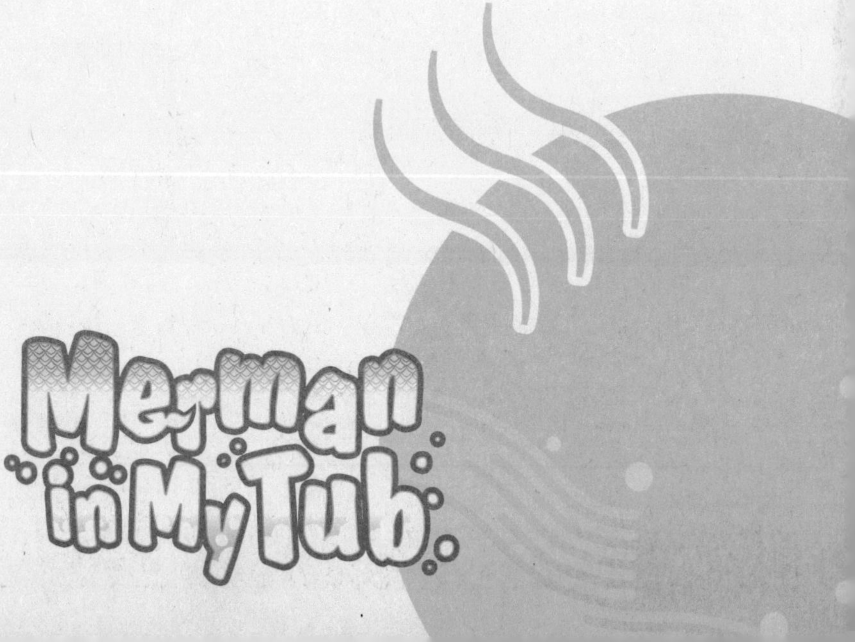

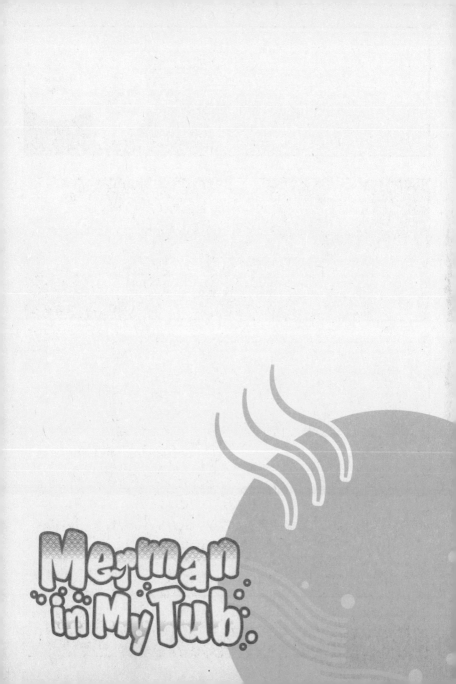

オレん家のフロ事情

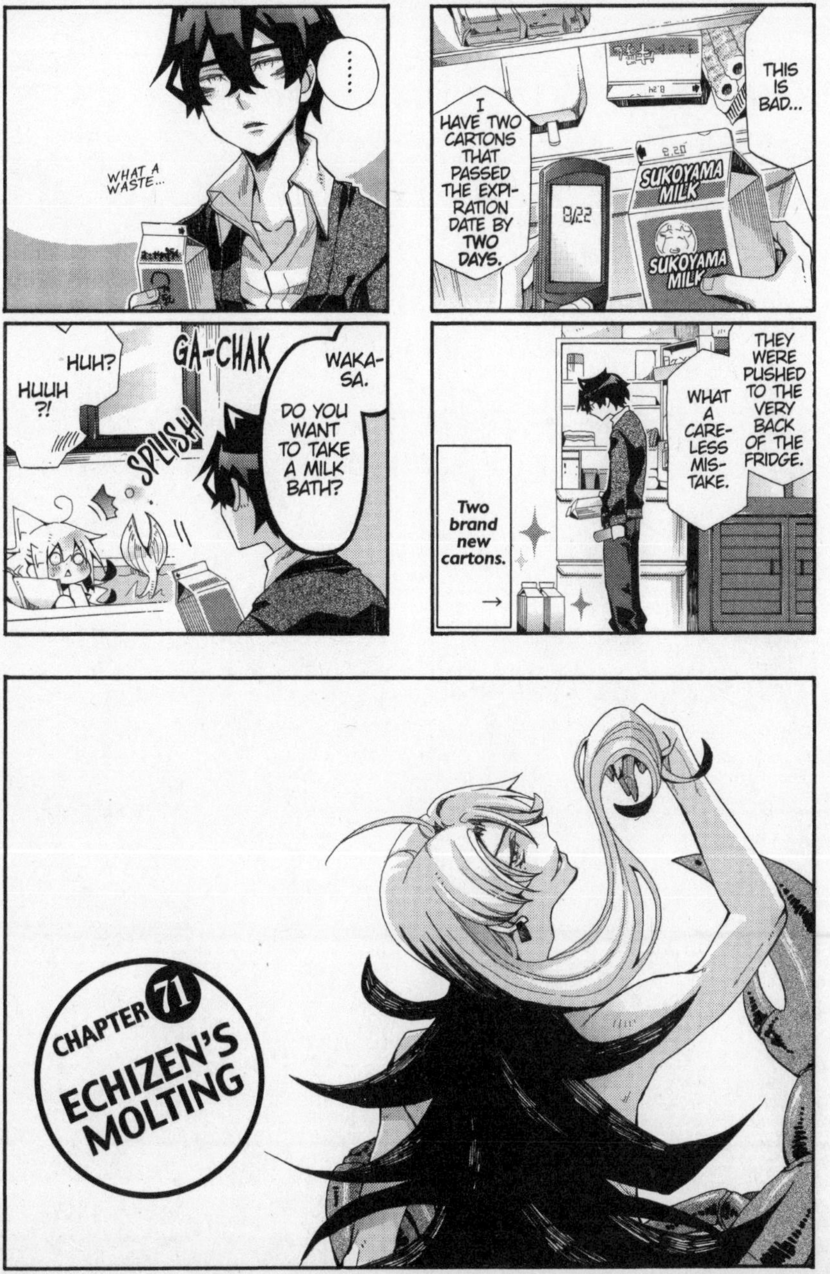
THIS IS BAD...
I HAVE TWO CARTONS THAT PASSED THE EXPIRATION DATE BY TWO DAYS.
8/22
SUKOYAMA MILK
SUKOYAMA MILK
......
WHAT A WASTE...
THEY WERE PUSHED TO THE VERY BACK OF THE FRIDGE.
WHAT A CARELESS MISTAKE.
Two brand new cartons. →
WAKASA.
DO YOU WANT TO TAKE A MILK BATH?
GA-CHAK
HUH?
HUUH?!
SPLISH
CHAPTER 71
ECHIZEN'S MOLTING

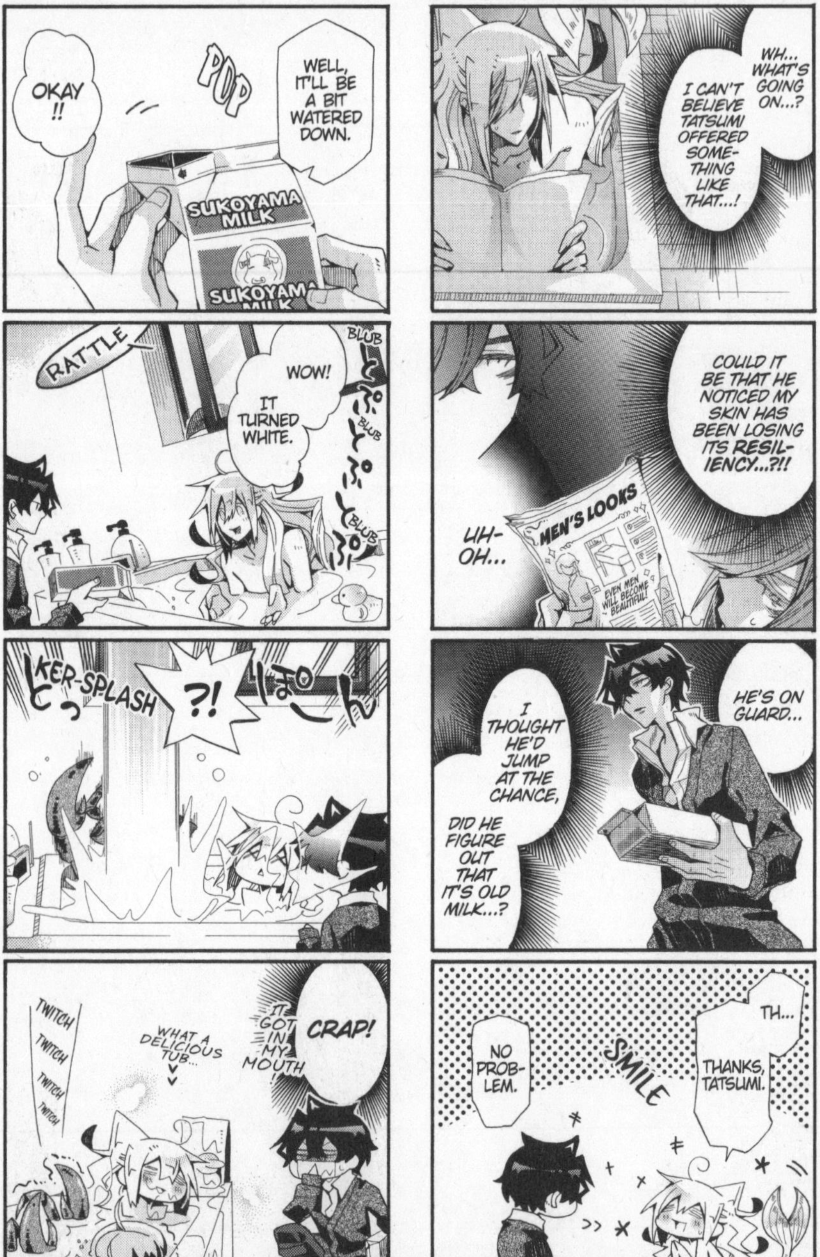
WH... WHAT'S GOING ON...?
I CAN'T BELIEVE TATSUMI OFFERED SOME-THING LIKE THAT...!
COULD IT BE THAT HE NOTICED MY SKIN HAS BEEN LOSING ITS RESIL-IENCY...?!!
UH-OH...
MEN'S LOOKS
EVEN MEN WILL BECOME BEAUTIFUL!
HE'S ON GUARD...
I THOUGHT HE'D JUMP AT THE CHANCE,
DID HE FIGURE OUT THAT IT'S OLD MILK...?
TH...
THANKS, TATSUMI.
SMILE
NO PROB-LEM.
WELL, IT'LL BE A BIT WATERED DOWN.
POP
OKAY!!
SUKOYAMA MILK
SUKOYAMA MILK
BLUB
WOW!
IT TURNED WHITE.
RATTLE
BLUB
BLUB
?!
KER-SPLASH
CRAP!
IT GOT IN MY MOUTH!
WHAT A DELICIOUS TUB...
TWITCH
TWITCH
TWITCH
TWITCH

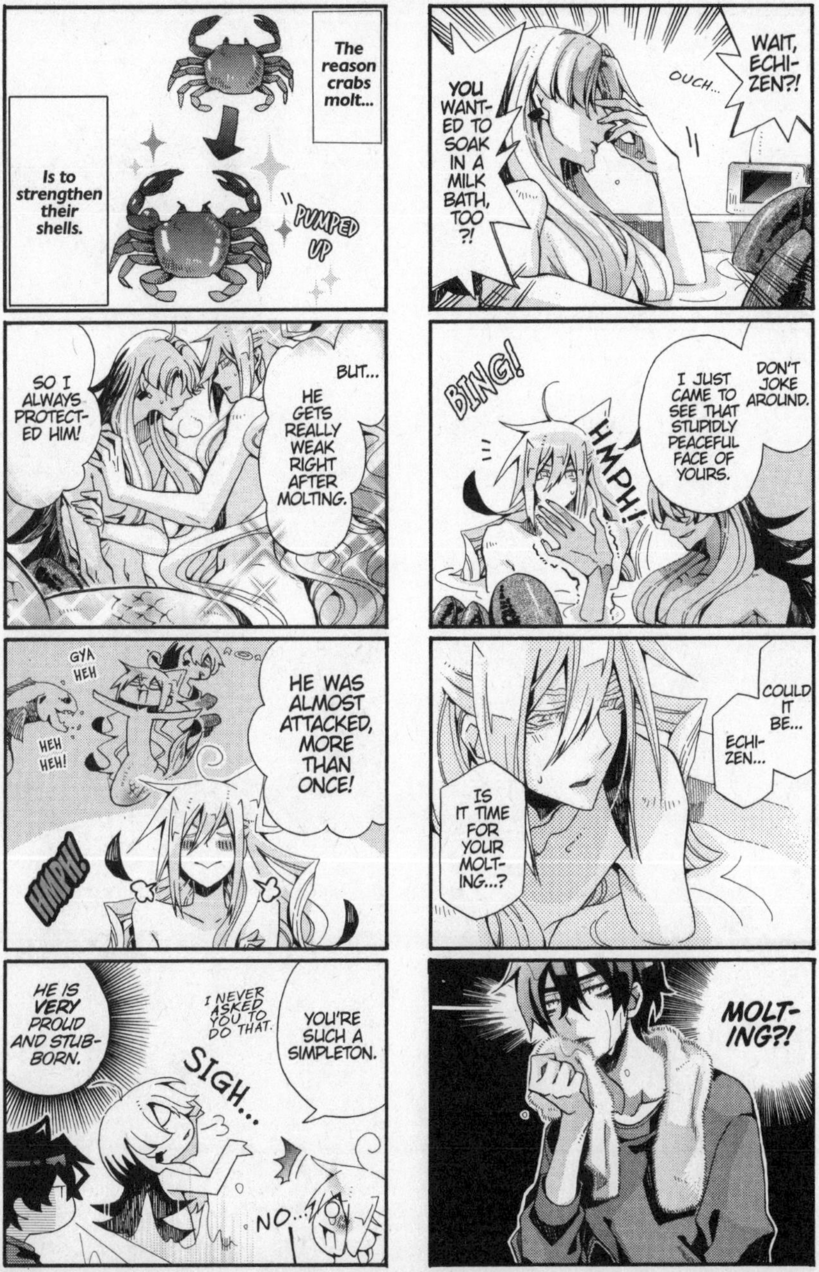
WAIT, ECHIZEN?!
OUCH...
YOU WANTED TO SOAK IN A MILK BATH, TOO?!
DON'T JOKE AROUND.
I JUST CAME TO SEE THAT STUPIDLY PEACEFUL FACE OF YOURS.
HMPH!
BING!
COULD IT BE... ECHIZEN...
IS IT TIME FOR YOUR MOLTING...?
MOLTING?!
The reason crabs molt...
PUMPED UP
Is to strengthen their shells.
BUT... HE GETS REALLY WEAK RIGHT AFTER MOLTING.
SO I ALWAYS PROTECTED HIM!
HE WAS ALMOST ATTACKED, MORE THAN ONCE!
GYA HEH
HEH HEH!
HMPH!
YOU'RE SUCH A SIMPLETON.
I NEVER ASKED YOU TO DO THAT.
HE IS VERY PROUD AND STUBBORN.
SIGH...
NO...

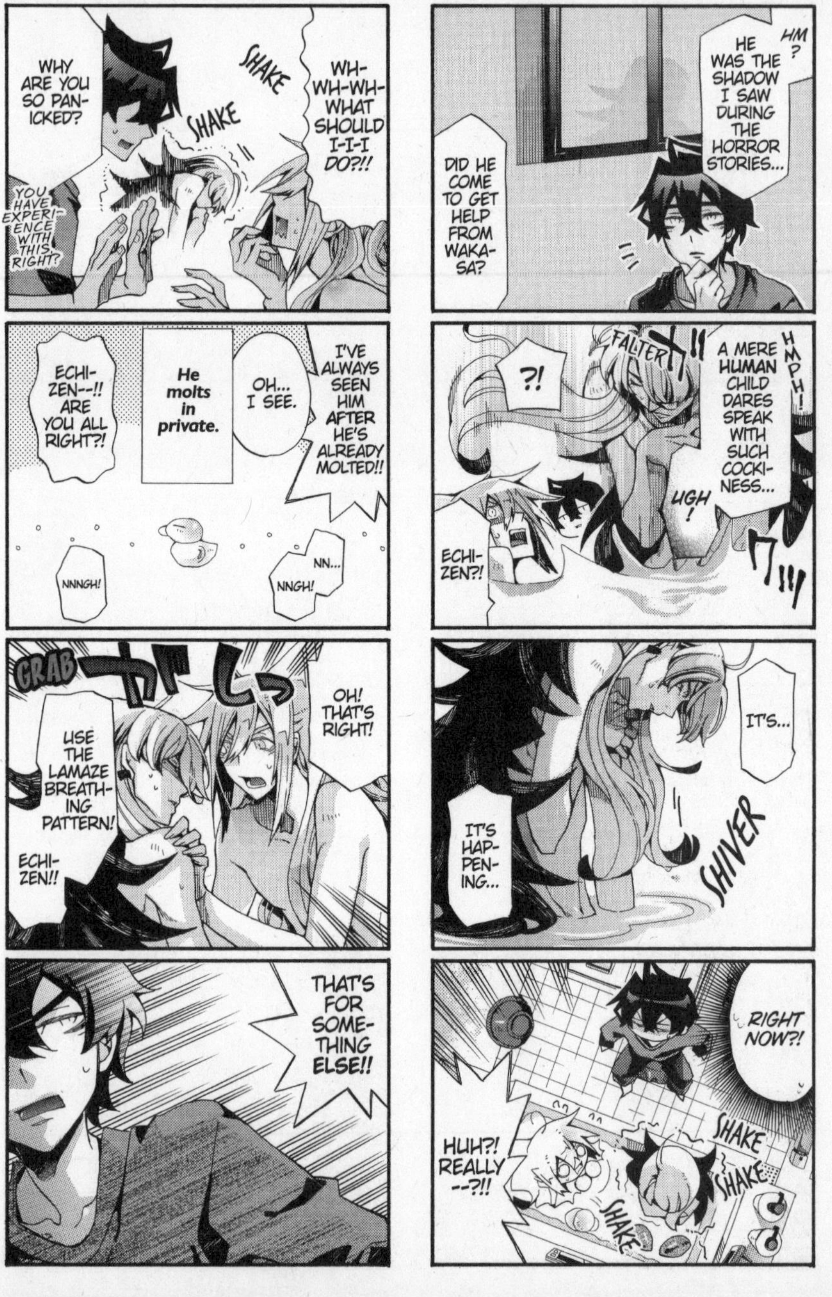
HM?
HE WAS THE SHADOW I SAW DURING THE HORROR STORIES...
DID HE COME TO GET HELP FROM WAKASA?
HMPH!
A MERE HUMAN CHILD DARES SPEAK WITH SUCH COCKINESS...
FALTER
?!
UGH!
ECHIZEN?!
IT'S...
SHIVER
IT'S HAPPENING...
RIGHT NOW?!
SHAKE
SHAKE
HUH?! REALLY--?!!
SHAKE
WH-WH-WH-WHAT SHOULD I-I-I DO?!!
SHAKE
SHAKE
WHY ARE YOU SO PANICKED?
YOU HAVE EXPERIENCE WITH THIS, RIGHT?
I'VE ALWAYS SEEN HIM AFTER HE'S ALREADY MOLTED!!
OH... I SEE.
He molts in private.
ECHIZEN--!! ARE YOU ALL RIGHT?!
NN...
NNGH!
NNNGH!
OH! THAT'S RIGHT!
GRAB
USE THE LAMAZE BREATHING PATTERN!
ECHIZEN!!
THAT'S FOR SOMETHING ELSE!!

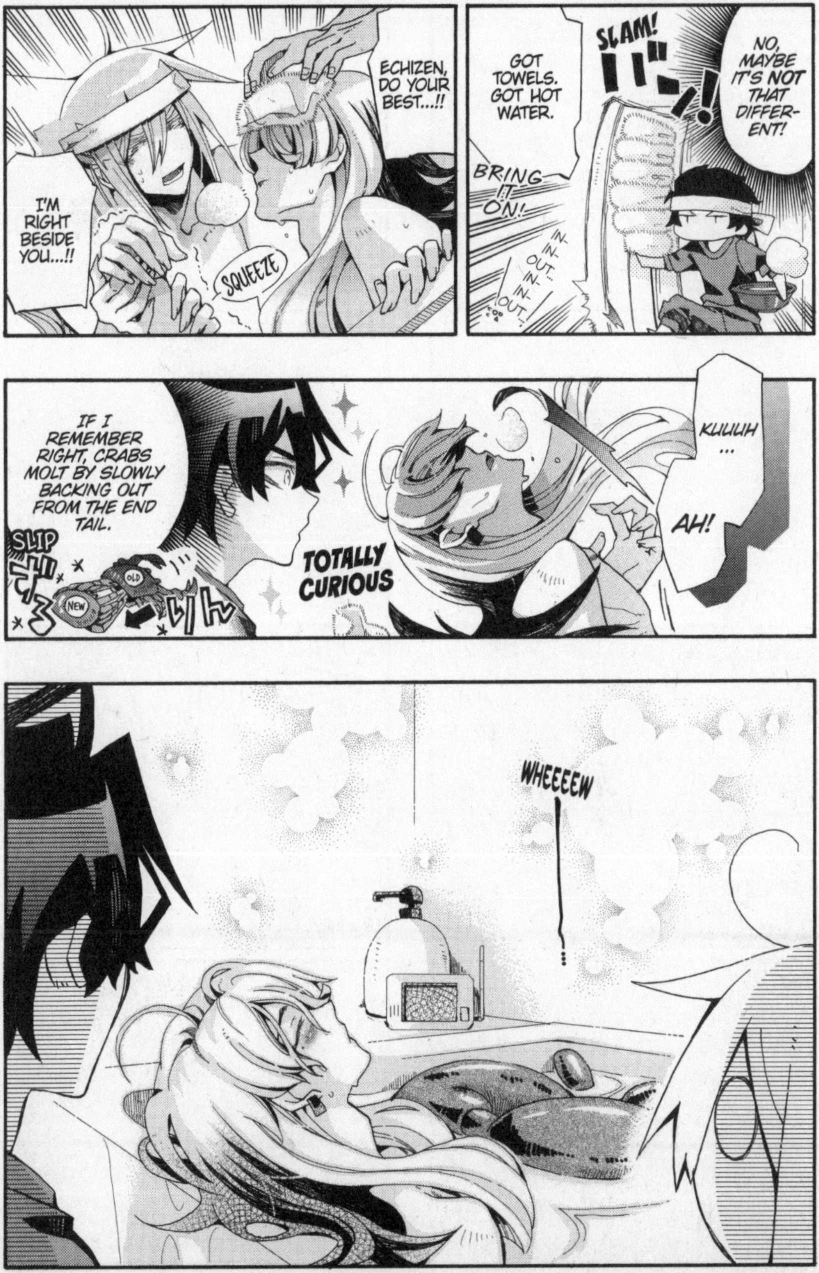
NO, MAYBE IT'S NOT THAT DIFFER-ENT!
SLAM!
GOT TOWELS. GOT HOT WATER.
BRING IT ON!
IN- IN- OUT... IN- OUT..!
ECHIZEN, DO YOUR BEST...!!
I'M RIGHT BESIDE YOU...!!
SQUEEZE
KUUUH ...
AH!
TOTALLY CURIOUS
IF I REMEMBER RIGHT, CRABS MOLT BY SLOWLY BACKING OUT FROM THE END TAIL.
OLD
NEW
SLIP
WHEEEEW

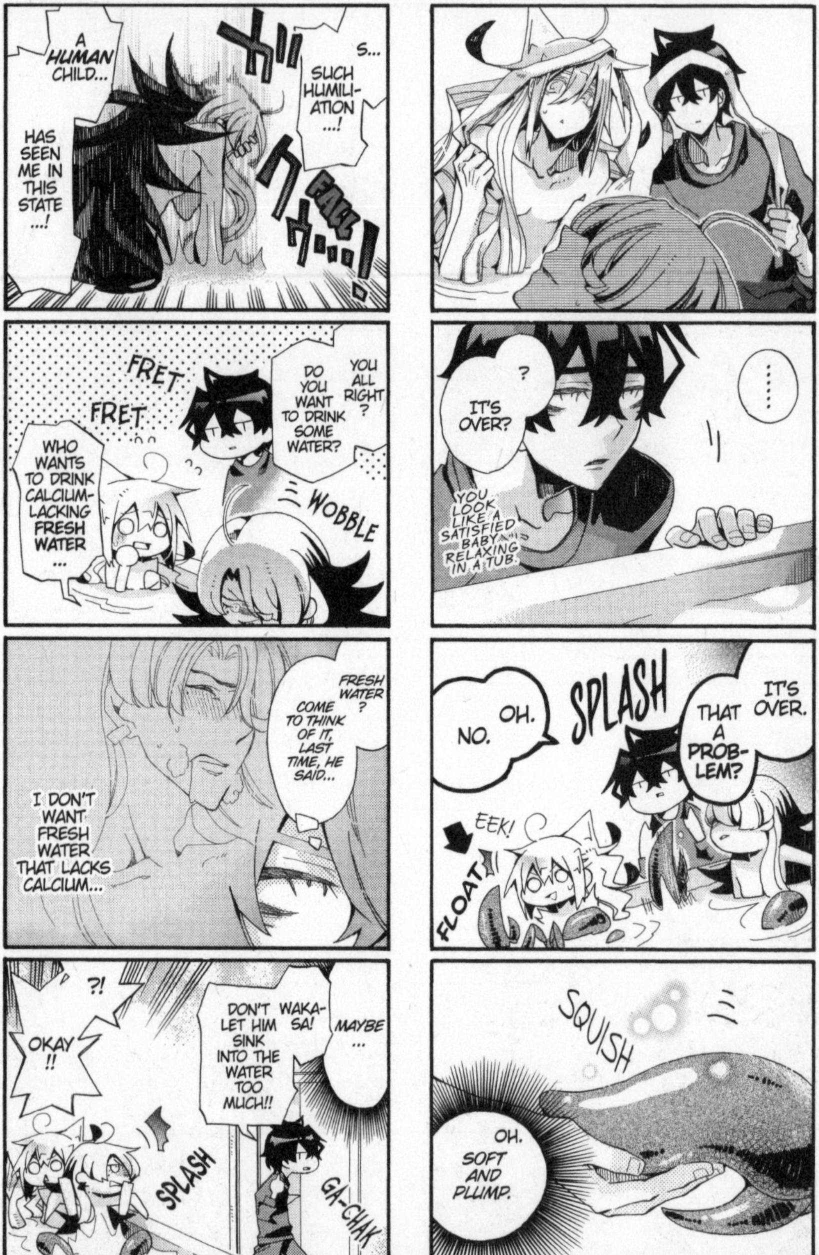
S...
SUCH HUMILIATION ...!
A HUMAN CHILD...
HAS SEEN ME IN THIS STATE ...!
......
?
IT'S OVER?
YOU LOOK LIKE A SATISFIED BABY RELAXING IN A TUB.
YOU ALL RIGHT?
DO YOU WANT TO DRINK SOME WATER?
FRET
FRET
WHO WANTS TO DRINK CALCIUM-LACKING FRESH WATER ...
WOBBLE
IT'S OVER.
THAT A PROBLEM?
SPLASH
OH.
NO.
EEK!
FLOAT
FRESH WATER?
COME TO THINK OF IT, LAST TIME, HE SAID...
I DON'T WANT FRESH WATER THAT LACKS CALCIUM...
SQUISH
OH. SOFT AND PLUMP.
MAYBE ...
WAKASA!
DON'T LET HIM SINK INTO THE WATER TOO MUCH!!
?!
OKAY!!
SPLASH
GA-CHAK

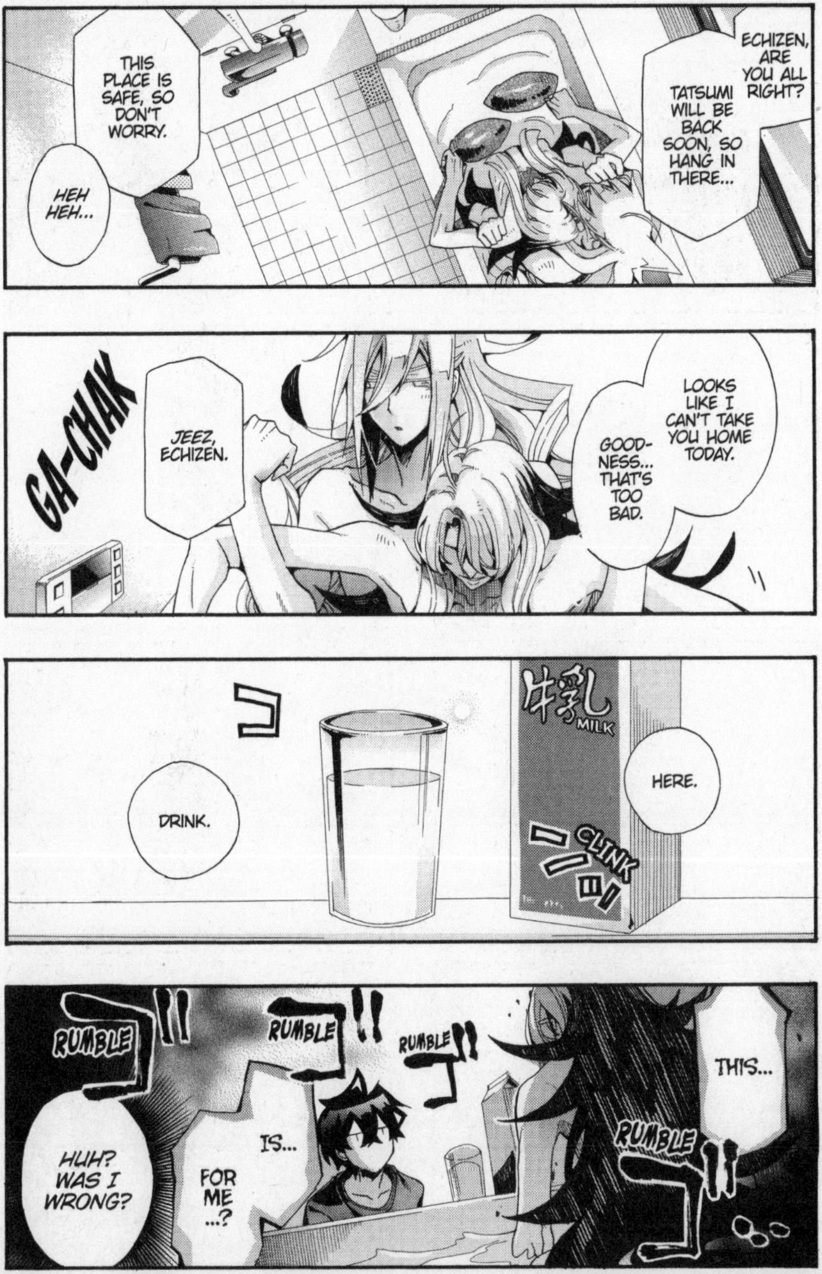
ECHIZEN, ARE YOU ALL RIGHT?
TATSUMI WILL BE BACK SOON, SO HANG IN THERE...
THIS PLACE IS SAFE, SO DON'T WORRY.
HEH HEH...
LOOKS LIKE I CAN'T TAKE YOU HOME TODAY.
GOOD-NESS... THAT'S TOO BAD.
JEEZ, ECHIZEN.
GA-CHAK
牛乳 MILK
HERE.
CLINK
DRINK.
THIS...
RUMBLE
RUMBLE
IS...
FOR ME ...?
RUMBLE
HUH? WAS I WRONG?
RUMBLE

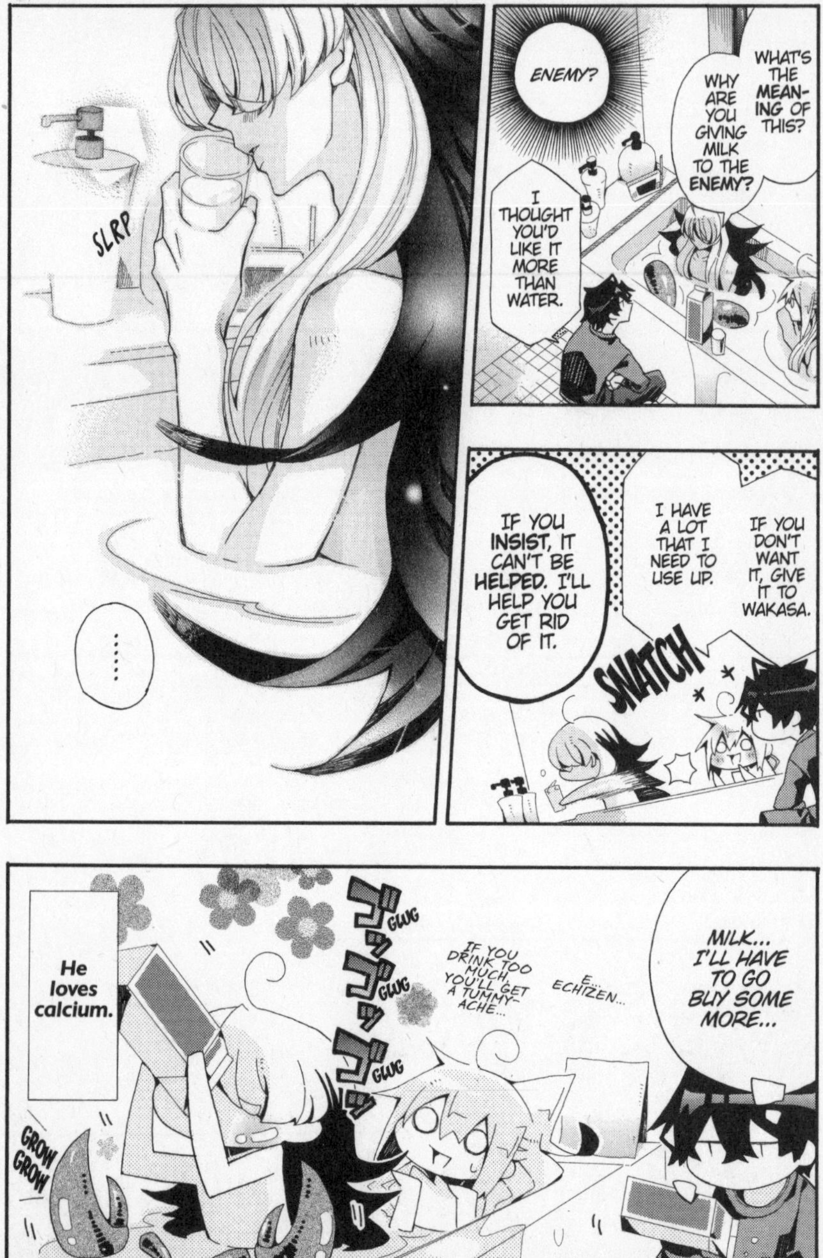
WHAT'S THE MEANING OF THIS?
WHY ARE YOU GIVING MILK TO THE ENEMY?
ENEMY?
I THOUGHT YOU'D LIKE IT MORE THAN WATER.
IF YOU DON'T WANT IT, GIVE IT TO WAKASA.
I HAVE A LOT THAT I NEED TO USE UP.
IF YOU INSIST, IT CAN'T BE HELPED. I'LL HELP YOU GET RID OF IT.
SNATCH
SLRP
......
MILK... I'LL HAVE TO GO BUY SOME MORE...
E... ECHIZEN...
IF YOU DRINK TOO MUCH, YOU'LL GET A TUMMY-ACHE...
ゴッ GWG
ゴッ GWG
ゴッ GWG
He loves calcium.
GROW GROW

Merman in My Tub

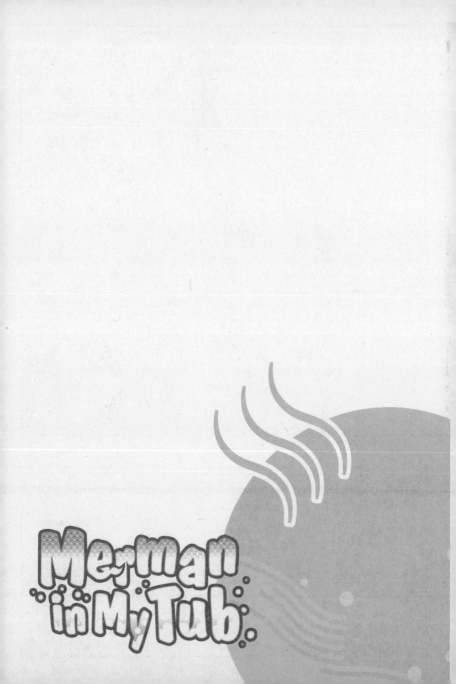

オレん家のフロ事情

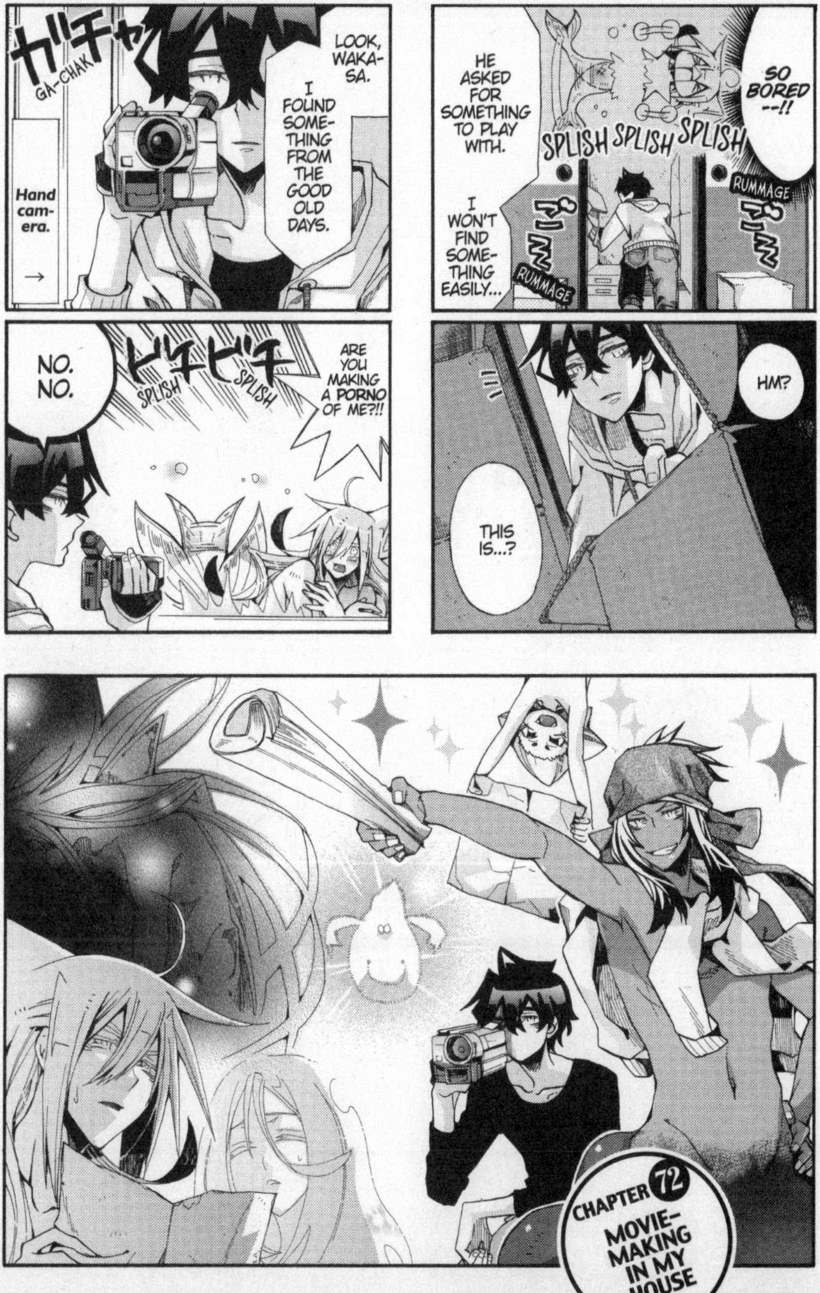
SO BORED --!!
HE ASKED FOR SOMETHING TO PLAY WITH.
SPLISH SPLISH SPLISH
RUMMAGE
I WON'T FIND SOMETHING EASILY...
RUMMAGE
ガチャ
GA-CHAK
LOOK, WAKASA.
I FOUND SOMETHING FROM THE GOOD OLD DAYS.
Hand camera.
→
HM?
THIS IS...?
ARE YOU MAKING A PORNO OF ME?!!
SPLISH SPLISH
NO. NO.
CHAPTER 72
MOVIE-MAKING IN MY HOUSE

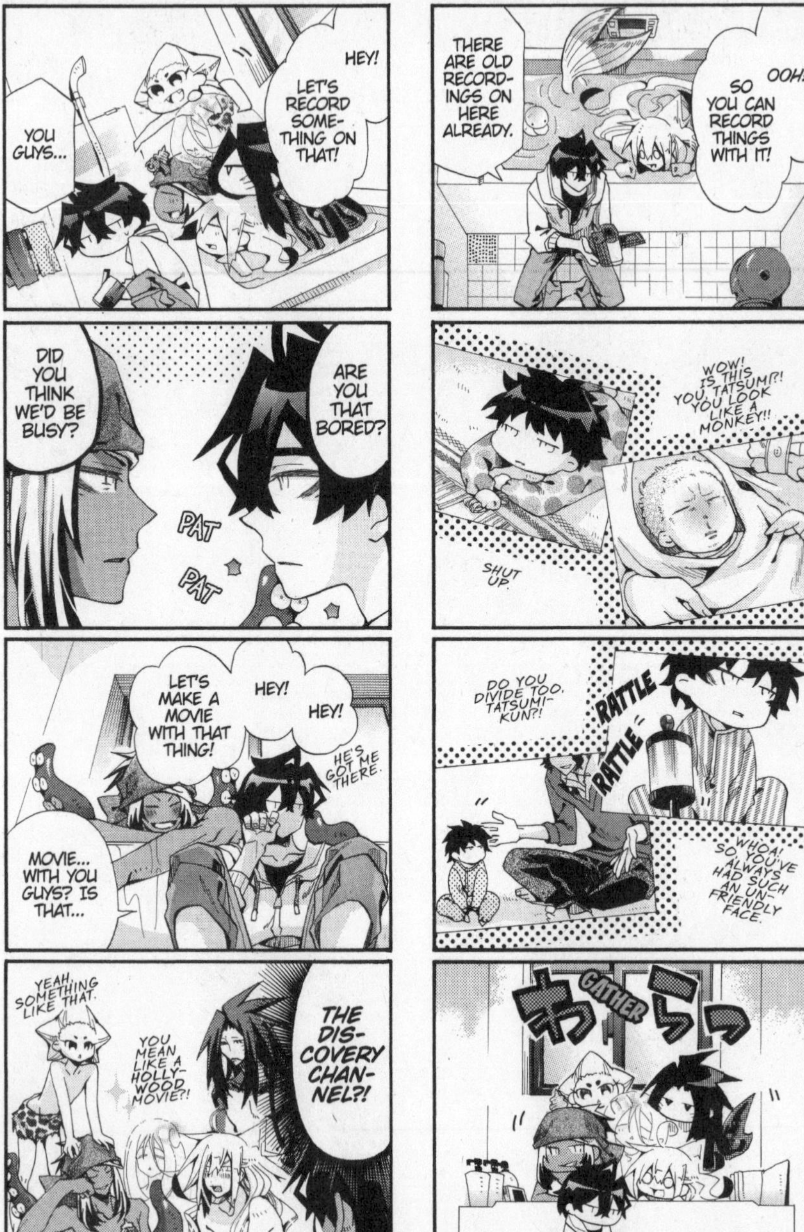
OOH!
SO YOU CAN RECORD THINGS WITH IT!
THERE ARE OLD RECORDINGS ON HERE ALREADY.
WOW! IS THIS YOU, TATSUMI?! YOU LOOK LIKE A MONKEY!!
SHUT UP.
DO YOU DIVIDE TOO, TATSUMI-KUN?!
RATTLE
RATTLE
WHOA! SO YOU'VE ALWAYS HAD SUCH AN UNFRIENDLY FACE.
わらっ
GATHER
HEY!
LET'S RECORD SOMETHING ON THAT!
YOU GUYS...
ARE YOU THAT BORED?
DID YOU THINK WE'D BE BUSY?
PAT
PAT
HEY!
HEY!
LET'S MAKE A MOVIE WITH THAT THING!
HE'S GOT ME THERE.
MOVIE... WITH YOU GUYS? IS THAT...
THE DISCOVERY CHANNEL?!
YOU MEAN LIKE A HOLLYWOOD MOVIE?!
YEAH, SOMETHING LIKE THAT.

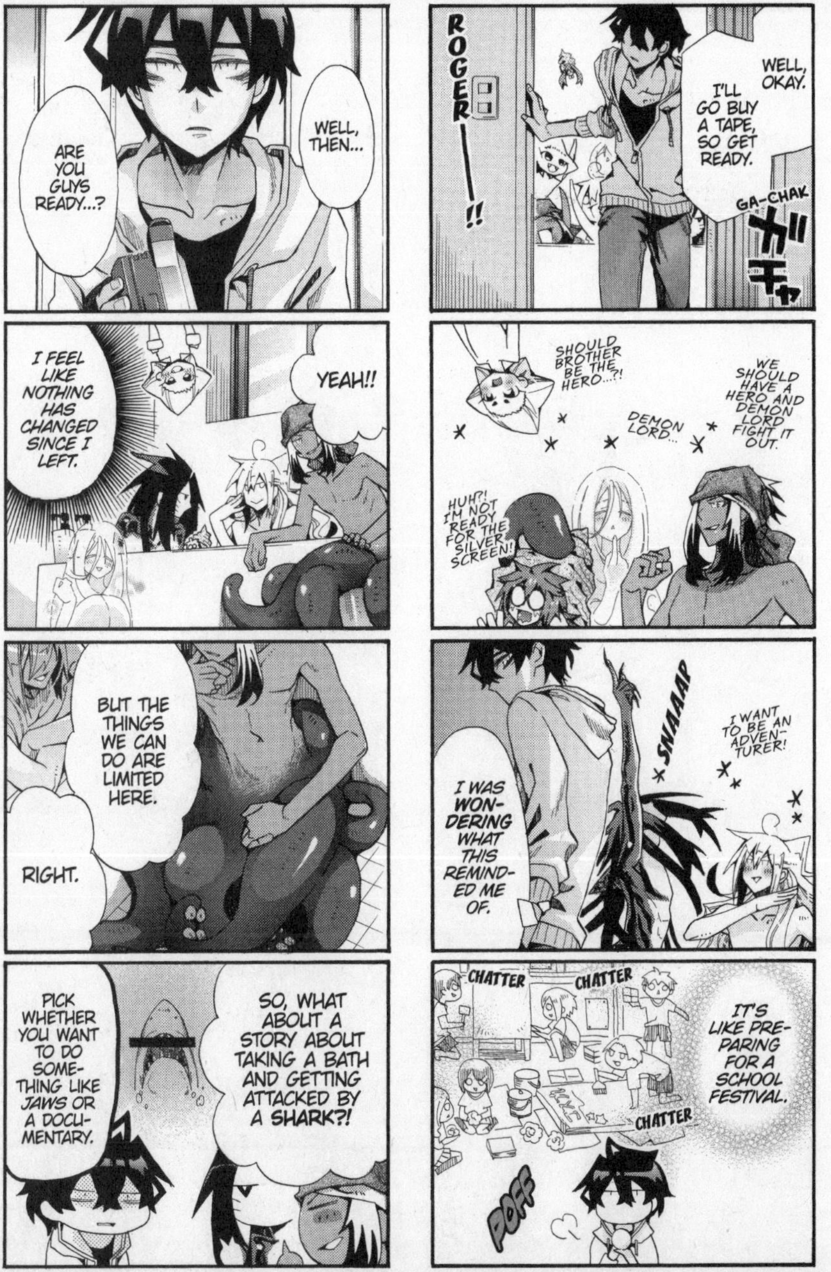
WELL, OKAY.
I'LL GO BUY A TAPE, SO GET READY.
GA-CHAK
ガチャ
ROGER—!!
WE SHOULD HAVE A HERO AND DEMON LORD FIGHT IT OUT.
DEMON LORD...
SHOULD BROTHER BE THE HERO...?!
HUH?! I'M NOT READY FOR THE SILVER SCREEN!
I WANT TO BE AN ADVENTURER!
SNAAAP
I WAS WONDERING WHAT THIS REMINDED ME OF.
CHATTER
CHATTER
IT'S LIKE PREPARING FOR A SCHOOL FESTIVAL.
CHATTER
POFF
WELL, THEN...
ARE YOU GUYS READY...?
YEAH!!
I FEEL LIKE NOTHING HAS CHANGED SINCE I LEFT.
BUT THE THINGS WE CAN DO ARE LIMITED HERE.
RIGHT.
SO, WHAT ABOUT A STORY ABOUT TAKING A BATH AND GETTING ATTACKED BY A SHARK?!
PICK WHETHER YOU WANT TO DO SOMETHING LIKE JAWS OR A DOCUMENTARY.

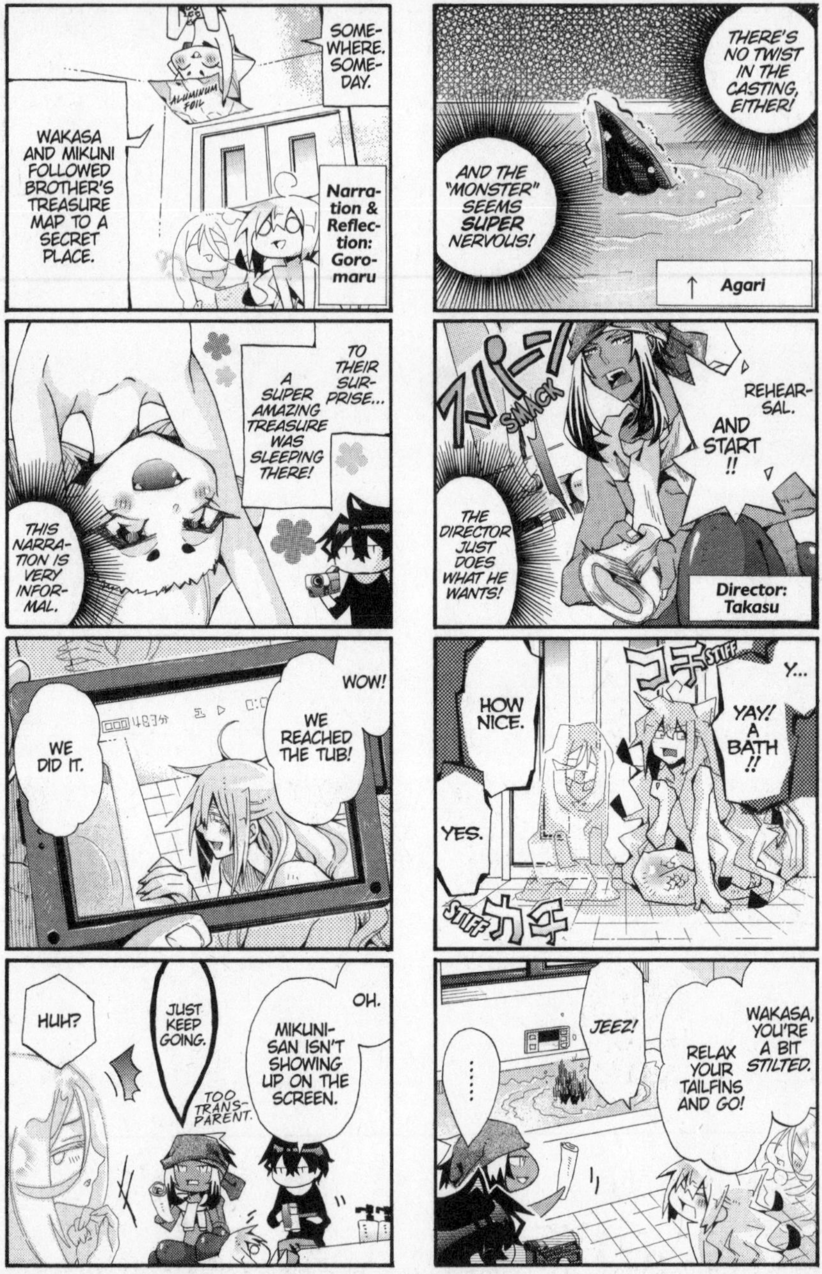
THERE'S NO TWIST IN THE CASTING, EITHER!
AND THE "MONSTER" SEEMS SUPER NERVOUS!
↑ Agari
REHEARSAL.
AND START!!
SMACK
THE DIRECTOR JUST DOES WHAT HE WANTS!
Director: Takasu
STIFF
Y...
YAY! A BATH!!
HOW NICE.
YES.
STIFF
WAKASA, YOU'RE A BIT STILTED.
RELAX YOUR TAILFINS AND GO!
JEEZ!
......
SOMEWHERE. SOMEDAY.
Narration & Reflection: Goromaru
ALUMINUM FOIL
WAKASA AND MIKUNI FOLLOWED BROTHER'S TREASURE MAP TO A SECRET PLACE.
TO THEIR SURPRISE...
A SUPER AMAZING TREASURE WAS SLEEPING THERE!
THIS NARRATION IS VERY INFORMAL.
WOW!
WE REACHED THE TUB!
WE DID IT.
OH.
MIKUNI-SAN ISN'T SHOWING UP ON THE SCREEN.
TOO TRANSPARENT.
JUST KEEP GOING.
HUH?

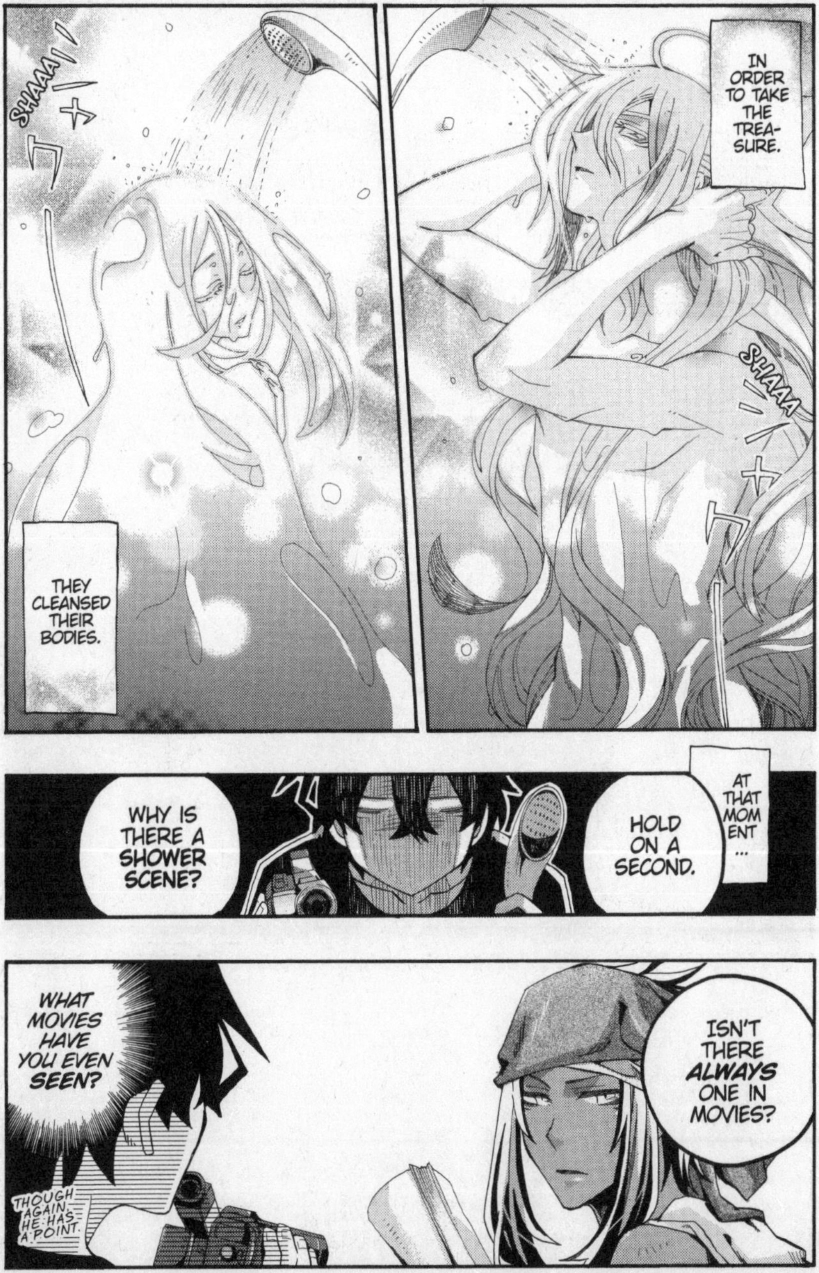
IN ORDER TO TAKE THE TREA-SURE.
SHAAA
SHAAAA
THEY CLEANSED THEIR BODIES.
AT THAT MOMENT...
HOLD ON A SECOND.
WHY IS THERE A SHOWER SCENE?
ISN'T THERE **ALWAYS** ONE IN MOVIES?
WHAT MOVIES HAVE YOU EVEN SEEN?
THOUGH AGAIN HE HAS A POINT.

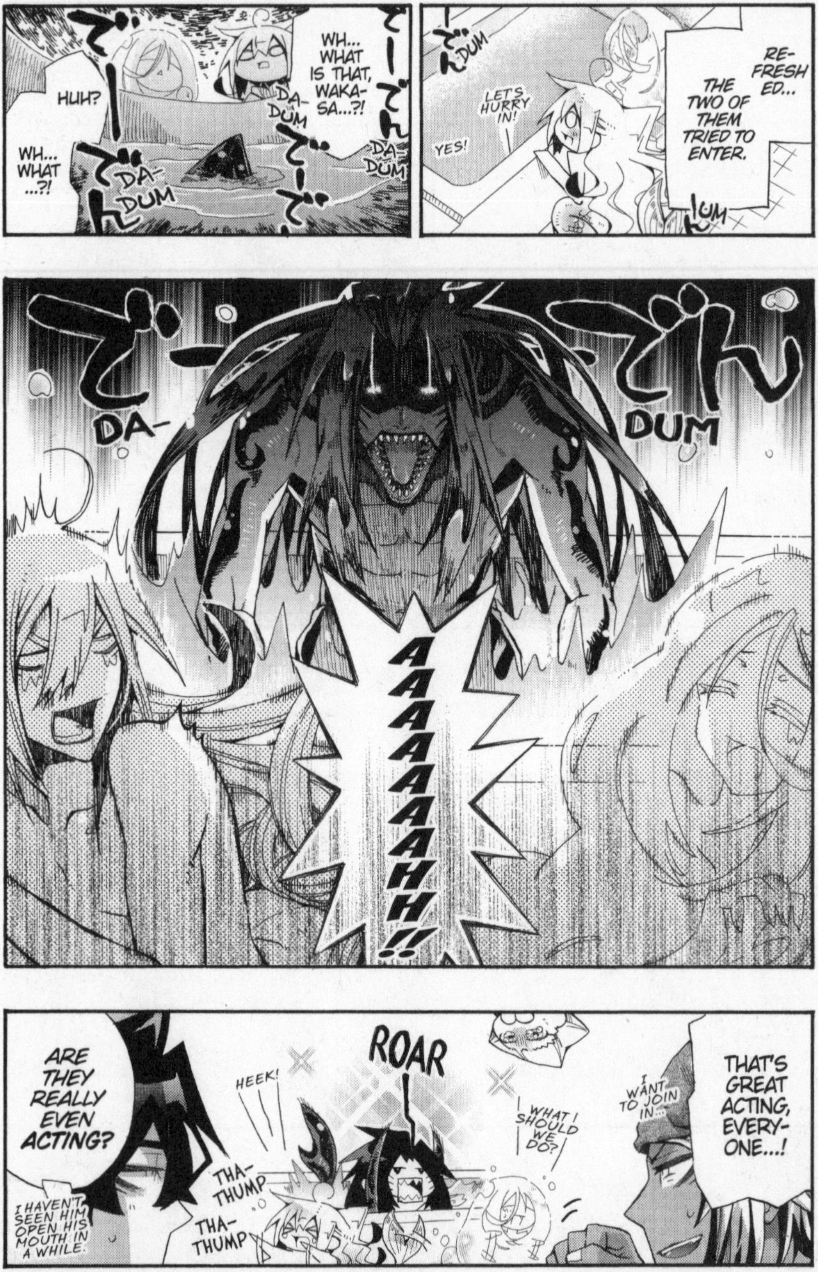
DUM
RE-FRESHED... THE TWO OF THEM TRIED TO ENTER.
LET'S HURRY IN!
YES!
UM
WH... WHAT IS THAT, WAKA-SA...?!
HUH?
DA-DUM
DA-DUM
WH... WHAT ...?!
DA-DUM
DA-
DUM
AAAAAAAAAHH!!
THAT'S GREAT ACTING, EVERY-ONE...!
I WANT TO JOIN IN...
WHAT SHOULD WE DO?
ROAR
HEEK!
ARE THEY REALLY EVEN ACTING?
THA-THUMP
THA-THUMP
I HAVEN'T SEEN HIM OPEN HIS MOUTH IN A WHILE.

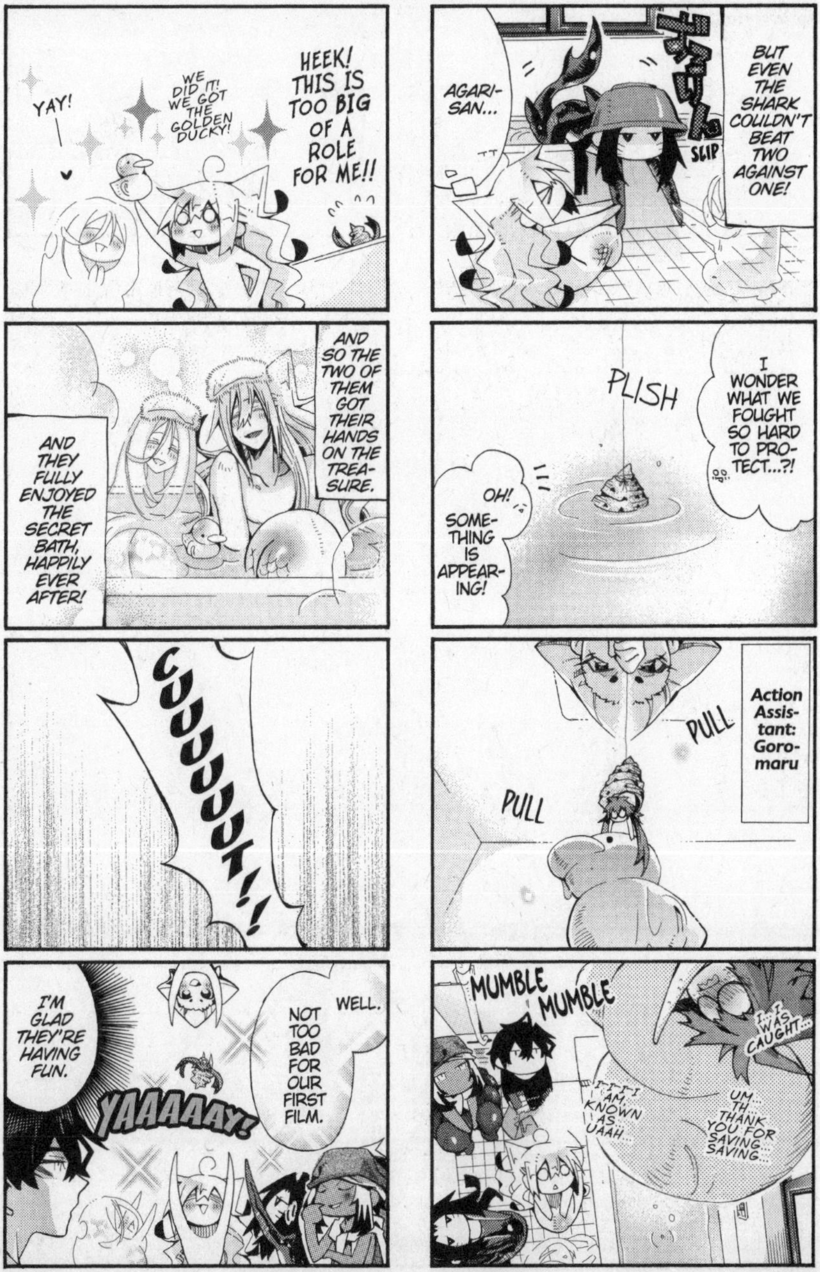
BUT EVEN THE SHARK COULDN'T BEAT TWO AGAINST ONE!
SLIP
AGARI-SAN...
HEEK! THIS IS TOO BIG OF A ROLE FOR ME!!
WE DID IT! WE GOT THE GOLDEN DUCKY!
YAY!
I WONDER WHAT WE FOUGHT SO HARD TO PROTECT...?!
PLISH
OH! SOMETHING IS APPEARING!
AND SO THE TWO OF THEM GOT THEIR HANDS ON THE TREASURE.
AND THEY FULLY ENJOYED THE SECRET BATH, HAPPILY EVER AFTER!
Action Assistant: Goromaru
PULL
PULL
CUUUUUUT!!
I... I WAS CAUGHT...
UM TH... THANK YOU FOR SAVING SAVING...
MUMBLE MUMBLE
I-I-I-I AM... KNOWN AS... UAAH...
WELL.
NOT TOO BAD FOR OUR FIRST FILM.
YAAAAAY!
I'M GLAD THEY'RE HAVING FUN.

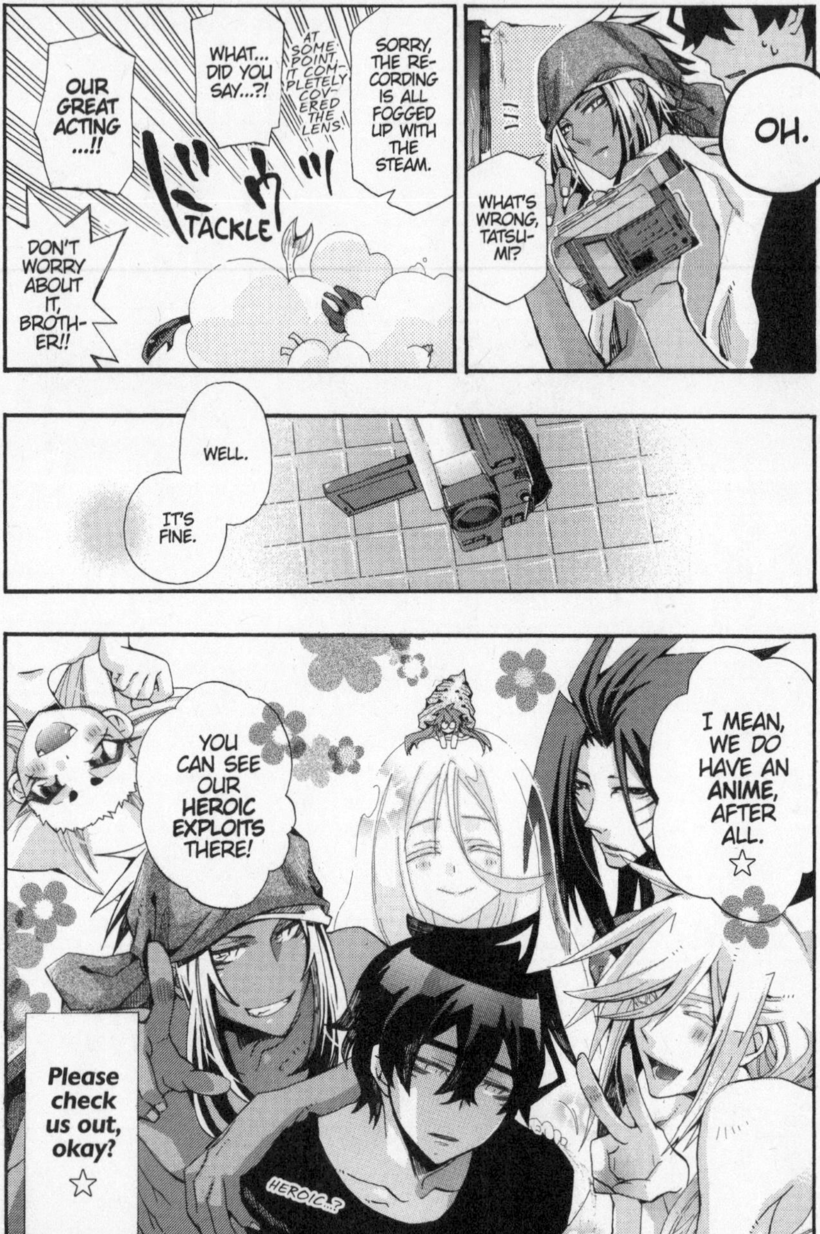
OH.
WHAT'S WRONG, TATSUMI?
SORRY, THE RECORDING IS ALL FOGGED UP WITH THE STEAM.
AT SOME POINT, IT COMPLETELY COVERED THE LENS.
WHAT... DID YOU SAY...?!
OUR GREAT ACTING ...!!
TACKLE
DON'T WORRY ABOUT IT, BROTHER!!
WELL.
IT'S FINE.
I MEAN, WE DO HAVE AN ANIME, AFTER ALL. ☆
YOU CAN SEE OUR HEROIC EXPLOITS THERE!
HEROIC...?
Please check us out, okay? ☆

To be continued...

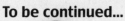

オレん家(ち)のウラ事情 special

THE BACKGROUND OF MY HOUSE

WE'RE GOING TO SHOW THE ILLUSTRATIONS AND QUESTIONS SENT IN AFTER OUR REQUEST IN VOLUME 4!!

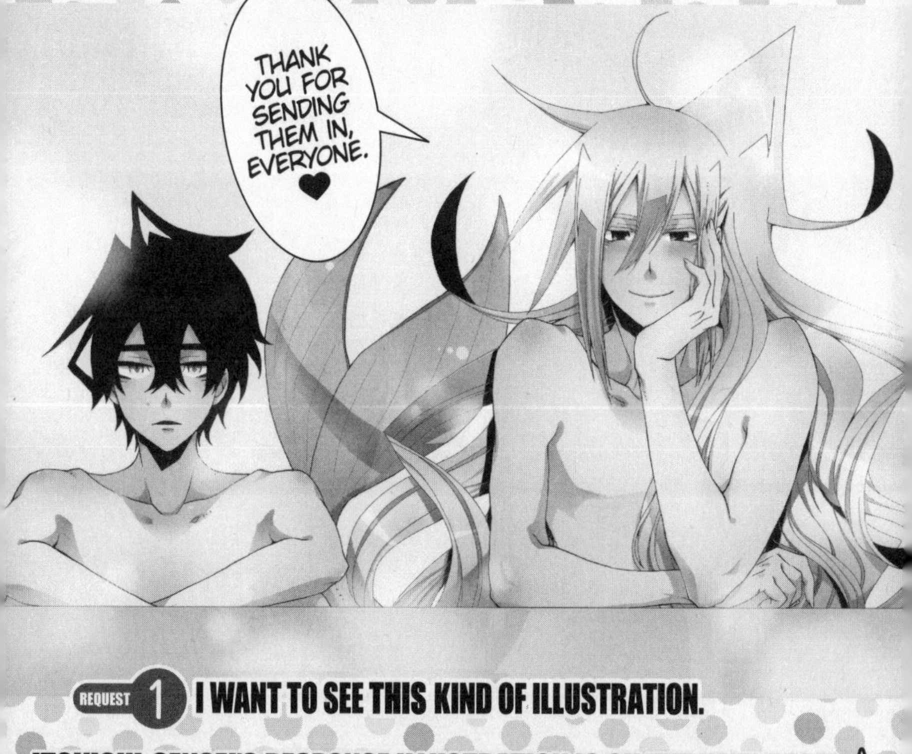
THANK YOU FOR SENDING THEM IN, EVERYONE. ♥

REQUEST 1 I WANT TO SEE THIS KIND OF ILLUSTRATION.

ITOKICHI-SENSEI'S RESPONSE ILLUSTRATION IS ON THE NEXT PAGE! ☆

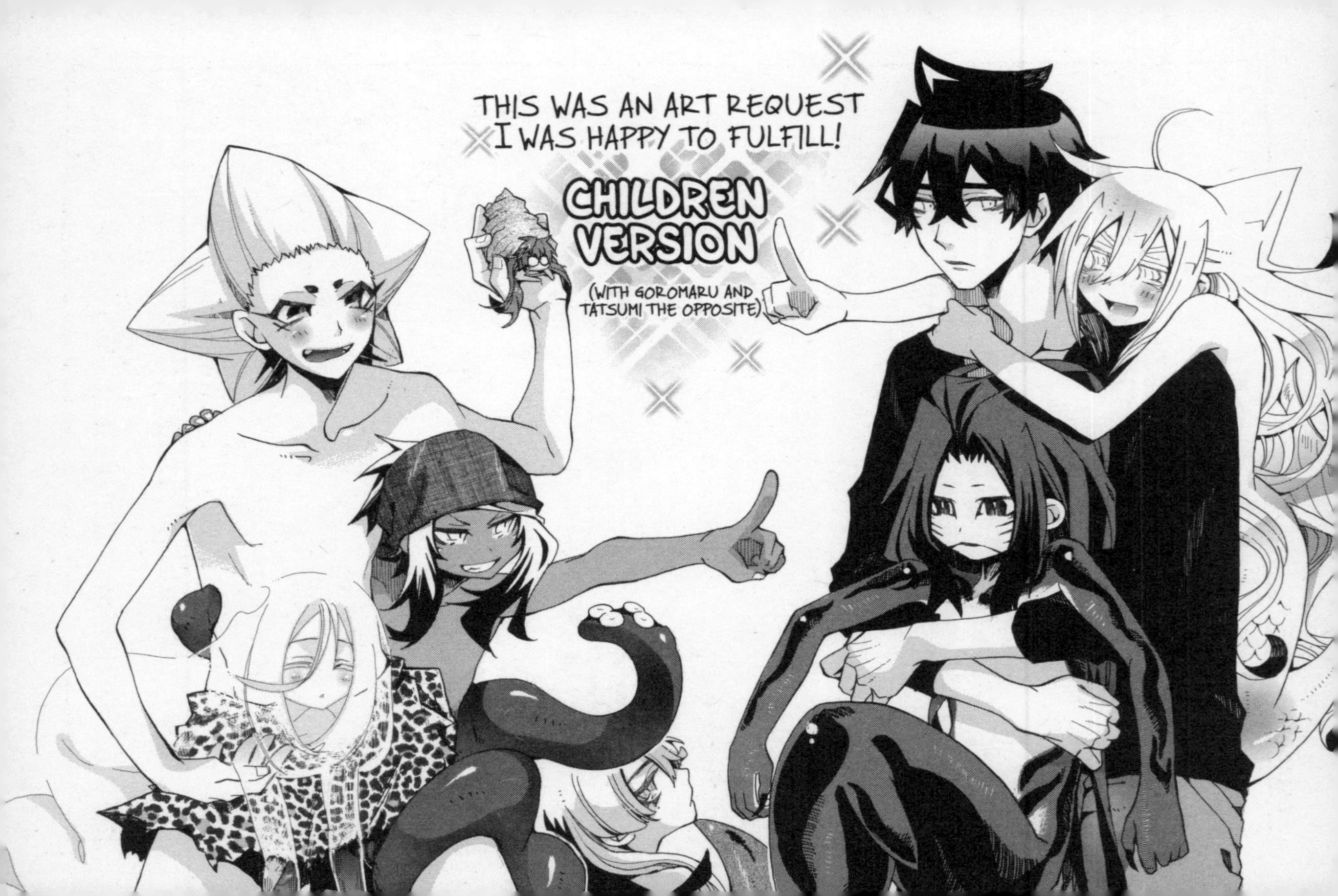
THIS WAS AN ART REQUEST I WAS HAPPY TO FULFILL!
CHILDREN VERSION
(WITH GOROMARU AND TATSUMI THE OPPOSITE)

OMAKE

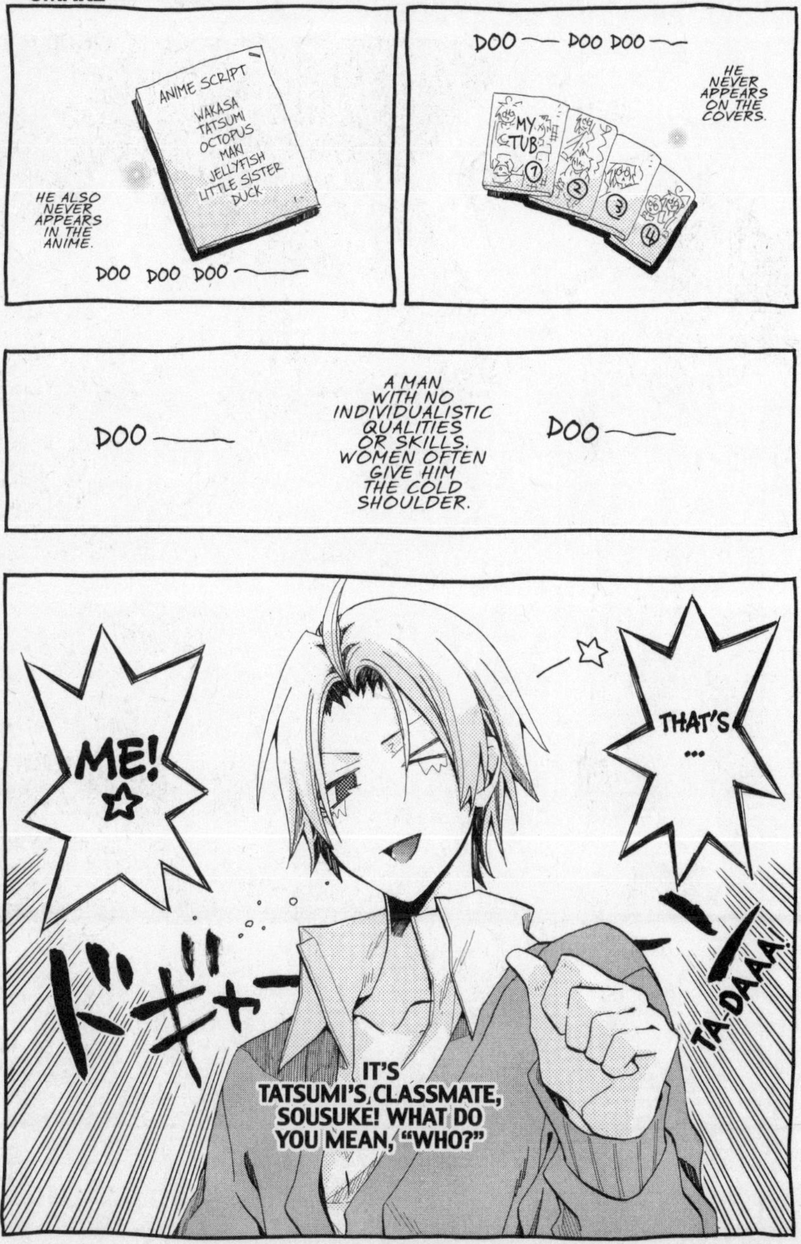
DOO — DOO DOO —
HE NEVER APPEARS ON THE COVERS.
MY TUB
ANIME SCRIPT
WAKASA
TATSUMI
OCTOPUS
MAKI
JELLYFISH
LITTLE SISTER
DUCK
HE ALSO NEVER APPEARS IN THE ANIME.
DOO DOO DOO —
DOO —
A MAN WITH NO INDIVIDUALISTIC QUALITIES OR SKILLS. WOMEN OFTEN GIVE HIM THE COLD SHOULDER.
DOO —
THAT'S ...
TA DAAA!
ME! ☆
ドギャー
IT'S TATSUMI'S CLASSMATE, SOUSUKE! WHAT DO YOU MEAN, "WHO?"

I'D LIKE TO SHOW YOU SOME OF THE WON-DERFUL *ART* PEOPLE HAVE SENT ME!!

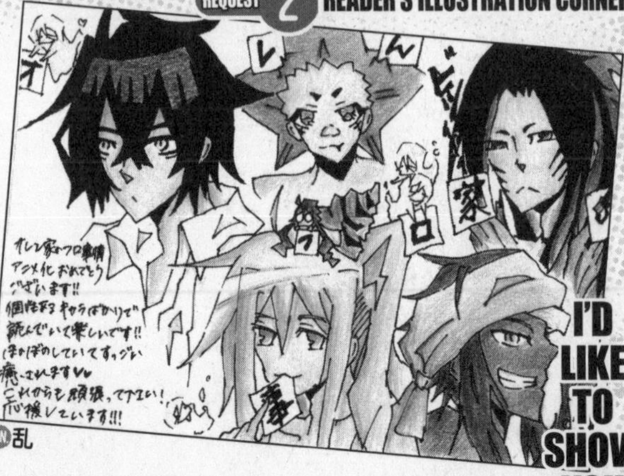
オ
レ
ん
家
フ
ロ
オレん家のフロ事情
アニメ化おめでとうございます!!
個性すぎるキャラばかりで読んでいて楽しいです!!
ほのぼのしていてすっごい癒されますv
これからも頑張って下さい!
応援しています!!!

P.N. 乱

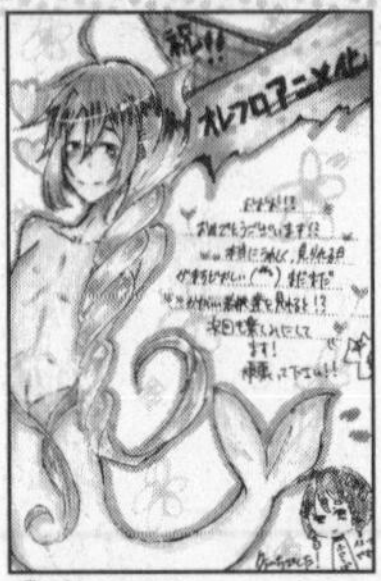
祝!!

P.N. 冬いち

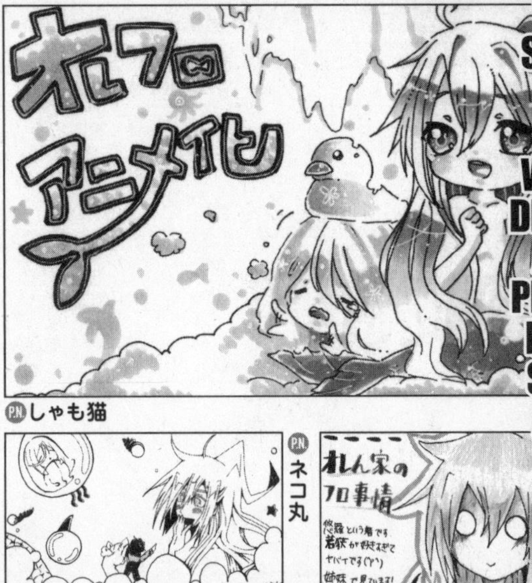

P.N. しゃも猫

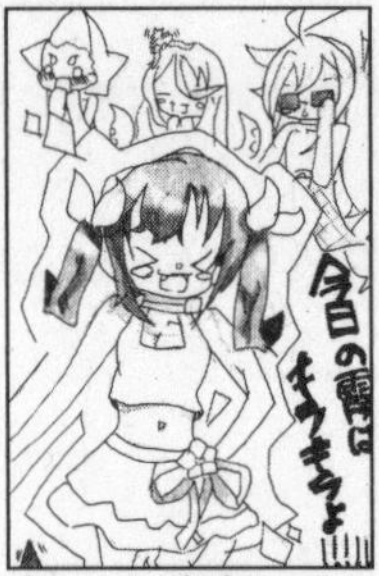

P.N. たん・ぽぽちゃん

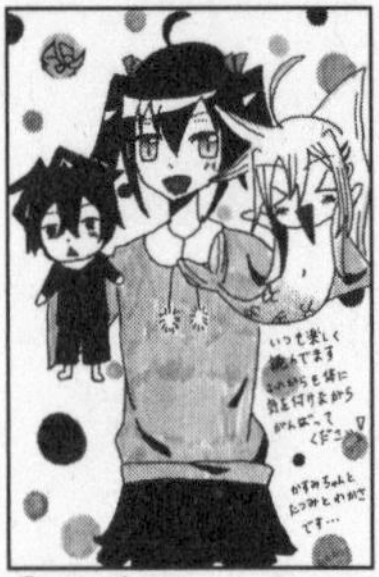

P.N. ログ

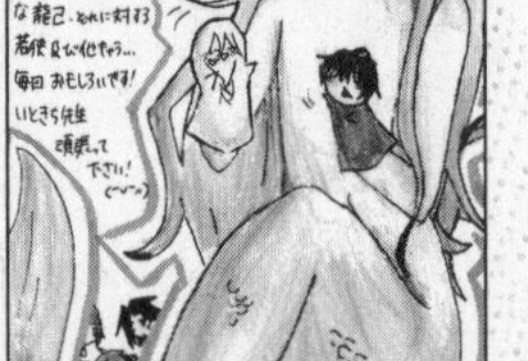
オレん家のフロ事情
いときち先生
頑張って下さい!

P.N. 悠羅

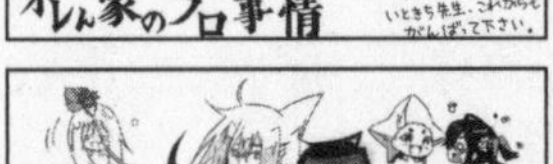
オレん家のフロ事情
三国さんにいつもいやされてます。大好きです。
いときち先生、これからもがんばって下さい。

P.N. ネコ丸

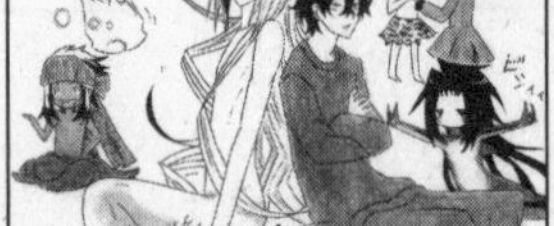

P.N. 黒須霊

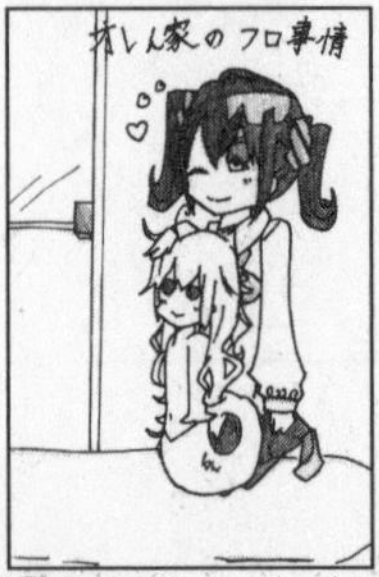
オレん家の フロ事情

P.N. うーり

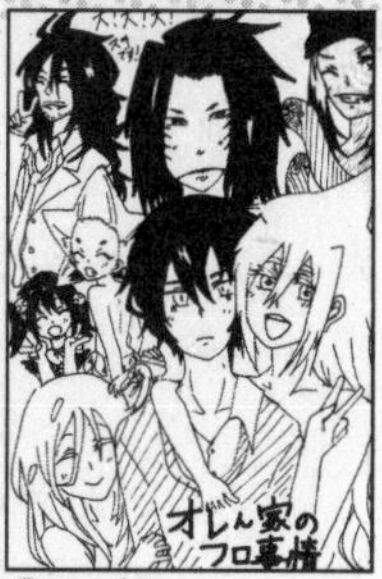
オレん家のフロ事情

P.N. めがね

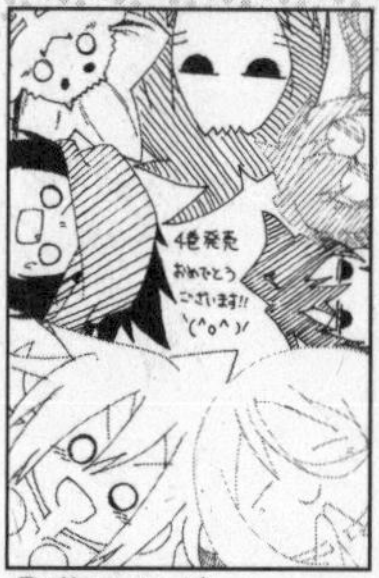
4巻発売
おめでとう
ございます!!
ヽ(^o^)ノ

P.N. 夢ウサギ

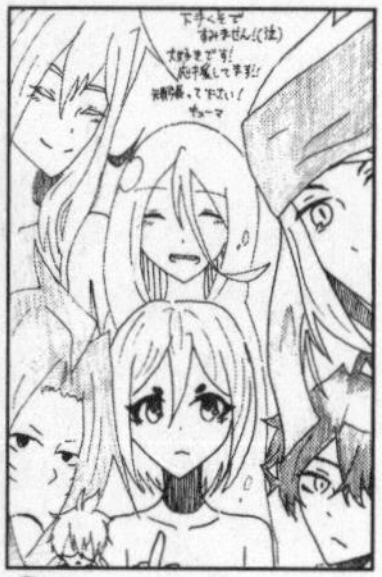
下手くそで
すみません!(汗)
大好きです!
応援してます!!
頑張って下さい!
キューマ

P.N. キューマ

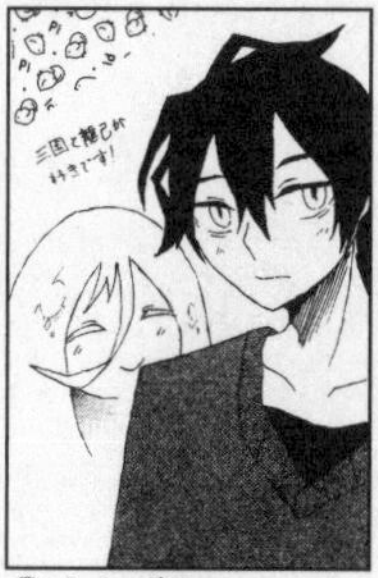
三国と雛己が
好きです!

P.N. まさずみ

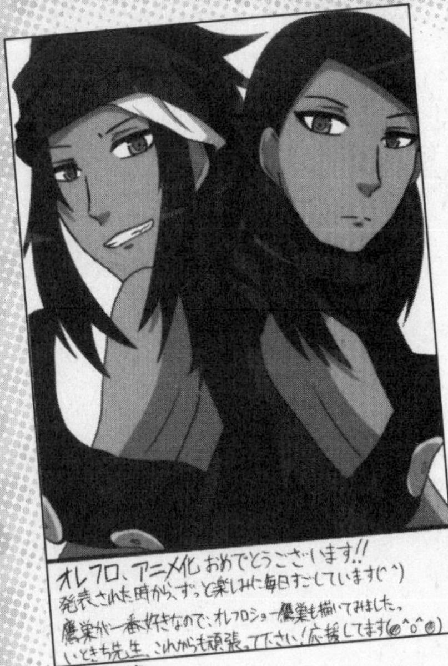
オレフロ、アニメ化おめでとうございます!!
発表された時から、ずっと楽しみに毎日すごしています(^^)
鷹巣が一番好きなので、オレフロショー鷹巣も描いてみました。
いときち先生、これからも頑張って下さい!応援してます(◎^o^◎)

P.N. 早池峰

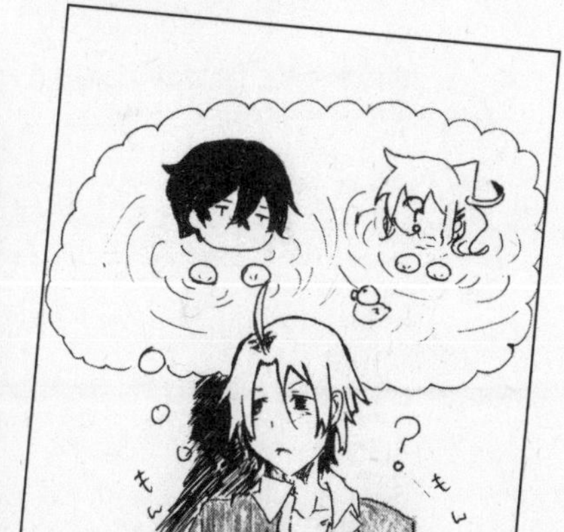
?
もん
もん

P.N. 食い意地犬

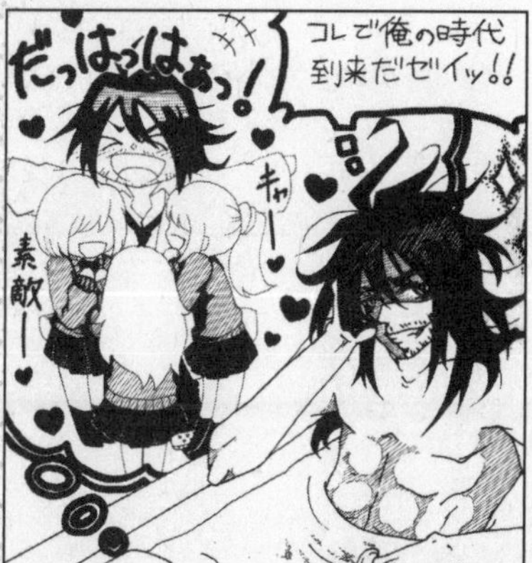
コレで俺の時代
到来だゼイッ!!
だっはっはぁっ!
キャー!
素敵ー!
ちゃぷん…
※注)
久虎さん作。
『イケメン風呂』w

P.N. 彰無契

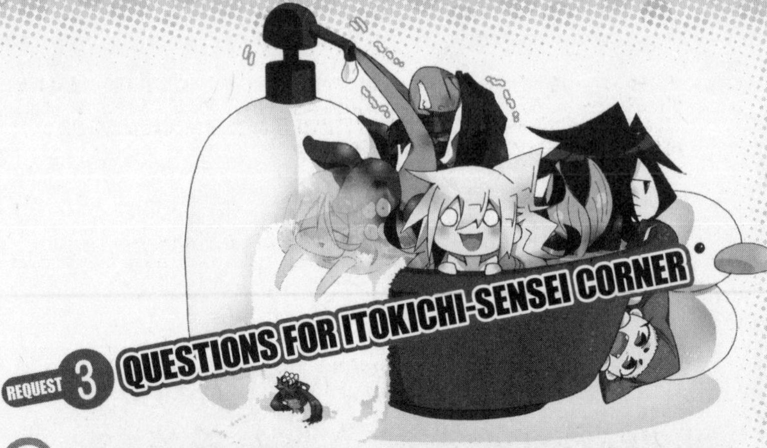

REQUEST 3 QUESTIONS FOR ITOKICHI-SENSEI CORNER

NICE TO MEET YOU! I ALWAYS ENJOY READING YOUR COMIC. I HAVE A QUESTION, WHAT IS AGARI-SAN'S BODY PATTERN? DEPENDING ON THE VOLUME, THE PATTERN ON HIS BODY IS DIFFERENT AND SOMETIMES IN COLOR IT IS GONE. I WOULD BE SO HAPPY IF YOU TOLD ME! (SEVEN MIST <3>)

That is a problem with my art skills. <Boom>
I try drawing shark skin in detail when inking sometimes and other times when I color him I think it'll be fine to just use a light color. ★ I'm always like this.
I see, it looks like body paint to you... I wish I had known this before I started coloring him. ^___^

A QUESTION FOR TATSUMI! WHO WOULD YOU RATHER CHANGE PLACES WITH? (KANAKANA)

Tatsumi: Why do I have to change places with these guys...?
Wakasa: So terrible! Don't be so mean!
Tatsumi: *Hmm...* Then I'd be Mikuni-san.
Wakasa: And why is that?
Tatsumi: I could spend my time relaxing and I can divide. And most of all, I wouldn't have to eat. It'd be nice not having to make meals.
Wakasa: Y-You can't change places!!

ITOKICHI-SENSEI, DO YOU HAVE CERTAIN WAYS THAT YOU ENJOY TAKING BATHS? LIKE BATH SALTS... (SATOU)

When I know I'm going to take a long bath, I bring music in with me. Also manga. I've wanted to try bath salts, but it is something my family hasn't used in generations, so... (laugh)

IF YOU CREATE A NEW CHARACTER, I THINK A NARWHAL WOULD BE GOOD. I THINK THEIR CANINE TOOTH PROTRUDING OUT LIKE A HORN IS UNIQUE AND MEMORABLE. WHAT DO YOU THINK? I THINK THE PERSONALITY SHOULD BE COLD AND WELL-INFORMED. (PECORO)

A narwhal...! Every time I see one on TV their long tooth puts me into high spirits! Cold and well-informed. What a wonderful personality... ^___^ I'll discuss it a bit with my editor.

HELLO!! (^__^) CONGRATULATIONS ON BECOMING AN ANIME!!! I CAN'T WAIT UNTIL IT'S RELEASED. (^O^) THERE IS ONLY ONE GIRL IN MERMAN IN MY TUB, KASUMI-CHAN. I WAS WONDERING IF WAKASA WOULD HAVE ANY FEMALE FRIENDS (A NEW CHARACTER) APPEAR? EXAMPLE) LIKE A SQUID. (SETSUNA)

Thank you for letting it become an anime!
It is because you all supported me so much! ^____^
Girl character... Well... There was a time I thought about it. But with Kasumi being the only girl, it's more delic... I mean, since Wakasa is a boy, he mainly hangs out with other boys. It's like he's in an all-boys school. It can't be... helped...

 I WAS SURPRISED TO FIND OUT THAT TATSUMI HAD CHUUNIBYOU!! WHAT HAPPENED TO HIM? (KURI)

Since the adults he had near him (Hisatora) are like that, they put such things into his mind. But since everyone has the ability to get chuunibyou, it can't be helped!

 THE WARM FEELINGS OF MERMAN IN MY TUB ALWAYS HELPS ME GET THROUGH THE WINTER. ♥ ITOKICHI-SENSEI, DO YOU HAVE A FAVORITE SEASON? (SHU-SHU)

It makes me happy that they do. ♥
My favorite season is the transition between fall and winter. It is before snow starts to fall, but there are no bugs or heat. It is also the time of year when food tastes the best!

 IF I HAD AN UNCLE LIKE HISATORA-SAN... IT'S FUNNY TO IMAGINE STUFF LIKE THAT. (LAUGH) DO YOU LOVE UNCLES? OR DO YOU LOVE BOYS?

I love uncles and grandpas. Lately I like boys, too.

 AREN'T TATSUMI'S MOM AND DAD LONELY THAT TATSUMI ISN'T AROUND? (YUKA)

I believe they are. But, they are watching over him lovingly, thinking about how quickly he's become an adult. Also, Kasumi has been giving them detailed information on how he is doing so it's all good!

TATSUMI WROTE THAT HE WANTED A GIRLFIRNED DURING THE STAR FESTIVAL, BUT WAS HE SERIOUS?! (YADA)

Of course! He's a healthy boy! After seeing the chests of men all the time, I'm sure he wants the healing powers of a female.

VOLUME 5 & ANIME RELEASE THANK YOU VERY MUCH!!

It's been three years since I've come into the care of the *Gene* editorial section. So much time has already passed...! I never expected that Wakasa would splash around the tub for this long! Thank you very much!!!

During that time, I've been waiting for the new Komichi photo collection, but recipe books I don't understand keep getting published instead. I have no relation with olive oil! I can only wet my pillow with tears every night in frustration. Just kidding. But I *am* waiting for the new collection.

Well, while things like that are happening, I continue drawing this bath manga. And please take a look at the anime where you can see and hear them splash around!!! ❤

TEE HEE!

TEE HEE!

ITOKISHI IS VERY HAPPY !!

TEE HEE!

SPECIAL THANKS

EVERYONE WHO FOLLOWED ME UNTIL NOW

FRIENDS AND FAMILY

PEOPLE AROUND ME

MY EDITOR

EVERYONE WHO ARE INVOLVED WITH THE ANIME

AND YOU!

ALL OF YOU GODS!

I HOPE THAT YOU CONTINUE TO READ THIS RUN-OF-THE-MILL BATH MANGA.

オレん家(ち)のフロ事情

SEVEN SEAS ENTERTAINMENT PRESENTS

Merman in My Tub.

story and art by **ITOKICHI**

volume **5**

TRANSLATION
Angela Liu

ADAPTATION
T Campbell

LETTERING
Laura Scoville

LOGO DESIGN
Meaghan Tucker

COVER DESIGN
Nicky Lim

PROOFREADER
Patrick King
Danielle King

PRODUCTION MANAGER
Lissa Pattillo

EDITOR-IN-CHIEF
Adam Arnold

PUBLISHER
Jason DeAngelis

MERMAN IN MY TUB VOL. 5
© Itokichi 2014
First published in Japan in 2014 by KADOKAWA CORPORATION, Tokyo.
English translation rights reserved by Seven Seas Entertainment, LLC.
under the license from KADOKAWA CORPORATION, Tokyo.

Seven Seas books may be purchased in bulk for promotional, educational, or
business use. Please contact your local bookseller or the Macmillan Corporate
and Premium Sales Department at 1-800-221-7945, extension 5442, or by
e-mail at MacmillanSpecialMarkets@macmillan.com.

Seven Seas and the Seven Seas logo are trademarks of
Seven Seas Entertainment, LLC. All rights reserved.

ISBN: 978-1-626923-56-0

Printed in Canada

First Printing: November 2016

10 9 8 7 6 5 4 3 2 1

FOLLOW US ON

READING DIRECTIONS

This book reads from **right to left**, Japanese style.
If this is your first time reading manga, you start
reading from the top right panel on each page and
take it from there. If you get lost, just follow the
numbered diagram here. It may seem backwards at
first, but you'll get the hang of it! Have fun!!

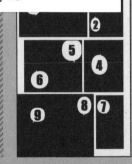